Students as Researchers of Culture and Language in Their Own Communities

Judith Green, editor

Preschoolers as Authors: Literacy Learning in the Social World of the Classroom
Deborah Wells Rowe

Shards of Glass: Children Reading and Writing Beyond Gendered Identities
Bronwyn Davies

Constructing Critical Literacies
Peter Freebody, Allan Luke and Sandy Muspratt

Children as Researchers of Culture and Language in Their Own Communities
Ann Egan-Robertson and David Bloome (eds.)

forthcoming

Learning Written Genres
Christine C. Pappas

Narrative Sign Making and Classroom Literacy
Joanne Golden

Reading to Children: Developing a Culture of Literacy
Carolyn Panofsky

Life in a Preschool
David P. Fernie and Rebecca Kantor

Early Childhood Classroom Processes: A View through an Ethnographic Lens
Rebecca Kantor and David P. Fernie (eds.)

Constructing Gender and Difference: Critical Research Perspectives on Early Childhood
Barbara Kamler (ed.)

Students as Researchers
of Culture and Language
in Their Own Communities

edited by
Ann Egan-Robertson
University of Wisconsin-Madison

David Bloome
Vanderbilt University

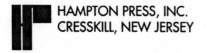
HAMPTON PRESS, INC.
CRESSKILL, NEW JERSEY

Printed in the United States of America

Library of Congress Cataloging-in-Publication Data

Students as researchers of culture and language in their own
   communities / edited by Ann Egan-Robertson, David Bloome.
         p.   cm. -- (Language and social processes)
   Includes bibliographical references and index.
   ISBN 1-57273-044-7. -- ISBN 1-57273-045-5 (pbk.)
      1. Language and culture--Research. 2. Students.   I. Egan
-Robertson, Ann.   II. Bloome, David. III. Series: Language & social
processes.
P35.S78   1997
306.44--dc21   97-39588
                                                                  CIP

Hampton Press, Inc.
23 Broadway
Cresskill, NJ 07626

[O]f all forms of scientific knowledge, ethnography is the most open, the most compatible with a democratic way of life, the least likely to produce a world in which experts control knowledge at the expense of those who are studied. The skills of ethnography are enhancements of skills all normal persons employ in everyday life. . . . As a discipline, ethnography adds a body of concepts and techniques that direct attention, relate observations, more systematically than community members would normally have occasion for doing. . . . [It] provide[s] for making explicit relationships and patterns that members leave implicit. . . . Ethnography, in short, is a disciplined way of looking, asking, recording, reflecting, comparing and reporting. It mediates between what members of a given community know and do, and accumulates comparative understanding of what members of communities generally have known and done.

A member of a given community, then, need not be merely a source of data, an object at the other end of a scientific instrument. He or she already possesses some of the local knowledge and access to knowledge that is essential to successful ethnography, and may have a talent for sifting and synthesizing it, special insight into some part of it. What he or she needs is the other part of disciplined ethnography, the comparative insight distilled over the decades. This can come in a variety of idioms, and does not require a graduate degree. Indeed, one might argue that an educational system devoted to a democratic way of life would provide this other part to every student, as a right and basis for citizenship. Not to do so is to withhold from citizens the best we have to offer them for the understanding of social experience, for coming to terms with it or changing it.
— Dell Hymes*

*From Dell Hymes (1981). Ethnographic monitoring. In H. Trueba, G. Guthrie & K. Au (Eds.), *Culture and the bilingual classroom: Studies in classroom ethnography* (p. 57). Rowley, MA: Newbury House.

Contents

Introduction   ix
Contributors   xxi

1. Students as Ethnographers, Thinking and Doing Ethnography
   A Bibliographic Essay   1
   Ann Egan-Robertson and Jerri Willett

**I COMMUNITY AS CURRICULUM: FOCUS ON CULTURE,
     WRITING, AND ACADEMIC LEARNING   33**

2. Learning To Write By Writing Ethnography   37
   Toby Curry and David Bloome

3. Celebrations and Letters Home: Research As An Ongoing
   Conversation Among Students, Parents, and Teacher   59
   Marceline Torres

4. When Young People From Marginalized Communities
   Enter The World Of Ethnographic Research:
   Scribing, Planning, Reflecting and Sharing   69
   Carmen I. Mercado

5. Life in Elementary School: Children's Ethnographic
   Reflections   93
   Rosi A.C. Andrade

6. Learning To See Learning In The Classroom:
   Developing An Ethnographic Perspective   115
   Beth Yeager, Ana Floriani, and Judith Green

**II COMMUNITY AS CURRICULUM: FOCUS ON
      LANGUAGE   141**

7. Investigating Language Practices in A Multilingual
   London Community   143
   Kit Thomas and Janet Maybin

8. Dialect Awareness And The Study of Language   167
   Walt Wolfram

9. Knowledge About Language in British Classrooms:
Children As Researchers   191
Jenny Cheshire and Viv Edwards

**III COMMUNITY AS CURRICULUM: FOCUS ON
SOCIAL ACTION**   **215**

10. Reclaiming Indigenous Cultures: Student-Developed
Oral Histories of Talamanca, Costa Rica   217
Martha Montero-Sieburth

11. Telling Stories With Ms. Rose Bell: Students As Authors
of Critical Narratives and Fiction   243
David Schaafsma

12. "We Must Ask Our Questions and Tell Our Stories":
Writing Ethnography and Constructing Personhood   261
Ann Egan-Robertson

Author Index   285
Subject Index   291

Series Preface

LANGUAGE AND SOCIAL PROCESSES

Judith Green, Editor
University of California at Santa Barbara

Associate Editors

Ginger Weade
University of Florida

Carol Dixon
University of California
at Santa Barbara

Language and Social Processes provides a forum for scholarly work that makes visible the ways in which everyday life is accomplished through discourse processes among individuals and groups. Volumes will examine how language-in-use influences the access of individuals and culturally, ethnically, and linguistically diverse groups to social institutions, and how knowledge construction and social participation across diverse social settings is accomplished through discourse.

Studies in education and other social institutions are invited from a variety of perspectives including those of anthropology, communication, education, linguistics, literary theory, psychology, and sociology. Manuscripts are encouraged that involve theoretical treatments of relevant issues, present in-depth analyses of particular social groups and institutional settings, or present comparative studies across social groups, settings or institution. Send inquiries to: Judith Green, Series Editor, Graduate School of Education, University of California, Santa Barbara, CA 93106, (805)893-4781.

Introduction

David Bloome
Vanderbilt University
Ann Egan-Robertson
University of Wisconsin-Madison

Over the past two decades, ethnographic and sociolinguistic research has become increasingly popular with educational researchers. But there have been only a small number of efforts at using ethnography and sociolinguistics as teaching tools in kindergarten through Grade 12 (K-12) schools. Yet, the relatively small number of efforts that have been made have been extraordinarily exciting in the new directions for classroom education that they have generated. In this book, we present new directions in classroom education generated by using ethnography and sociolinguistics as teaching tools, the theory behind these efforts, and the classroom practices involved.

But this book is more than a description of educational projects. Engaging students as ethnographic and sociolinguistic researchers involves fundamental questions about the knowledge base of classroom learning, about the nature of ethnographic and sociolinguistic research, and about the nature of writing. In this introduction we highlight some of these questions, so that they may serve as a second framework for reading the chapters that follow. (Readers who are unfamiliar with ethnographic and sociolinguistic research may first want to read Chapter 1, "Students as Ethnographers, Thinking and Doing Ethnography: A Bibliographic Essay" by Ann Egan-Robertson and Jerri Willett. It is an introduction to ethnographic and sociolinguistic research.)

STUDENTS AS RESEARCHERS

Students at all grade levels are typically asked by their teachers to engage in "research" projects. Often, this means researching a topic by going to the library. Research skills are limited to organizing note cards, generating an outline, and learning bibliographic formats. Perhaps it is to create distance from such definitions of research that science teachers and others often engage students in "inquiry" projects where students do hands-on experiments and explore natural phenomena. We mean neither term when we refer to *students as researchers*.

Research that is bounded by classroom and library walls, in which students are expected to reproduce the knowledge printed in authoritative texts, is little more than legitimized plagiarism. Inquiry that is designed so that students find the knowledge or insight predetermined by their teachers is little more than a teaching trick, just a more effective and motivating classroom strategy for doing the same thing as classroom and library research. It is not that classroom experiments and library books are not useful sources of knowledge, rather what typically occurs in K-12 classrooms under the rubric of research and inquiry is neither.

Research requires the generation of new knowledge and the production of new texts through which the new knowledge is shared. Research also requires a new "looking," a new search: Familiar phenomena viewed and understood in a new way, and unfamiliar phenomena newly encountered and understood both on their own terms and in familiar terms. Research involves a search and an understanding that is systematic, based on a history of thought about principles of inquiry and how they are related to various types of knowledge. And, in the sense of looking for alternative explanations and counter-evidence, inquiry is only research when it is rigorous and self-skeptical.

Research then, can never be bounded by classroom or library walls, the walls of teacher knowledge, or even the walls of extant disciplinary knowledge. As researchers, students—like any researcher—must have access to the freedom to go beyond what is already known and to go beyond the ways in which knowledge is traditionally generated. Thus, to invite students to be researchers is to invite them into a new relationship with the teacher and a new relationship with academic knowledge.

These new relationships are especially highlighted in the chapters by Yeager, Floriani and Green (Chapter 6) and Curry and Bloome (Chapter 2). Curry and Bloome are interested in moving students beyond text reproduction as a mode of academic engagement to text production. Students were reluctant to view their own knowledge and the knowledge in their own communities as valuable in school and in academic work. Curry and Bloome used student ethnographic projects as a way to help students understand what knowledge was available in their families and communities and how that knowledge might be used for academic writing and learning. In their chapter, Yeager, Floriani, and Green redefine academic knowledge from an ethnographic perspective. They begin by defining both the classroom and academic disciplines as types of communities. The question they posed for the students was: What is the nature of these communities (including the classroom community) and what does it take to be an effective member in those communities? Students were required to be ethnographers both of their own classroom community and of the various academic disciplines they were studying, and in the process they were able to restructure their relationships to classroom dynamics (e.g., how to interact with the teacher, peers, classroom tasks, etc.) and to academic bodies of knowledge.

Andrade (Chapter 5) focuses attention on another dimension of student as researcher. Noting the absence of student perspectives both on themselves and on their schools and communities, Andrade views an ethnographic perspective as a way to get at how young people see the worlds in which they live. Andrade, like many other educational ethnographers, views ethnographic research not as a set of techniques for doing research, but as a perspective, a way of getting at understanding that young people themselves hold. Andrade's chapter can be viewed as part of the ongoing debate about the relationship of the researcher to the researched. Through the use of dialogue journals and other techniques, Andrade is able to employ an ethnographic perspective to help young people reflect on school, family, themselves, and other aspects of their world, in order to express their particular view as young people. The distinction between researcher and researched is blurred in Andrade's chapter, and the ethnographic perspective unusual both in the way it is used and in the results, expressions, it provides.

The restructuring of relationships includes the relationship of young people and parents and parents and the school. As the chapter by Torres (Chapter 3) highlights, parents are potential informants for student research, collaborators, and an audience for research reports. The research in which students engage can bring parents and young people closer together, breaking down the traditional relationship in which parents are often left with only the distasteful role of ensuring that homework has been completed and enforcing their children's motivation and good behavior in school. By emphasizing the knowledge that exists in family and community domains, by focusing attention on the particular histories and experiences that families and people in the community have lived, what students do in school brings the community and family into the school. And, as occurred in the project described in the chapters by Torres and by Mercado (Chapter 4), parents come to the school to participate in the research process, providing much greater common ground—intellectually, academically, emotionally, and physically—with students and the community than is usually the case.

In summary, to engage students as researchers is to reconstitute what it means to be a student. The question, "What is it that the young people are students of?" can no longer be simply answered by pointing to a set of authoritative texts, a curriculum document, or a particular discipline. At the same time, what has come to be defined as *research* and *inquiry* in schools is defenestrated and redefined as the generation of new knowledge and new texts to share that knowledge. New relationships are created between students and teachers, between students and their parents, between parents and the school, and between students and academic knowledge, learning, and writing.

RESEARCHING CULTURE AND LANGUAGE

There are at least two dimensions to studying culture. The first is to study the culture of a particular group of people and describe it. Such ethnographic studies provide information that might otherwise be unknown about a group of people, about a way of life that may be different from our own. Descriptions derive only in part from what researchers see, hear, and learn. Descriptions depend as well on the principles and interpretive frameworks used to guide the "seeing," "hearing," "learning," and "describing." Ethnographic and sociolinguistic descriptions are guided by principles and frameworks derived from the history of inquiry and the ongoing debates in cultural and social anthropology, the ethnography of communication, anthropological linguistics, sociolinguistics, and related fields (a discussion of these principles, frameworks, and debates can be found in Chapter 1).

A second dimension to studying a culture concerns the nature of culture itself: how culture is transmitted across generations; how culture changes over time; what happens when different cultures come into contact with each other; how culture influences how people think, feel, believe, use language, and act; how it gives meaning to both social and naturally occurring activities; and so forth. So too with the study of language—we can study a particular language and we can study the nature of language, itself.

The ethnographic and sociolinguistic studies conducted by the students in the various chapters covered both dimensions. In the chapters by Torres (Chapter 3), Schaafsma (Chapter 11), and Montero-Sieburth (Chapter 10) students are creating descriptions of aspects of the cultural life of particular cultures in New York, Detroit, and Talamanca, respectively. In some cases, they are describing aspects of their own cultural life; in other cases they are describing aspects of others' cultural lives. Because students live in a world in which cross-cultural contact is increasingly routine, especially for students who live in areas that are already ethnically and linguistically diverse, the particular knowledge they acquire from their ethnographic and sociolinguistic studies is important because it is part of the immediate social context in which they live.

In Chapter 7 by Thomas and Maybin the focus is on the particular language variations that make up the students' lives. Beginning with what it means to "talk proper," the sociolinguistic research the students conducted helped students examine who used what language (English, Urdu, Panjabi, Gujerati, etc.) and what registers and dialects, when, where, and with what feelings and attitudes. Next, the students engaged in language autobiographies, tracing their use of languages and their memories about language attitudes and language discrimination. Understanding the particulars of the dynamics of language in their own lives and histories helped them understand the relationship of power and language.

Wolfram's chapter (Chapter 8) also focused attention on what students implicitly knew about language, but began with a study of language variation beyond the students' immediate experience. By looking at the systematicity of language variation rules in Appalachian English and Boston English, students were able to raise questions that then could be used to examine their own dialects in relationship to so-called Proper English. In so doing, they learned both about the particulars of various dialects of English as well as an abstract understanding of how language variation operates.

The chapters by Thomas and Maybin and by Wolfram provide alternatives to the traditional study of Proper English, usually characterized by prescriptive Proper English Grammar exercises. It makes little sense for educators to proclaim educational philosophies based on building on what the child already knows and on respect for the child's home culture, when explicitly or implicitly the language they speak is disrespected or ignored in the study of language component of the language arts curriculum. When the study of language revolves around the prescription of so-called Proper English, how can children ignore the insult to the way they speak outside of school or to the way their families speak? Of course, one cannot ignore the power of access that speaking Proper English may provide to some students. What Maybin and Thomas and Wolfram provide is a way for students to build a knowledge base about language variation, language in general, and a context for learning so-called Proper English, that recognizes the cultural and political contexts of language use while emphasizing respect for language variations and for the young person as a student of language.

Cheshire and Edwards push the study of language along the same lines as Thomas and Maybin and Wolfram, but add a twist. The project in which they engaged students involved a collaborative relationship between themselves as sociolinguistic researchers and the students as sociolinguistic researchers, yielding needed data for the study of language use and variation. That is, although there were educational benefits to the students, the students were real researchers contributing real data to an ongoing program of sociolinguistic studies.

Any study of culture or language involves writing. Writing is an integral part of the research as well as a means for sharing findings and interpretations. Although building on so-called "process" and "developmental" approaches to writing instruction, the writing students learn to do as part of their ethnographic and sociolinguistic inquiry provides them with a different framework for writing than they might otherwise have learned. In part, they learn to do a wide variety of different kinds of writing—field notes, transcripts, charts, diagrams, maps, lists, reports, stories, among other genres—and they learn the power of various kinds of writing to synthesize, generate, and transform knowledge. Further, as Mercado shows in Chapter 4, the students become writers, many of them carrying their journals and field notebooks around with them as part of their identity kit.

Ethnographic and sociolinguistic writing also requires students to bring together different domains of knowledge. As highlighted in Chapter 2 by Curry and Bloome, this might include bringing together new knowledge (what they have learned from their inquiry) with old knowledge (what they knew before or what was in their textbooks) or bringing together knowledge about the community they were studying with knowledge about a community others were studying. Further, because the reports they write are not just for getting grades, but are themselves important ethnographic and sociolinguistic products that become part of the corpus of studies in the field and available to the community, their writing takes on a different character and status.

One of the difficult issues that ethnographers must face concerns the genres in which they will write their reports. There have been numerous discussions about this topic in the field covering issues ranging from the use of technical jargon to use of first person narratives. In some cases, researchers have included "fictionalized" descriptions, either to protect the identity and safety of the people they are studying or because only through "fiction" can the author accurately portray and communicate key issues. Thus, for example, in Myerhoff's (1978) ethnographic study of a Jewish senior citizen center, she included autobiographical information, an imaginary conversation with a long-time friend and informant who had died before the study had been completed, and a dream she had during the study. The issues are no different for students as ethnographers. In Chapter 11 by Schaafsma, the students create "true" stories about the lives of people in the area in which they live and go to school. Telling stories as a genre for reporting their findings makes sense because stories are what they were told as they met and learned from people in the community. The choice to create stories and use drama by the students described in Chapter 12 by Egan-Robertson was grounded in what students had learned from local artists about how to fight racism. Through their inquiry and interviews, the students had learned that local artists and community activists were using drama and fiction as a way to make visible the stories, knowledge, wisdom, and experience of people in their community, as a way to assert their personhood and as a way to fight racism. For one student, the choice to fictionalize her report was based on the need to protect people and to protect herself.

Writing becomes a resource for students to use and to manipulate as they go about researching and sharing what they have found and the new knowledge they have generated. They may learn how various genres of writing are used in the communities in which they live, in school, and in various academic disciplines. They may learn how writing can bring people together, as coworkers and coresearchers, how it can create bonds between authors and readers, and how it can provide themselves with both an academic and community identity. Perhaps most importantly, they may learn that writing is not a set of rules to be followed—another "brick in the wall" to borrow a phrase from the rock group Pink Floyd—but a set of resources that they can use to pursue their agendas, a set of resources that have a history and a presence within their own communities, a set of resources for going beyond the walls of the classroom.

IN THEIR OWN COMMUNITIES

In the work that Curry and Bloome have done together (Chapter 2), one of the hardest tasks for students was to define and locate their community, to distinguish community from neighborhood and family. Rather than give them a specific definition to apply, the students needed to grapple with the problems inherent in a term like *community*. But the students are not the only ones to note the difficulties inherent in trying to define community. For example, Williams (1983) began his definition of community by tracing some of its historical senses—a community of goods, a sense of common identity and characteristics, "an attempt to distinguish the body of direct relationships from the organized establishment of *realm* or *state*," noting that by the nineteenth century community had the "sense of immediacy or locality strongly developed in the context of larger and more complex industrial societies" (p. 75, emphasis in original). Williams continued:

> The complexity of *community* thus relates to the difficult interaction between the tendencies originally distinguished in the historical development: on the one hand the sense of direct common concern; on the other hand the materialization of various forms of common organization, which may not adequately express this. *Community* can be the warmly persuasive word to describe an existing set of relationships, or the warmly persuasive word to describe an alternative set of relationships. What is most important, perhaps, is that unlike all other terms of social organization (*state, nation, society,* etc.) it seems never to be used unfavourably, and never to be given any positive opposing or distinguishing term." (p. 77, emphasis in original).

In this volume, *community* is used to describe neighborhoods, ethnic groups, religious groups, classrooms, and professional academic groups (e.g., mathematicians). Whatever its use, the assumption of community as a positive term permeates the uses of community throughout the chapters in the book, as does the use of the term elsewhere. Indeed, one might suggest that applying the term *community* to social organizations not usually thought of as communities (e.g., classrooms, academic professions) may be an attempt either to reshape those social organizations as communities or perhaps only to create a public relations image by coopting the positive sense of community.

Yet, despite the positive sense of community, throughout the book there is a faint but nonetheless visible negative tint to the term as well. For example, Chapter 12 by Egan-Robertson begins by noting the alienation that adolescents often feel from their classrooms, schools, families, and local communities. In many ways, the project in which the students engaged was an attempt to overcome that alienation. Although not directly noted, there is a similar sense of alienation in nearly every chapter.

Communities—whether they are neighborhoods, ethnic groups, religious groups, classrooms, academic professions, and so on—are not necessarily the warm, nurturing, and caring entities suggested in Williams's definition, but neither are they necessarily negative nor is adolescent alienation inherent. Communities are what we make them. Several of the chapters highlight the social action that students took with regard to their communities. In chapter 12, the students oriented their work to fight racism among their peers and in their community; in Chapter 11, the students published a book telling the stories of local people in the community and what they had done to build the community and help people care for each other; and, in Chapter 10 by Montero-Sieburth, the students resisted the erosion of their people's heritage, history, and culture and their work was disseminated throughout Costa Rica. In these three chapters, the social action taken by students was highlighted; yet, in each chapter students are engaged in social action that transforms the communities and social contexts in which they live. There is no separation between education and action or between learning and doing.

THE ORGANIZATION OF THE VOLUME

The chapters in this volume could have been organized in several different ways to highlight different key educational issues. We could have organized the book by age and grade levels, to show how students as researchers of culture and language can be encouraged across the grade levels. Or, we could have organized the book to emphasize the different definitions of ethnography and sociolinguistics employed. We have chosen to organize the book to highlight three issues of recent concern to K-12 educators: how student ethnographic and sociolinguistic research can be used to enhance academic learning and academic writing (Section I), how sociolinguistic inquiry can be used to supplant or enhance the study of language component of the traditional language arts curriculum (Section II), and how student ethnographic and sociolinguistic research can be linked with social action to improve students' lives and their communities (Section III).

The first part of the book contains this introduction, a list of contributors and their addresses, and the bibliographic essay written by Egan-Robertson and Willett. We have provided the addresses of the contributors to encourage you to write to them, to share your experiences, to ask questions, and so on. The bibliographic essay provides an excellent introduction to ethnographic and sociolinguistic research with a useful list of recommended further readings.

Section I contains five chapters, each of which highlights the integration of students as researchers of culture and language in their own communities with concerns for academic learning. Each chapter lays out what happened in the students' specific project, allowing readers to follow both the planning and implementation process. However, none of the chapters provide a recipe to follow. Educators who are interested in engaging their students as researchers of culture and language may build on the models and experiences described in the chapters in the book, but each educator and each group of students needs to construct their own model, their own set of definitions and goals, their own praxis.

Section II contains three chapters. Each chapter describes a project in which students studied language as sociolinguists. Two of the chapters describe projects in England where there has been much debate and politicking about the content of the study of language component of the language arts curriculum. The third chapter describes a project in the United States where questions about the appropriateness of grammar instruction have not become part of national government debate and policy. Nonetheless, sentiments may run very strong among educators and parents. Each chapter provides an alternative to the traditional study of language component that was based on the direct instruction of the prescriptive grammar of so-called Proper English (called Received Pronunciation or BBC English in the United Kingdom, and Standard English in the United States). But as important, they describe a mode of inquiry about language that has far-reaching effects for students. Students acquire a way of thinking about and analyzing language, in addition to knowledge about the systematicity of language variation. And accompanying the knowledge and modes of inquiry students acquire are changes in the attitudes and values they hold about both their own language and the languages of others.

Section III contains three chapters, each of which describes how students' research on issues of culture and language was either part of or led to their taking social action. Almost all of the chapters in this book could have been included in this fourth section. The three chapters that were included were written in a manner that highlighted the community social action taken by students, and thus they provide a way to highlight an important dimension of engaging students as researchers of culture and language in their own communities.

Using ethnographic and sociolinguistic inquiry as a K-12 teaching tool requires a change in perspective about the nature of curriculum, instruction, knowledge, and educational goals. It is not just a matter of placing student inquiry at the center of the curriculum. Through their inquiry, students become anthropologists and sociolinguists helping to define and explain how culture and language work. In so doing, they not only learn about culture and language, and how they vary, but more importantly, they come to have new understandings of their own communities (both their neighborhood/ ethnic community and their classroom community), their language or languages, and their own cultural and linguistic identities. Through their ethnographic and sociolinguistic inquiry students do more than learn and acquire skills; the work they produce (like the work of any ethnographer or sociolinguist) has value for themselves, for other students (as ethnographers and sociolinguists), for members of the community, and for the broader field of cultural and social anthropology and sociolinguistics. In brief, students are not just doing to learn or learning to do, they are learning and doing.

REFERENCES

Myerhoff, B. (1978). *Number our days*. New York: Simon & Schuster.
Williams, R. (1983). *Keywords: A vocabulary of culture and society*. London: Fontana Press.

1

Students as Ethnographers, Thinking and Doing Ethnography: A Bibliographic Essay

Ann Egan-Robertson
University of Wisconsin, Madison
Jerri Willett
University of Massachusetts, Amherst

What is ethnographic and sociolinguistic inquiry, how is it done, and what can be learned from it? In this chapter we recommend readings to help readers explore these questions. We also provide a sketch of the major ideas and debates shaping the field of ethnographic and sociolinguistic inquiry.

There are many debates in the field of sociolinguistic and ethnographic inquiry, especially so about the concept underpinning inquiry. One reason for this lack of consensus is that researchers believe that theories should change as a result of what they learn from the groups they study. Each study helps researchers to examine their assumptions about the nature of culture and language and how it should be studied. Part of engaging in ethnographic and sociolinguistic inquiry is to join these ongoing debates and reflections.

Another difficulty that readers will face is the fact that there is no standard way of characterizing the practice of ethnography. There are, however, a number of key ideas that are continually debated. Reading about these ideas will provide insights into the nature of ethnography. We suggest reading books and articles by several different authors because they configure key ideas in different ways. Each reading, together with your own research experiences, will contribute to a more nuanced understanding of ethnography and sociolinguistic research.

A final difficulty that readers may face is the heavy theoretical focus of many of the recommended readings. Why bother with so much theory? Why not just get on with the doing, especially because we are advocating using ethnography and sociolinguistics as teaching tools in K-12 schools? There are two major reasons for such a focus. First, theory shapes the way that ethnographic and sociolinguistic research is conducted. This theory comes from the ongoing scholarly discussions about the nature of culture in general, the researcher's emerging ideas about the local culture, and folk theories held by members of the local culture about their social worlds. Second, without conscious and systematic reflection on our personal theories and constant comparison with the theories of others, we may inappropriately interpret the behavior of others.

Although we reference many books and journal articles and although we purposefully include diverse perspectives, our discussion is not intended to be comprehensive and necessarily reflects at least in part how we view the field. We list readings with author, title of book or articles, and date, in the margin. Full bibliographic information can be found at the end of the chapter.

WHAT IS ETHNOGRAPHIC AND SOCIOLINGUISTIC INQUIRY?

A fundamental debate in the field of ethnographic and sociolinguistic inquiry centers around the question, "What counts as ethnographic and sociolinguistic inquiry?" One way to answer this question is to examine the history of ethnographic and sociolinguistic research and how their traditions of inquiry have developed and evolved.

Hymes. "What is Ethnography?" 1982.

Wolcott. "On Ethnographic Intent." 1987.

Although some scholars trace the beginning of ethnographic research back to Malinowski and his study of the Trobriand Islanders, others suggest that the first ethnography was done by Du Bois and his study of African-American life in Philadelphia. It is helpful to read some of the early ethnographic studies both to understand the kinds of questions the researchers were asking as well as the theoretical and methodological problems these studies raised. In many ways, it has been by reflecting on the problems

Malinowski. Argonauts of the Western Pacific. 1932.

Du Bois. The Philadelphia Negro. 1899.

Mead. Coming of Age in Samoa. 1961.

Benedict. Patterns of Culture. 1934.
Sapir. Language, Culture, and Personality. 1970.

encountered while conducting or writing ethnographic and sociolinguistic research that new directions and approaches have been developed.

There are a number of books and articles that provide helpful overviews of ethnographic and sociolinguistic research. We recommend reading several to get a sense of the range of perspectives employed. It is also important to read across national boundaries. For example, there are differences in emphasis, some people claim, between American and British ethnographic and sociolinguistic inquiry into education. *Life in Schools, Classrooms and Staffrooms,* and *Researching Language and Literacy in Social Contexts,* all produced by the Open University in the United Kingdom, are excellent sources for getting a sense of the range of perspectives and emphases in British and other ethnographic and sociolinguistic studies of education. Each contains a series of articles and excerpts from often classic ethnographic and sociolinguistic studies.

Sociolinguistic studies cover a broad range of topics. Some studies describe variations in the phonology, grammar, and semantics of the various dialects of a language. In many countries and societies, there is a prestige dialect. In the United States it is Standard American English, in the United Kingdom the prestige dialect is called "Received Pronunciation" or more popularly, "BBC English." These prestige dialects are dominant dialects in the sense that they constitute "correctness" in language and variations from them are often viewed as inferior language and the speakers of nonstandard dialects unfortunately and outrageously judged as uneducated, unintelligent, and inferior. Sociolinguistic studies have shown that nondominant

Firth. We, the Tikopia. 1936.

Hammersly & Atkinson. Ethnography: Principles and Practices. 1983.

Agar. The Professional Stranger. 1980.

Hammersly. Reading Ethnographic Research. 1990.

Hammersly & Woods (eds). Life in Schools. 1984.

Graddol, Maybin, & Stierer (eds). Researching Language and Literacy in Social Contexts. 1994.

Hargreaves & Woods (eds.). Classrooms and Staffrooms. 1984.

Labov. Language in the Inner City. 1972a.

Montgomery. An Introduction to Language and Society. 1986.

Newsum. Class, Language, and Eduction: Class Struggle and Sociolinguistics in an African Situation. 1990.

Ferguson & Heath (eds.). Language in the USA. 1981.

Grillo. Dominant Languages. 1989.

dialects are rule-governed and vary in ways that are systematic and sensitive to the situation, to the people involved in the event, and to subtle but important intentions of meaning—as is true of all dialects and languages. The once-popular belief that Black English (more formally called African-American Vernacular English [AAVE]) was an inferior, incomplete, and lazy language was shown by sociolinguistic researchers to be completely false. Despite this research and court decisions to support the use of this research in schools, many people including teachers, pupils, and parents, still believe that AAVE is an inferior language. Educational efforts are needed to correct these wrong beliefs and to reshape education so that these wrong beliefs are not promulgated.

Trudgill. Accent, Dialect and the School. 1975.

Labov. Sociolinguistic Patterns. 1972b.

Smitherman. Talkin' and Testifyin'. 1977.

Wolfram & Christian. Dialects and Education: Issues and Answers. 1989.

Smitherman. "'What go round come round': King in perspective." 1981.

Stubbs & Hillier (eds.). Readings on Language, Schools and Classrooms. 1983.

In addition to studies of variation in phonology, grammar, and semantics, sociolinguists have studied variation in how people use language. In the United States, many of these studies have occurred under the rubric of sociolinguistic ethnography, which is another term for the ethnography of communication. These studies are discussed later. Other sociolinguistic studies of variation in how people use language have been carried out under the rubric of applied linguistics, pragmatics, and interactional sociolinguistics. Many of these studies have looked at the use of multiple languages and bilingualism, both in and outside of education. Like the studies of dialect, these studies show that what appeared to be laziness, randomness, or inadequate ways of using language were instead systematic and competent variations revealing linguistic sensitivity and appropriate responsiveness to the situation, to the topic, and to the people being addressed.

Garcia. Bilingual Education. 1991.

Although sociolinguistic research and ethnographic research have had their own histories and traditions of inquiry, in many studies the two are brought together and many people view the two as complementary.

Zaharlick & Green. "Ethnographic Research." 1991.

Typically, ethnography is defined as having three goals:

1. *to describe in rich detail and interpret the cultural life of particular social groups,*
2. *to contribute to our general knowledge about the kinds of life-worlds humans create and the nature of the cultural processes operating to create these worlds, and*
3. *to help people imagine and create better worlds*

Heath. "Ethnography in Education: Defining the Essentials." 1982a.

Ethnography is usually defined as having the following characteristics:

1. *it is holistic, contextual, and comparative;*
2. *it is systematic but uses multiple, nonstandard, and recursive methods; and*
3. *it elicits the group member view of reality.*

Each of these characteristics is discussed here.

First, observed behaviors are not taken out of context, but are interpreted within the holistic context. For example, a classroom ethnographer would not venture an interpretation of the comments by a teacher or a student or speculate on the meaning of a particular activity or organizational structure without understanding the full social, cultural, and educational context. What happened before, during, and after? How do these phenomena fit into the broader contexts of the school and community? The broader social context?

Green & Wallat (eds.). Ethnography and Language in Educational Settings. 1981.

Researchers constantly compare what they are observing and experiencing with other situations within and across groups and settings. There is a constant search for ways to construct comparisons and to learn from them. Comparisons can be made through coordinated efforts across cultural groups or by juxtaposing studies conducted in different areas of the world. The purpose of cross-cultural comparison is not just to better understand foreign or different cultures (sometimes called studying "the other") or to just document the variation that exists in the world, but to better understand and reveal the taken-for-granted and nearly invisible cultural assumptions that drive the worlds in which the researchers themselves live.

Second, researchers engage in a recursive and cyclical process of research. Selecting problems and questions, collecting and recording data, analyzing and interpreting data are processes that occur over and over again throughout the study. Questions asked shape data collection but data collection engenders more questions. Writing stimulates further analyses and helps to refine questions.

Researchers keep systematic records of their data, interpretations, and procedures. They systematically look for evidence to disconfirm their interpretations and they check many sources to ensure that the information they get is valid and reliable. Most important, they select multiple methods of data collection that are appropriate to the context.

Third, group member perspectives are elicited and respected. Sometimes this is called capturing an "emic" perspective and compared with an outsider's perspective called an "etic" perspective. The major task of an ethnographer is to understand the

Shultz, Erickson, & Florio. "Where's the floor?" 1982.

Spindler & Spindler (eds.). Interpretive Ethnography of Education: At Home and Abroad. 1987a.

Whiting & Edwards. Children of Different Worlds. 1988.

Saravia-Shore & Arvizu (eds.). Cross-cultural Literacy: Ethnographies of Communication in Multiethnic Classrooms. 1992.

Cole (ed.). Anthropology for the Nineties. 1988.

culture as the natives do and to reflect on how one's own conceptions influence what is understood. That is why informants are not called subjects.

One issue debated by some ethnographers, particularly those working in the tradition of critical ethnography, is that the third goal—to help people imagine and create better worlds—is too often ignored. They argue that by merely describing the cultural life of a group, ethnographers may contribute to maintaining the existing power relationships in a group, relationships that my be oppressive to some members of the community. Brodkey (1987b) stated the case as follows:

Anderson. "Critical Ethnography in Education." 1989.

> The only way to fight a hegemonic discourse is to teach ourselves and others alternative ways of seeing the world and practice [than traditional ethnographic narrative]. While such an approach will not persuade those who are not committed to other understandings of the meaning and value of scholarship, it should be possible to enter critical ethnographic narratives into the academic record and thereby sustain the conversation on hegemonic practices. (p. 75)

Brodkey. Academic Writing as Social Practice. 1987a.

Brodkey. "Writing Critical Ethnographic Narratives." 1987b.

WHAT IS CULTURE?

Embedded in the ongoing debate about what counts as ethnography is the question, "What is culture and how is it created and learned?" Culture and the language by which culture is constructed are important topics of debate, not only because describing culture is one of the goals of ethnography, but also because our understandings of culture and language shape every aspect of doing ethnography: the question we ask, the ways we collect and record data, the kinds of interpretations we use to make sense of our descriptions, and the ways we represent our understandings about others.

Peacock's (1988) *The Anthropological Lens: Harsh Light, Soft Focus* provides a short and interesting introduction to the major themes and assumptions debated in anthropology, the parent discipline of ethnography. Drawing on the work of well-known anthropologists, he began with a working definition of culture: "The taken-for-granted but powerfully influential understandings and codes that are learned and shared by members of a group" (p. 7). Then, giving concrete examples from ethnographies and his own experiences, he explored questions such as:

- What is the difference between nature and culture?
- What is the relationship between individuals and communities, individuals and culture, communities and culture?
- What is the relationship between the parts of culture and the whole of culture?
- If culture is more than the sum of its parts but culture is encountered in parts, how is the whole grasped?
- What is the relationship between society and culture?
- How can one see these abstract concepts working in everyday life?

Although Peacock's introduction provides a good grounding to these theoretical questions, it is important to remember that answers to these questions differ according

Peacock. The Anthropological Lens: Harsh Light, Soft Focus. 1988.

to the theoretical orientation of the research. Many of the ethnographers and theorists Peacock reviewed are from theoretical orientations sometimes called *structuralism* and *functionalism*. These orientations view culture and language as holistic, unified, and coherent systems. Researchers are concerned with how these systems are structured and how they function. For example, such ethnographers might describe how adolescent rite-of-passage rituals function to ensure that young people remain loyal to traditional ways of running society. There are, of course, other orientations to ethnography that eschew structuralist and functionalist assumptions, and we discuss some of these other orientations later.

To get a feel for the range of issues raised in debates about culture and how it influences ethnography, we recommend reading a broad range of theorists from the traditions of cognitive anthropology, interpretive anthropology, social anthropology, critical theory, poststructural theory, psychological anthropology, and native anthropology theory, among other perspectives. In the following pages we provide a brief overview of some of these various orientations. However, please keep in mind that few ethnographers are "purists" in the sense of drawing from only one definition of culture; most draw on several perspectives.

One important perspective, especially in the United States, has been that of cognitive anthropology. In his book, *Culture, Language, and Society*, Goodenough (1981), a cognitive anthropologist, argued that: "culture consists of whatever it is one has to know or believe in order to 'operate in a manner acceptable to [society's] members'" (p. 109).

Spindler & Spindler (eds.). Interpretive Ethnography of Education At Home and Abroad. 1987a.

Eckert. Jocks and Burnouts. 1989.

Varenne. Americans Together. 1977.

Whiting & Edwards. Children of Different Worlds. 1988.

Ogbu. Minority Education and Caste. 1979.

Jones. "Towards a Native Anthropology." 1988.

Goodenough. Culture, Language and Society. 1981.

Holland & Quinn (eds.). Cultural Models in Language and Thought. 1987.

In other words, culture is the shared ideas, expectations, and standards we hold in our heads about how to act, feel, think, believe, and use language in our group. Our concepts are like "road maps" that guide our interactions with others in the group.

A different view of culture is given by Geertz. Geertz did not locate culture in the mind but in the meaningfulness of the material world, which includes people's interactions, language, and the social and natural environment. In explaining his view of culture and of ethnography, which is sometimes called interpretive ethnography or materialist ethnography, Geertz used many metaphors. He described culture as the "webs of significance [humankind] has spun" and as an "acted document" visible to everyone. People signal to one another how they are interpreting behavior by how they act. In turn, others react to these actions, which signals their interpretations. In the process, they weave webs of significance. Over time, we build up expectations about the kinds of interpretations that are typically made in a particular group and the kinds of consequences that result and we act on the basis of our expectations. Through careful and systematic observation and description of everyday action where meaning is acted out, ethnographers can make plausible interpretations about what is significant to the group. Geertz described ethnography as similar to reading a manuscript. The manuscript, in this case, is cultural action, and there are many interpretations of this action. In the process of negotiating interpretations, cultural meanings gradually change. The concern from this perspective is to ground interpretations in "thick description" of cultural action.

Geertz. The Interpretation of Culture. 1973

Geertz. Local Knowledge. 1983.

Holland & Quinn (eds.). Cultural Models in Language and Thought. 1987.

The view of culture described by Geertz frames the work of many interpretive sociolinguists and ethnographers of communication, who are interested in how language is used in particular contexts to construct and interpret meanings, identities, and relationships. Researchers from these traditions believe that is is impossible to examine culture without examining the linguistic processes through which culture is constructed. The work of Gumperz and Hymes starting in the 1960s laid out much of the early theoretical work in the ethnography of communication. A good introduction to the ethnography of communication is Saville-Troike's (1982), *The Ethnography of Communication: An Introduction.*

One of the contributions of studies in the ethnography of communication is detailed descriptions of how communicative practices—speaking, telling a story, joking, using written language, and so on—vary across cultures and across situations. This research has led to studies that have helped explicate how miscommunication may occur when people from different cultural groups interact. Another contribution comes from studies often conducted under the rubric of language socialization studies. These studies detail how children are socialized *through* language as well as to language.

Critical theorists provide yet another view of culture. Critical theorists believe that previous views of culture fail to take into account the power relations inherent in cultural production. Some groups have more power to impose the meanings that best serve their own interests, interests that are frequently oppressive to subordinate groups. Dominant groups maintain their power at least in two ways: They create social structures that prevent access to

Gumperz. Discourse Strategies. 1982a.

Hymes. Foundations of Sociolinguistics: The Ethnography of Communication. 1974.

Gumperz & Hymes (eds). Directions in Sociolinguistics: The Ethnography of Communication. 1972.

Bauman & Sherzer (eds.). Explorations in the Ethnography of Speaking. 1989.

Saville-Troike. The Ethnography of Communication: An Introduction. 1982.

Tannen. Talking Voices. 1989.

Shuman. Storytelling Rights. 1986.

Gumperz (ed.). Language and Social Identity. 1982b.

Schieffelin & Ochs (eds.). Language Socialization Across Cultures. 1986.

Giroux. Ideology, Culture and the Process of Schooling. 1981.

Giroux. Theory and Resistance in Education. 1983.

Apple. Education and Power. 1982.

knowledge and power and they control meanings, part of which justifies the position of those in power. However, subordinate groups continually resist dominant meanings and this resistance can be the basis of cultural and social change. The concern from this perspective is to analyze power relationships, often hidden from the consciousness of informants, and to ask who benefits from the cultural meanings governing behavior. Critical theorists argue that merely interviewing informants to elicit cultural categories, such as one might do from the perspective of structuralist or functionalist anthropology may only tap into the dominant meaning system without revealing power relations shaping meaning. Data collection, data analysis, reporting, and disseminating must occur through the lens of critical theory. Moreover, critical theorists argue that research should be undertaken in collaboration with those affected by the dominant power structures. The goal is to change existing structures in order to free individuals from sources of oppression and domination.

An example of an ethnography from this tradition is Everhart's (1983) *Reading, Writing and Resistance: Adolescence and Labor in a Junior High School*. By thickly describing the cultural life of a junior high, Everhart illustrated how schooling attempts to control and impose meanings acquired by students through its hierarchical structures, modes of knowledge, and social action. These meanings are needed for the roles students will play later in the labor force, such as recognition of authority, ability to follow direction, punctuality, and acceptance of being restricted in the use of their abilities. Students, on the other hand, resist this

McLaren. Schooling as a Ritual Performance. 1986.

Everhart. Reading, Writing and Resistance. 1983.

Willis. Learning to Labour. 1977.

control. They goof off, attempt to derail the routine and beat the system. More importantly, these behaviors work to create solidarity among the students, giving their resistance more power. Everhart concluded his study by envisioning a different kind of schooling in which power relations are restructured to empower students rather than to subordinate them.

Another ethnography from this tradition is Fine's (1991) *Framing Dropouts*. Her study examined how the social realities of African-American and Hispanic students are excluded from talk in schools, and instead they are treated with a steady diet of rhetoric about equal opportunity that obscures the unequal distribution of power and resources. Fine suggested that dropping out is a form of resistance to the systematic silencing of their voices in schools. She argued that schools miss opportunities to allow students to examine and problematize the conditions that contribute to gender, race, and class stratification and that they miss opportunities to engage students in changing the society that oppresses them.

Fine. Framing Dropouts. 1991.

Building on the social theories of Habermas and other European social theorists rather than on American critical theorists, a critical approach to the study of language has been developed by linguists at Lancaster University and elsewhere in the United Kingdom, Australia, and Europe. Sometimes known as critical language awareness or critical discourse analysis, this approach emphasized understanding how power relationships are embedded in and manifested through how we use language, both in our daily lives and in institutional settings like schools.

Fairclough (ed.). Critical Language Awareness. 1992a.

Fairclough. Discourse and Social Change. 1992b.

Another perspective on culture that has guided some ethnographic and sociolinguistic studies is poststructuralism. Many people find poststructuralist theory difficult to read. This may be because its purpose is to disrupt our taken-for-granted notions about what is real, who we are, and how we know things, and the stability of our understanding of "reality." One idea that seems common to much poststructuralist theorizing and research is that reality, including personhood and culture, is created by language. Language, here, includes more than vocabulary, grammar, and pronunciation. Language, or discourse as it is sometimes called, includes ways of thinking, believing, talking, and behaving. Individuals can only know (perceive, think about, talk about, etc.) the world through language or discourse. As we acquire language, we are able to give meaning to experiences. Consequently, language or discourse shapes what we can think and say, and who we can be, as well as locates power in some places and instills control in others. A second major idea associated with poststructuralist theory is that language is not tied to the things to which it refers and it is not unified, logical, consistent, or stable. Rather, meaning slips and slides as we use it. A corollary notion about language being inherently unstable and contradictory is that because we understand reality through language, reality itself is not stable and claims to truth are always suspect. One consequence of this view is that many of the "regimes of truth" that have oppressed particular groups can be exposed.

Weedon. Feminist Practice and Poststructural Theory. 1987.

Solomon. The Signs of Our Time: The Secret Meanings of Everyday Life. 1988.

Davies. Shards of Glass. 1993.

Gilbert. Gender, Literacy, and the Classroom. 1989.

Brodkey. "Articulating Poststructural Theory in Research on Literacy." 1992.

Foucault. The Archaeology of Knowledge. 1972.

THE CONTRIBUTION OF ETHNOGRAPHIC AND SOCIOLINGUISTIC RESEARCH TO EDUCATION

One of the most exciting changes in education is the renewed interest in examining the theoretical assumptions we all bring to education. Our ideas about education, about teaching and learning are impacted profoundly by the perspectives we hold about culture and language. Once we start looking at our educational practices as cultural practices and our educational system as a cultural system, we find that the kinds of questions we ask lead us in new directions that are invigorating and productive.

Redefining Education

When most people—including researchers and educators—use the word *education* they mean schooling. It is this equation of *schooling = education* that ethnographic and sociolinguistic studies call into question and that provides some of their most important contributions to education. Spindler and Spindler (1987b), education anthropologists, defined education as: "A calculated intervention in the learning process" (p. 3). This definition is important because it locates education in many places inside and outside of school, including: families, religious organizations, workplaces, peer groups, sports activities, shops, school cafeterias, detention halls, classrooms, the principal's office, playgrounds, street corners, as well as in thousands of other places. A broadened view of where education takes place raises questions about the relationship of the many locations of education to each other. One view has been school-centered, asking questions about

Spindler & Spindler. "Issues and Applications in Ethnographic Methods." 1987b.

Solsken. Literacy, Gender, and Work in Families and in School. 1993.

how the many sites of education affect learning in school. For example:

> How do the ways that language is used in a community affect young children's participation in language arts activities in the classroom? How does it affect their learning to read and write in school?
>
> How do children's cultural backgrounds affect how they interact with the teacher?
>
> How might children be able to employ the cultural knowledge they have from their community and family in the classroom?

A second view of the relationship among the various sites of education has been community-centered, asking questions about how academic learning and participation in school affect family and community life. For example:

> How does learning to read and write in school affect children's relationships with their parents? How does it affect the organization of family life?
>
> How does the social and cultural organization of school learning affect young people's cultural identity · and participation in community life?
>
> How does academic learning in school affect young people's understanding of what counts as knowledge and what knowledge is valuable?
>
> How does schooling affect young people's and their community's use of and feelings toward different language and dialects?
>
> How does schooling contribute to cultural reproduction and to the

Heath. "What No Bedtime Story Means." 1982b.

Philips. Invisible Culture: Communication in Classroom and Community on the Warm Springs Indian Reservation. 1983.

Willett & Bloome. "Literacy, Language, School and Community: A Community-Centered View." 1993.

Gibson. Accommodation Without Assimilation: Sikh Immigrants in an American High School. 1988.

Trueba, Jacobs & Kirton. Cultural Conflict and Adaptation. 1990.

reproduction of social and economic classes?

The Spindlers' definition is also important because it focuses attention on cultural transmission, the transmission of cultural knowledge from one generation to the next. Questions can be asked about what is transmitted? When? Where? How? By whom? To whom? But questions can also be asked about the nature of education and cultural transmission. Clearly, cultural transmission does not happen just because an older generation teaches a younger one. Educational processes, both those that happen during school instruction and at other times and places, are complex and involve the active participation of both educators (whether formally defined as teachers or not) and learners (whether in the role of student, apprentice, child, newcomer, or other). What gets learned is neither an exact reproduction of what was nor is the learning completely explicit.

Harkness, Super, & Keefer. "Learning To Be An American Parent: How Cultural Models Gain Directive Force." 1992.

Although schools sometimes admit that one of their functions is to socialize students, they almost always emphasize the teaching of academics. They characterize the work they do—including their socialization efforts—as neutral, as not promoting a specific cultural ideology or bias.

Yet, a broad range of ethnographic and sociolinguistic studies has shown that overwhelmingly schools do promote a cultural bias, a bias that in the United States has sometimes been call *Eurocentric*. Although sometimes this bias can be found explicit in the content studied (e.g., studying Columbus's "discovery" of the "New World"), often the cultural bias is entrenched in the organization and nature of knowledge, the types and nature of thinking and learning promoted and allowed, and the use of language in instruction.

Ethnographic and sociolinguistic studies have been successful at revealing the nature of cultural bias in school so that it can be addressed. Studies have shown how some schools and educational programs have successfully moved toward a multicultural basis. One set of studies has focused on how schools have reorganized instruction, its content, nature, and language, to help students bring their cultural background, knowledge, and language into the classroom and how they have made such knowledge a foundation for academic learning. Another direction has been to describe educational programs whose explicit agenda has been to fight the oppression of nondominant cultural, linguistic, and economic groups.

Included in the directions described here are ethnographic studies of gender and schooling. These studies have sought to point out the inequities that women and girls often face, and the underlying cultural biases that rationalize such inequities. Part of the effort has involved unpacking taken-for-granted definitions and assumptions about gender, about the activities in which some women and girls engage (e.g., reading so-called romance novels), redefining perspectives and presenting alternatives to male-centered perspectives, and linking specific and particular events and conditions to broader cultural, social, political, and economic contexts.

Studies of educational programs involved in changing the monocultural bias of schooling are useful, but it is through attempting to change the status quo that the nature, complexity, and embeddedness of a cultural ideology is revealed.

Dei. "Afrocentricity: A Cornerstone of Pedagogy." 1994.

Au. "Participation Structures in a Reading Lesson with Hawaiian Children." 1980.

Moll & Diaz. "Teaching Writing As Communication: The Use of Ethnographic Findings in Classroom Practice." 1987.

Foster. "Sociolinguistics and the African-American Community: Implications for Literacy." 1992.

Rockhill. "Gender, Language and the Politics of Literacy." 1993.

Davies. Frogs, and Snails, and Feminist Tales: Preschool Children and Gender. 1989.

Gilbert & Taylor. Fashioning the Feminine: Girls, Popular Culture and Schooling. 1991.

Moss. Unpopular Fictions. 1989.

Lather. Getting Smart: Feminist Research and Pedagogy With/In The Postmodern. 1991.

Ernst, Statzner, & Trueba (eds.). Alternative Visions of Schooling: Success Stories in Minority Settings. 1994.

Walsh (ed.). Literacy as Praxis. 1991.

Ladson-Billings. "Reading Between the Lines and Beyond the Pages: A Culturally-Relevant Approach to Literacy Teaching." 1992.

Redefining Literacy

Understanding education as being more than schooling, as involving multiple sites, as involving cultural transmission, and as always involving a stance toward cultural ideology (monocultural or multicultural), gives a warrant for redefining many concepts related to education, such as reading, writing, and literacy. Rather than view reading, writing, and literacy as a set of decontextualized, cognitive skills, ethnographic and sociolinguistic studies define reading, writing, and literacy as social and cultural. For example, Bloome (1985) defined reading as follows:

> In addition to being a communicative process, reading is also a social process. . . . That is, reading involves social relationships among people: among teachers and students, among students, among parents and children, and among authors and readers. The social relationships involved in reading include establishing social groups and ways of interacting with others; gaining or maintaining status and social position; and acquiring culturally appropriate ways of thinking, problem-solving, valuing, and feeling. (p. 134)

In addition to focusing on social relationships, ethnographic and sociolinguistic studies have focused on literacy events (events involving or related to the use of written language) and literacy practices (culturally shared ways of using and interpreting written language in specific situations, including situations in which it is or is not appropriate to use written language). One of the findings of ethnographic and sociolinguistic studies is that there is a wide range of literacy practices and that these practices vary both

Basso. "The Ethnography of Writing." 1974.

Willinsky. The New Literacy. 1990.

Street. Literacy in Theory and Practice. 1984.

Bloome. "Reading as a Social Practice." 1985.

Bloome. "Reading as a Social Process in a Middle School Classroom." 1987.

Heath. Ways with Words. 1983.

Street (ed.). Cross-cultural Studies of Literacy. 1993.

Maybin (ed.). Language and Literacy in Social Practice. 1994.

Scollon & Scollon. Narrative, Literacy, and Face in Interethnic Communication. 1981.

Boyardin. The Ethnography of Reading. 1992.

Hamilton, Barton, & Ivanic (eds.). Worlds of Literacy. 1994.

across and within cultures. Variations in literacy practices include how to structure written text, how to interpret it, who is or may be involved in various literacy events, when to use written language, how to value it, who can use which literacy practices, when, and for what purposes. One consequence of these findings is that it is impossible to create a single list of cognitive-linguistic skills that constitute literacy. Becoming literate involves learning (and learning how to adapt) the appropriate literacy practices expected within one's community (whether that community is an ethnic group, a profession, a classroom, or other). Another consequence is to ask questions about how some literacy practices become privileged over others and how other literacy practices become so marginalized that they may not even be recognized by the people involved as literacy activities. These questions lead directly to questions about the relationship of literacy practices to the exercise of power.

Cross-cultural studies of literacy practices had led scholars to question the "Great Divide" theory. In brief, the Great Divide theory suggested that there were profound differences between preliterate and literate societies, and that these differences included education, government, economic development, ways of thinking, knowledge accumulation, and cultural organization. Similarly, some scholars had suggested that the development or acquisition of literacy has cognitive consequences (benefits) both for groups and for individuals.

A series of important ethnographic studies have shown compelling evidence that the Great Divide theory is not tenable. First, whatever consequences accrue are

Gadsden. "Giving Meaning to Literacy: Intergenerational Beliefs About Access." 1992.

Erickson. "School Literacy, Reasoning, and Civility." 1984.

Elsasser & Irvine. "English and Creole: The Dialects of Choice in a College Writing Program." 1985.

Sola & Bennett. "The Struggle for Voice: Narrative, Literacy and Consciousness in an East Harlem School." 1985.

Goody & Watt. "The Consequences of Literacy." 1968.

Ong. Orality and Literacy. 1982.

Ong. The Presence of the Word. 1967.

Graff. The Legacies of Literacy. 1987.

more a result of the cultural practices in which a person or group engages than anything inherent to literacy per se. Second, cultural groups are as likely to adapt imported literacy practices to their own cultural way of life and needs as they are likely to adapt their way of life to accommodate those literacy practices. Third, what may appear to teachers and other educators as illiterate, underliterate or uneducable communities of children and adults may be little more than the school's cultural bias. Such biases often influence how children from low-income families, from communities of color, and from communities of nondominant languages (e.g., Standard English), are evaluated and educated.

Over the last two decades, there have been an increasing number of ethnographic studies of community and family literacy practices that can give educators an understanding of the variety of literacy practices found in the diverse communities in the United States and elsewhere. These studies challenge taken-for-granted assumptions about educability, how people learn to read and write, what reading and writing mean to people, how reading and writing fit into people's lives and what people use reading and writing for. Perhaps most importantly, they have challenged the way that educators have defined reading, writing, and literacy and the cultural bias often built in reading and writing instruction.

Redefining Classroom Practice

Instructional practices are typically judged as either effective or not effective in students' achievement of academic goals. Ethnographic and sociolinguistic studies of instructional practice provide a different way to view instructional practice. Rather

Street. Literacy in Theory and Practice. 1984.

Scribner & Cole. The Psychology of Literacy. 1981.

Tierney & Rogers. "Exploring the Cognitive Consequences of Variations in the Social Fabric of Classroom Literacy Events." 1989.

Michaels. "Sharing Time: Children's Narrative Styles and Differential Access to Literacy." 1981.

Moss (ed.). Literacy Across Communities. 1994.

Taylor & Dorsey-Gaines. Growing Up Literate. 1988.

Taylor. Family Literacy. 1983.

Schieffelin & Gilmore (eds.). The Acquisition of Literacy: Ethnographic Perspectives. 1986.

Barton & Ivanic (eds.). Writing in the Community. 1991.

Reder & Wikelund. "Literacy Development and Ethnicity: An Alaskan Example." 1993.

Bloome. "Anthropology and Research on Teaching the English Language Arts." 1991.

McDermott & Hood. "Institutionalized Psychology and the Ethnography of Schooling." 1982.

that asking, "Is it effective?" the question asked is, "What is it effective at doing?" That is, ethnographers ask, "What is happening educationally? Culturally? and Socially? And how has what happened during instructional events occurred?"

One approach has been to examine how language in the classroom is used to create a cultural context (the classroom culture) and how the cultural context of the classroom influences the use of language for learning, for social interaction, and for exploring both the social and material worlds in which students live. A number of studies have examined how the language of the classroom marginalizes and alienates some students, especially students from nondominant cultural and linguistic communities. Other studies have documented variation in how language is used both within and across classrooms, providing new understandings of classroom and what their possibilities are for creating new approaches to learning.

One of the key issues to emerge from studies of language in the classroom as well as from other ethnographic and sociolinguistic studies of education is the issue of access. Some students get valued educational opportunities, whereas other students get other choices. Differential distribution of educational opportunities is not necessarily in and of itself bad. What ethnographers and sociolinguists ask is, "What is the basis on which the distribution occurs? How does it occur? And what are the social and cultural consequences of its occurrence?" Researchers have shown that access to appropriate educational opportunities is too often denied to students on the basis of their cultural or linguistic background, gender, or race.

Delamont & Galton. Inside the Secondary Classroom. 1986.

Green. "Research On Teaching as a Linguistic Process: A State of the Art." 1983.

Cazden, John, & Hymes (eds.). Functions of Language in the Classroom. 1972.

Mehan. Learning Lessons. 1979.

Edwards & Furlong. The Language of Teaching. 1978.

Cazden. Classroom Discourse. 1988.

Trueba. "English Literacy Acquisition: From Cultural Trauma to Learning Disabilities in Minority Students." 1989.

Santa Barbara Classroom Discourse Group. A special issue of Linguistics and Education. 1993.

Gilmore. "Sulking, Stepping, and Tracking: The Effects of Attitude Assessment on Access to Literacy." 1987.

Cook-Gumperz (ed.). The Social Construction of Literacy. 1986.

Foster. "Sociolinguistics and the African-American Community: Implications For Literacy." 1992.

Eder. "Differences in Communicative Styles Across Ability Groups." 1982.

Access may also be denied because the organization of instruction may inherently require access to be denied to some. For example, there have been a number of ethnographic and sociolinguistic studies of ability-grouping and tracking (also known as streaming). These studies have shown that students in the low groups and tracks are disadvantaged in many ways, and that the different groups take on their own "culture" and that students are socialized to that culture. As a result, the groups and tracks become even more rigid than they might otherwise be and students take on the identity of the group or track. Further, the organization of the groups and tracks affects social relationships both among students and between students and teachers. One of the questions asked by ethnographic and sociolinguistic research of tracking and other instructional organizations is how such organizational practices are related to the social and cultural life of the broader community. Although it is always the case that the broader social and cultural context influences classroom and school life, a number of ethnographic and sociolinguistic studies have shown how instructional organizations and what happens in schools and classrooms also help maintain and reproduce (or perhaps more accurately, reconstruct) that broader social and cultural context.

It is important to point out that teachers and other educators may not be consciously aware that access is inappropriately being denied to students or that the organization of instruction in schools and classrooms is helping to maintain a broader social context (about which they themselves may be unhappy). Ethnographic and sociolinguistic studies

Hart. "Analyzing the Social Organization for Reading in One Elementary School." 1982.

McDermott. "Social Relations as Contexts for Learning in School." 1977.

Borko & Eisenhart. "Reading Ability Groups as Literacy Communities. 1987.

Eckert. Jocks and Burnouts. 1989.

Cummins. Empowering Minority Students: A Framework for Intervention. 1986.

can be helpful in making educators aware of the ways that they might be denying access and ways in which they might recreate classroom life to benefit all students.

FINAL COMMENTS

There is often a sense of challenge in many ethnographic and sociolinguistic studies, especially studies of classrooms and schools. In part this is because ethnographic and sociolinguistic studies emphasize new and different ways to understand classroom life. The sense of challenge may also derive because ethnographic and sociolinguistic inquiry has a history of concern for educational equity in the context of cultural and linguistic diversity. Good research— whether it is ethnographic, sociolinguistic, or other—should always challenge the thinking and practice of both educators and researchers. But this sense of challenge does not need to create divisions or tensions between educators and researchers. Rather, it is a challenge that should be jointly shared and promoted.

It is important to note that ethnographic and sociolinguistic research continues to change and evolve. Once limited to the study of "foreign" cultures, ethnographic research is now prominent in the study of ourselves and our way of life. Once the exclusive domain of university-based scholars, ethnographic and sociolinguistic research is now conducted by a broad range of people—teachers, administrators, other educators, university researchers, and as shown in this book, students across the grade levels—who often work in teams. The writing up of ethnographic and sociolinguistic research

Heath & Branscombe. "'Intelligent Writing' in an Audience Community." 1986.

Corridors: Stories From Inner City Detroit. 1989

Reflections: Expressions From Inner City Detroit. 1990.

has also changed. Once limited to "scientific" and "academic" genre, a greater range of writing styles and genres is being employed, with conscious awareness that how one writes and who one writes for are as important as the conduct of the study itself. As Hymes (1981) wrote:

> Of all forms of scientific knowledge, ethnography [and sociolinguistic inquiry] is the most open, the most compatible with a democratic way of life, the least likely to produce a world in which experts control knowledge at the expense of those who are studied. (p. 57)

REFERENCES

Agar, M. (1980). *The professional stranger: An informal introduction to ethnography.* San Diego: Academic Press.

Anderson, G. (1989). Critical ethnography in education. *Review of Educational Research, 59*(3), 249-270.

Apple, M. (1982). *Education and power.* London: Routledge & Kegan Paul.

Au, K. (1980). Participation structures in a reading lesson with Hawaiian children. *Anthropology and Education Quarterly, 11,* 91-115.

Barton, D., & Ivanic, R. (Eds.). (1991). *Writing in the community.* Newbury Park, CA: Sage.

Basso, K. (1974). The ethnography of writing. In R. Bauman & J. Sherzer (Eds.), *Explorations in the ethnography of speaking* (pp. 425-432). Cambridge: Cambridge University Press.

Bauman, R., & Sherzer, J. (Eds.). (1989). *Explorations in the ethnography of speaking* (2nd ed.). Cambridge: Cambridge University Press.

Benedict, R. (1934). *Patterns of culture.* New York: Mentor.

Bloome, D. (1985). Reading as a social process. *Language Arts, 62*(2), 134-142.

Bloome, D. (1987). Reading as a social process in a middle school classroom. In D. Bloome (Ed.), *Literacy and schooling* (pp. 123-199). Norwood, NJ: Ablex.

Bloome, D. (1991). Anthropology and research on teaching the English language arts. In J. Flood, J. Jensen, D. Lapp, & J. Squires (Eds.), *Handbook of research on teaching the English language arts* (pp. 46-56). New York: Macmillan.

Borko, H., & Eisenhart, M. (1987). Reading ability groups as literacy communities. In D. Bloome (Ed.), *Classrooms and literacy* (pp. 107-134). Norwood, NJ: Ablex.

Boyarin, J. (Ed.). (1992). *The ethnography of reading.* Berkeley: University of California Press.

Brodkey, L. (1987a). *Academic writing as social practice.* Philadelphia: Temple University Press.

Brodkey, L. (1987b). Writing critical ethnographic narratives. *Anthropology & Education Quarterly, 18*, 67-76.

Brodkey, L. (1992). Articulating poststructural theory in research on literacy. In R. Beach, J. Green, M. Kamil, & T. Shanahan (Eds.), *Multidisciplinary perspectives on literacy research* (pp. 293-318). Urbana, IL: National Conference on Research in English.

Cazden, C. (1988). *Classroom discourse.* Portsmouth, NH: Heinemann.

Cazden, C., John, V., & Hymes, D. (Eds.). (1972). *Functions of language in the classroom.* New York: Teachers College Press.

Cole, J. (Ed.). (1988). *Anthropology for the nineties: Introductory readings.* New York: The Free Press.

Cook-Gumperz, J. (Ed.). (1986). *The social construction of literacy.* Cambridge: Cambridge University Press.

Cummins, J. (1986). Empowering minority students: A framework for intervention. *Harvard Educational Review, 56*, 18-36.

Davies, B. (1989). *Frogs, and snails, and feminist tales: Preschool children and gender.* Sydney, Australia: Allen & Unwin.

Davies, B. (1993). *Shards of glass: Children reading & writing beyond gendered identities.* Cresskill, NJ: Hampton Press.

Dei, G. (1994). Afrocentricity: A cornerstone of pedagogy. *Anthropology and Education Quarterly, 25*(1), 3-28.

Delamont, S., & Galton, M. (1986). *Inside the secondary classroom.* London: Routledge & Kegan Paul.

Du Bois, W.E.B. (1989). *The Philadelphia negro.* Philadelphia: University of Pennsylvania Press. (Original work published 1899).

Eckert, P. (1989). *Jocks and burnouts: Social categories and identity in the high school.* New York: Teachers College Press.

Eder, D. (1982). Differences in communicative styles across ability groups. In L. Wilkinson (Ed.), *Communicating in the classroom* (pp. 245-264). New York: Academic Press.

Edwards, A., & Furlong, V. (1978). *The language of teaching.* London: Heinemann.

Elsasser, N., & Irvine, P. (1985). English and creole: The dialects of choice in a college writing program. *Harvard Educational Review, 55*(4), 399-415.

Erickson, F. (1984). School literacy, reasoning and civility: An anthropologist's perspective. *Review of Educational Research, 54*(4), 525-546.

Ernst, G., Statzner, E., & Trueba, H. (Eds.). (1994). Alternative visions of schooling: Success stories in minority settings [special issue]. *Anthropology and Education Quarterly, 25*(4), 199-393.

Everhart, R.B. (1983). *Reading, writing, and resistance: Adolescence and labor in a junior high school.* Boston: Routledge & Kegan Paul.

Fairclough, N. (Ed.). (1992a). *Critical language awareness*. London: Longman.

Fairclough, N. (1992b). *Discourse and social change*. Cambridge: Polity Press.

Ferguson, C., & Heath, S. (Eds.). (1981). *Language in the USA*. Cambridge: Cambridge University Press.

Fine, M. (1991). *Framing dropouts*. Albany, NY: SUNY Press.

Firth, R. (1936). *We, the Tikopia*. Boston: Beacon Press.

Foster, M. (1992). Sociolinguistics and the African-American community: Implications for literacy. *Theory Into Practice, 31*(4), 303-311.

Foucault, M. (1972). *The archaeology of knowledge*. London: Tavistock.

Gadsden V. (1992). Giving meaning to literacy: Intergenerational beliefs about access. *Theory Into Practice, 31*(4), 328-336.

Garcia, O. (Ed.). (1991). *Bilingual education*. Philadelphia: John Benjamins.

Geertz, C. (1973). *The interpretation of culture*. New York: Basic Books.

Geertz, C. (1983). *Local knowledge*. New York: Basic Books.

Gibson, M. (1988). *Accommodation without assimilation: Sikh immigrants in an American high school*. Ithaca, NY: Cornell University Press.

Gilbert, P. (1989). *Gender, literacy and the classroom*. Carlton South, Victoria: Australian Reading Association.

Gilbert, P., & Taylor, S. (1991). *Fashioning the feminine: Girls, popular culture and schooling*. North Sydney, Australia: Allen & Unwin.

Gilmore, P. (1987). Sulking, stepping, and tracking: The effects of attitude assessment on access to literacy. In D. Bloome (Ed.), *Literacy and schooling* (pp. 98-120). Norwood, NJ: Ablex.

Giroux, H. (1981). *Ideology, culture and the process of schooling*. Philadelphia: Temple University Press.

Giroux, H. (1983). *Theory and resistance in education*. S. Hadley, MA: Bergin & Garvey.

Goodenough, W. (1981). *Culture, language, and society*. Menlo Park, CA: Cummings.

Goody, J., & Watt, I. (1968) The consequences of literacy. In J. Goody (Ed.), *Literacy in traditional societies* (pp. 27-68). Cambridge: Cambridge University Press.

Graddol, D., Maybin, J., & Stierer, B. (Eds.). (1994). *Researching language and literacy in social contexts*. Clevedon, England: Multilingual Matters.

Graff, H. (1987). *The legacies of literacy: Continuities and contradictions in western culture and society*. Bloomington: University of Indiana Press.

Green, J. (1983). Research on teaching as a linguistic process: A state of the art. In E. Gordon (Ed.), *Review of research in education* (Vol. 10, pp. 152-252). Washington, DC: American Educational Research Association.

Green, J., & Wallat, C. (Eds.). (1981). *Ethnography and language in educational settings*. Norwood, NJ: Ablex.

Grillo, R. (1989). *Dominant languages: Language and hierarchy in Britain and France*. Cambridge: Cambridge University Press.

Gumperz, J. (1982a). *Discourse strategies*. Cambridge: Cambridge University Press.

Gumperz, J. (Ed.). (1982b). *Language and social identity*. Cambridge: Cambridge University Press.

Gumperz, J., & Hymes, D. (Eds.). (1972). *Directions in sociolinguistics: The ethnography of communication*. New York: Holt, Rinehart & Winston.

Hamilton, M., Barton, D., & Ivanic, R. (Eds.). (1994). *Worlds of literacy*. Clevedon, England: Multilingual Matters.

Hammersly, M. (1990). *Reading ethnographic research*. Harlow: Longman.

Hammersly, M. & Atkinson, P. (1983). *Ethnography: Principles and practices*. London: Routledge.

Hammersly, M., & Woods, P. (Eds.). (1984). *Life in school: The sociology of pupil culture*. Milton Keynes: Open University Press.

Hargreaves, A., & Woods, P. (Eds.). (1984). *Classrooms & staffrooms: The sociology of teachers and teaching*. Milton Keynes: Open University Press.

Harkness, S., Super, C., & Keefer, C. (1992). Learning to be an American parent: How culture models gain directive force. In R. D'Andrade & C. Strauss (Eds.), *Human motives and cultural models* (pp. 163-178). New York: Cambridge University Press.

Hart, S. (1982). Analyzing the social organization for reading in one elementary school. In G. Spindler (Ed.), *Doing the ethnography of schooling* (pp. 410-439). New York: Holt, Rinehart & Winston.

Heath, S. (1982a). Ethnography in education: Defining the essentials. In P. Gilmore & A. Glatthorn (Eds.), *Children in and out of school* (pp. 33-58). Washington, DC: Center for Applied Linguistics.

Heath, S. (1982b). What no bedtime story means: Narrative skills at home and school. *Language in Society, 11*, 49-76.

Heath, S. (1983). *Ways with words*. Cambridge: Cambridge University Press.

Heath, S., & Branscombe, A. (1986). "Intelligent writing" in an audience community: Teacher, student and researcher. In S. Freedman (Ed.), *The acquisition of written language: Response and revision* (pp. 16-34). Norwood, NJ: Ablex.

Holland, D., & Quinn, N. (Eds.). (1987). *Cultural models in language and thought*. New York: Cambridge University Press.

Hymes, D. (1974). *Foundations of sociolinguistics: The ethnography of communication*. Philadelphia: University of Pennsylvania Press.

Hymes, D. (1981). Ethnographic monitoring. In H. Trueba, G. Guthrie, & K. Au (Eds.), *Culture and the bilingual classroom: Studies in classroom ethnography.* Rowley, MA: Newbury House.

Hymes, D. (1982). What is ethnography? In P. Gilmore & A. Glatthorn (Eds.), *Children in and out of school* (pp. 21-32). Washington, DC: Center for Applied Linguistics.

Jones, D. (1988). Towards a native anthropology. In J. Cole (Ed.), *Anthropology for the nineties: Introductory readings.* New York: The Free Press.

Labov, W. (1972a). *Language in the inner city.* Philadelphia: University of Pennsylvania Press.

Labov, W. (1972b). *Sociolinguistic patterns.* Philadelphia: University of Pennsylvania Press.

Ladson-Billings, G. (1992). Reading between the lines and beyond the pages: A culturally-relevant approach to literacy teaching. *Theory Into Practice, 31*(4), 312-320.

Lather, P. (1991). *Getting smart: Feminist research and pedagogy with/in the postmodern.* New York: Routledge.

Malinowski, B. (1961). *Argonauts of the western Pacific.* New York: Dutton. (Original work published 1932)

Maybin, J. (Ed.). (1994). *Language and literacy in social practice.* Clevedon, England: Multilingual Matters.

McDermott, R. (1977). Social relations as contexts for learning. *Harvard Educational Review, 47*(2), 198-213.

McDermott, R., & Hood, L. (1982). Institutionalized psychology and the ethnography of schooling. In P. Gilmore & A. Glatthorn (Eds.), *Children in and out of school* (pp. 232-249). Washington, DC: Center for Applied Linguistics.

McLaren, P. (1986). *Schooling as a ritual performance.* London: Routledge & Kegan Paul.

Mead, M. (1961). *Coming of age in Samoa: A psychological study of primitive youth for western civilization.* New York: Morrow.

Mehan, H. (1979). *Learning lessons.* Cambridge, MA: Harvard University Press.

Michaels, S. (1981). "Sharing time": Children's narrative styles and differential access to literacy. *Language In Society, 10*(3), 423-442.

Moll, L., & Diaz, R. (1987). Teaching writing as communication: The use of ethnographic findings in classroom practice. In D. Bloome (Ed.), *Literacy and schooling* (pp. 193-221). Norwood, NJ: Ablex.

Montgomery, M. (1986). *An introduction to language and society.* London: Methuen.

Moss, B. (Ed.). (1994). *Literacy across communities.* Cresskill, NJ: Hampton Press.

Moss, G. (1989). *Unpopular fictions.* London: Virago.

Newsum, H.E. (1990). *Class, language & education: Class struggle and sociolinguistics in an African situation.* Trenton, NJ: Africa World Press.

Ogbu, J. (1979). *Minority education and caste.* New York: Academic Press.

Ong, W. (1967). *The presence of the word.* New Haven, CT: Yale University Press.

Ong, W. (1982). *Orality and literacy: The technologizing of the word.* London: Methuen.

Peacock, J. (1988). *The anthropological lens: Harsh light, soft focus.* Cambridge: Cambridge University Press.

Philips, S. (1983). *Invisible culture: Communication in classroom and community on the Warm Springs Indian Reservation.* New York: Longman.

Reder, S., & Wikelund, K. (1993). Literacy development and ethnicity: An Alaskan example. In B. Street (Ed.), *Cross-cultural approaches to literacy* (pp. 176-197). Cambridge: Cambridge University Press.

Rockhill, K. (1993). Gender, language and the politics of literacy. In B. Street (ed.), *Cross-cultural approaches to literacy* (pp. 156-174). Cambridge: Cambridge University Press.

Santa Barbara Classroom Discourse Group. (1993). *Linguistics and Education: An International Research Journal* [Special issue]. 5(3 & 4), 231-410.

Sapir, E. (1970). *Language, culture and personality: Selected essays* (D.G. Mandelbaum, Ed.). Berkeley: University of California Press.

Saravia-Shore, M., & Arvizu, S. (Eds.). (1992). *Cross-cultural literacy: Ethnographies of communication in multiethnic classrooms.* New York: Garland.

Saville-Troike, M. (1982). *The ethnography of communication: An introduction.* Oxford: Basil Blackwell.

Schieffelin, B., & Gilmore, P. (Eds.). (1986). *The acquisition of literacy: Ethnographic perspectives.* Norwood, NJ: Ablex.

Schieffelin, B., & Ochs, E. (Eds.). (1986). *Language socialization across cultures.* Cambridge: Cambridge University Press.

Scollon, R., & Scollon, S. (1981). *Narrative, literacy and face in interethnic communication.* Norwood, NJ: Ablex.

Scribner S., & Cole, M. (1981). *The psychology of literacy.* Cambridge, MA: Harvard University Press.

Shultz, J., Erickson, F., & Florio, S. (1982). Where's the floor? Aspects of the cultural organization of social relationships in communication at home and in school. In P. Gilmore & A. Glatthorn (Eds.), *Children in and out of school* (pp. 88-123). Washington, DC: Center for Applied Linguistics.

Shuman, A. (1986). *Storytelling rights: The uses of oral and written texts by urban adolescents.* Cambridge: Cambridge University Press.

Smitherman, G. (1981). "What go round come round": King in perspective. *Harvard Educational Review, 51*(1), 40-56.

Smitherman, G. (1977). *Talkin' and testifyin': The language of Black America.* Boston: Houghton-Mifflin.

Sola, M., & Bennett, A. (1985). The struggle for voice: Narrative, literacy and consciousness in an East Harlem school. *Journal of Education, 167*(1), 88-110.

Solomon, P. (1988). *The signs of our time: The secret meanings of everyday life.*

Solsken, J. (1993). *Schools, literacy, gender and work in families and in school.* Norwood, NJ: Ablex.

Spindler G., & Spindler, L. (Eds.). (1987a). *Interpretive ethnography of education at home and abroad.* Hillsdale, NJ Erlbaum.

Spindler, G., & Spindler, L. (1987b). Issues and applications in ethnographic methods. In G. Spindler & L. Spindler (Eds.), *Interpretive ethnography of eduction at home and abroad* (pp. 1-10). Hillsdale, NJ: Erlbaum.

Street, B. (1984). *Literacy in theory and practice.* Cambridge: Cambridge University Press.

Street, B. (Ed.). (1993). *Cross-cultural studies of literacy.* Cambridge: Cambridge University Press.

Stubbs, M., & Hillier, H. (Eds.). (1983). *Readings on language, schools and classrooms.* London: Methuen.

Tannen, D. (1989). *Talking voices.* Cambridge: Cambridge University Press.

Taylor, D. (1983). *Family literacy.* Exeter, NH: Heinemann.

Taylor, D., & Dorsey-Gaines, C. (1988). *Growing up literate: Learning from inner-city families.* Portsmouth, NH: Heinemann.

Tierney, R., & Rogers, T. (1989). Exploring the cognitive consequences of variations in the social fabric of classroom literacy events. In D. Bloome (Ed.), *Classrooms and literacy* (pp. 250-263). Norwood, NJ: Ablex.

Trudgill, P. (1975). *Accent, dialect and the school.* London: Edward Arnold.

Trueba, H. (1989). English literacy acquisition: From cultural trauma to learning disabilities in minority students. *Linguistics and Education, 1*(2), 125-152.

Trueba, H. Jacobs, L., & Kirton, E. (1990). *Cultural conflict and adaptation: The case of Hmong children in American society.* London: The Falmer Press.

Varenne, H. (1977). *Americans together.* New York: Teachers College Press.

Walsh, C. (Ed.). (1991). *Literacy as praxis*. Norwood, NJ: Ablex.

Weedon, C. (1987). *Feminist practice and poststructural theory*. Oxford: Blackwell.

Whiting, B., & Edwards, C. (1988). *Children of different worlds*. Cambridge, MA: Harvard University Press.

Willinsky, J. (1990). *The new literacy: Redefining reading and writing in the schools*. New York: Routledge.

Willis, P. (1977). *Learning to Labour*. Aldershot, England: Gower.

Willett, J., & Bloome, D. (1993). Literacy, language, school and community: A community-centered view. In A. Carrasquillo & C. Hedley (Eds.), *Whole language and the bilingual learner* (pp. 35-60). Norwood, NJ: Ablex.

Wolcott, H.F. (1987). On ethnographic intent. In G. Spindler & L. Spindler (Eds.), *Interpretive ethnography of eduction at home and abroad* (pp. 37-60). Hillsdale, NJ: Erlbaum.

Wolfram, W., & Christian, D. (1989). *Dialects and education: Issues and answers*. Englewood Cliffs, NJ: Prentice-Hall.

Zaharlick, A., & Green, J. (1991). Ethnographic research. In J. Flood, J. Jensen, D. Lapp, & J. Squire (Eds.), *Handbook of research on teaching the English language arts* (pp. 205-225). New York: Macmillan.

Section I

Community as Curriculum: Focus on Culture, Writing, and Academic Learning

The chapters in this section highlight the integration of students as researchers of culture and language in their own communities with concerns for academic learning.

In the first chapter, Curry and Bloome describe a project in which students learned to conduct ethnographic inquiry of their own communities as a way to improve their academic writing. Their observations of previous student writing revealed that students primarily engaged in text reproduction—reproducing the texts of "authoritative" sources such as textbooks, encyclopedias, and teachers. Students engaged in little reflection on the knowledge they were reproducing and they did not employ the knowledge they had or that was in their communities to help them compose their academic writing or to challenge authoritative knowledge. By learning to write ethnographic reports of their own communities, the students had to define their families and communities as sources of knowledge that could be employed in academic learning. One of the components of the project Curry and Bloome implemented was to help students synthesize the academic knowledge learned at school with the knowledge that students could find in their communities.

The chapters by Torres and Mercado should be read as complementary chapters. Torres and Mercado worked together in planning, discussing, implementing, and researching the student ethnography project—one model of how educators in K-12 classrooms and educators based at universities can collaborate as co-researchers. Their chapters focus on different dimensions. Torres describes how the student ethnographic research created a new set of connections among students, parents, and teacher. Like the work reported by Curry and Bloome, the students came to view their parents and their communities as sources of knowledge, pertinent both to community life and to academic learning. The chapter by Torres also raises themes picked up later in the book by Egan-Robertson—how ethnographic inquiry and writing can be used to fight the alienation that so many young people feel from school and even from their families and communities. The chapter by Mercado shows how this same project engaged students in the use of a broad range of genres of writing. Although students did have to pay some formal attention to the features of the genres they were using, they learned the various genres and their features by using them for the real purposes involved in ethnographic inquiry. But as important, the students also became writers, people who saw writing and inquiry as part of their identity.

The question of identity is picked up in the chapter by Andrade, who is concerned about how teachers and researchers view their students, how students get defined both in classrooms and in professional articles and books. Her concern is an important one because it is a fundamental assumption of ethnographic inquiry that great caution should be exercised in how the people being studied are defined and how their behavior is interpreted. Yet, there has been little attention to the ways in which students in our own classrooms get defined. Part of what Andrade proposes is both a perspective on dialogue journal writing and a way of interpreting of reading student writing based on principles of ethnographic research.

The last chapter in this part is written by a classroom teacher-researcher (Yeager) and two university-based researchers (Floriani and Green), who are part of a larger group of classroom teacher-researchers and university-based researchers called the Santa Barbara Classroom Discourse Group. In this chapter, the three educator-researchers join with student-researchers in exploring the nature of the classroom community and the nature of the academic communities that are the focus of the curriculum (e.g., historians, scientists, anthropologists). As part of this inquiry, the educators and the students are constantly engaged in critically examining the language and languages that are being used both in the classroom and in the academic disciplines they are studying. One focus of attention is how language influences the nature and generation of knowledge, and how students can gain access to the language they need to engage in the various social and academic activities in the classroom. The chapter by Yeager, Floriani, and Green provides an important complement to the earlier chapters by Curry and Bloome, Torres, and Mercado with regard to how "community" is defined. Students (and educators) live in many "communities" including their home and neighborhood communities, their ethnic and religious communities, as well as their classroom and academic communities. Yeager, Floriani, and Gree view the students as new or initiate members of the various disciplinary communities that make up the academic curriculum. In so doing, the students' ethnographic inquiry provides them with a systematic understanding of the "culture" of these disciplinary communities and encourages them to see academic disciplines as made up of people, rather than as inert bodies of knowledge. As importantly, the students reposition themselves as members—albeit new or novice members—of these academic communities.

2
Learning to Write by Writing Ethnography*

Toby Curry
Detroit Public School System
David Bloome
Vanderbilt University

Midway School (pseudonym) is a K-8 school in the heart of a major urban area in Michigan. Like many urban schools, it serves an ethnically and linguistically diverse population. But in many ways, Midway School is different. Threatened with being closed by a school board short of funds, parents in the local neighborhood rallied to support the school, proposing it become a part-magnet school and part-neighborhood school, emphasizing linguistic, cultural, and economic diversity—an "international" school. The parents succeeded.

Outside of Midway School is a large mural, three stories tall, painted by a local artist. The mural shows a large tree on whose branches sit children of different races and cultures. Inside, the main corridor is draped by flags from around the world. In other corridors, hanging on the walls are hand-drawn pictures of students, each with the country of their origin or heritage—Nigeria, India, Nepal, China, the United States, among others. The staff is also diverse: African-American, Chinese, Chinese-American, Filipino, Irish-American, Jewish, other White European-American backgrounds, among other backgrounds.

We began to work together because we were both interested in new ways of promoting reading and writing development. At the time, most educators, teacher educators, and educational researchers saw

*The research reported in this chapter was supported, in part, by an Elva Knight Research Grant from the International Reading Association. However, the statements and opinions expressed here do not necessarily reflect the policies or opinions of the International Reading Association.

diversity as a problem. We saw it as a potential resource and as a joy. Toby was experimenting with whole language, probing what it had to offer, and trying out adaptations of various activities and approaches. Dave was trying to better understand the diverse ways people had of reading and writing, and thought there was much to learn from what Midway School was already doing. We began working together each thinking there was much to learn from the other, but each doubting we had much to offer

Dave spent the first year studying the diverse ways that reading and writing were used in the many ethnic communities from which students came to Midway School and he spent a lot of time sitting in the back of Toby's classroom, helping out when he could.[1] From the community study, we learned that the issues raised in previous studies of diversity did not always make sense in the Midway communities. Although there was great diversity in the ways people used reading and writing and the family histories in which reading and writing were embedded, mismatch between ways of reading, writing, and languaging across home and school settings was not a pertinent issue. Although each family viewed schooling, reading, and writing in slightly different ways, they did not expect school to be like home or community. Based on their own historical experience and cultural understanding of schooling and of how to learn academics, each family found ways to support their children's school learning. For many families—especially immigrant families and non-White non-middle-class families—supporting their children's school learning was difficult and in some cases painful. In one family, the children refused to speak to their parents in Chinese although the parents knew very little English. Yet, their father worked double shifts at low-paying jobs while their mother worked full time at another low-paying job whose hours allowed her to supervise the doing of homework and to take the children regularly to the library during the few free hours she had. In another family, a single mother worked at a day-care center while an older brother cut back on his own education and activities to care for the younger children. When the mother came home, she then supervised their homework, limiting play until after homework was completed, carefully monitoring who the children played with and what trouble they might be in danger of getting into. Despite difficulties, pain, and frequent exhaustion, no parent complained about the work or sacrifice involved in supporting their children's school learning. (See Bloome, 1989, for a partial report of the findings of the community study.)

At the same time as the community study was occurring, the experiments with whole-language activities were often frustrating. The

---

[1]Lin Wong and Sylvia Twymon were co-researchers in the study of reading and writing in the community and school.

educational goals Toby had for learning, thinking, reading, and writing were not shared by enough of the students and some of them tried to subvert the intent of an activity. Activities that were intended to build on student knowledge and to help students develop confidence and see themselves as sources of knowledge and competence were sometimes undercut by students who constructed themselves as unknowledgeable, passive, and as having little to contribute. (See Bloome, 1989, for a description of how a group of students in the class constructed themselves as unknowledgeable and unable to complete a brainstorming task.)

One activity, which is still painful for us to describe, captures our frustration. Each year the school chose a region of the world on which to focus. During the first year of our study, South Asia was the chosen area. In early spring, Toby began a unit on the South Asian countries. She placed the names of various South Asian countries in a bowl and students blindly selected one. There were several reasons Toby chose to organize the study of South Asia in this way. For most of the year, she had been guiding students on how to research a topic and write a report. She also wanted students to focus on different topics, so that they could investigate a topic in depth and so that they could learn from each other. After the students had chosen their topic/country, Toby conducted several lessons in which she and the students discussed how to go about researching their topic/country, how to identify a particular subtopic, theme, or issue on which to focus, how to locate resources, and how to write up the report (with several drafts, peer review, revision, etc.). She repeatedly emphasized using each other and their own families as resources; after all several of the students in the class and many students in the school had come from the very countries they were studying. As chance would have it, one of the students from India picked India as his topic/country. He had attended primary school there, learning Hindi Punjabi, and English. He had attended Midway School for a few years and he was a very capable student. In his home there were many books on India, and his family—mother, father, aunt—could have provided a great deal of information for his report. Yet, his report was mainly copied from an out-of-date *World Book Encyclopedia* that contained information he knew was wrong (the edition he used was so old that it did not have Bangladesh as a separate country)—but he included that out-of-date and wrong information anyway. It was not just that the information was wrong and out of date; Toby had literally begged him to write a personal narrative about what it was like growing up in India, but instead he conducted his investigation and report as if he knew nothing about the topic and that the only legitimate sources of knowledge were textbooks, encyclopedias, and the like. He was not the only student to do so.

Based on our observations of classroom activities and our concerns about students' school reading and writing (including how their school academics affected their family life), we developed some concepts that helped us understand what was happening or might be in the classroom. The first concept was *procedural display*. Dave (along with Pamela Puro and Erine Theodorou) had generated this concept from his earlier ethnographic studies of learning to read in a junior high school (see Bloome, Puro, & Theodorou, 1989). Formally defined, procedural display is

> (a) the display by teacher and students, to each other, of a set of academic and interactional procedures that themselves count as the accomplishment of a lesson, and (b) the enactment of a lesson is not necessarily related to the acquisition of intended academic or nonacademic content or skills but is related to the set of cultural meanings and values held by the local education community for classroom education. (p. 272)

Although the metaphor is not perfect, procedural display can be compared to a group of actors who know how to perform their parts in a play, know their lines and how and when to say them, but who may have little or no understanding of the substantive meaning or significance of the play.

The concept of procedural display was helpful in two ways. First, it helped us better understand students' orientation to classroom lessons. It was not that they were resistant to Toby's lessons; Toby's classes were an overwhelming favorite of almost all the students. Indeed, the students were actively cooperating in making the lessons go smoothly. We were all "actors" performing "classroom lessons." It would be wrong to suggest that the students had not been learning anything; they had. But the kinds of things we wanted them to learn—to see themselves, their families, their communities, and each other as sources of knowledge, to be critical of the knowledge they find in "authoritative" sources, to view knowledge as created and constructed rather than as given, and to see themselves as creators of knowledge—required moving beyond procedural display.

There is a warning in the concept of procedural display that is important to heed. Classroom education is a cultural activity. If the activities that occur in a classroom do not take the cultural forms that teachers, students, and parents can identify as "academic learning" then what occurs in the classroom is liable to be dismissed as unimportant or worse. For example, the year after the project was completed, Toby had a parent who could not understand her teaching practice tell her that, "I don't call what you do teaching." With the student's journal, learning log, and reading folder in hand, Toby went to her administrator and informed her that she would not confer with the parent without an administrator present. The following school year (when the student had moved on to another teacher), this same parent became one of Toby's biggest advocates, but only after months of reflection and a critical look at his son's then dismal performance in a traditional skills-based middle school classroom.

However, acknowledging that classroom lessons involve culturally driven sets of expectations does not mean that we are limited to the traditional cultural forms of activity already taken as academic learning. We can all—teachers, students, parents, researchers—learn to critique our assumptions about what should go on in a classroom. Nonetheless, it is dangerous to assume that anyone can unilaterally change cultural assumptions about classroom academic learning without risking students and parents viewing the changes as eschewing academic learning. Thus, when students copied out of authoritative texts and failed to be creative, insightful, or to heed Toby's recommendations to use each other, their families, and other sources of knowledge, their behavior needed to be viewed not as resistance or as an inability to be creative or insightful, but rather as cooperative behavior in maintaining what they held as the classroom culture (in a general sense) and as what they held as cultural forms of activity that represent academic learning and academic achievement within that classroom culture.

The second concept that was helpful in reflecting on what was happening in the classroom was *text reproduction* versus *text production*. Text reproduction is, as its name suggests, the reproduction of a text. Text reproduction includes writing down oral language (e.g., writing down what the teacher says), copying in writing what is written elsewhere (e.g., copying from an encyclopedia), orally rendering a written text (e.g., reading aloud from a textbook), and orally copying what has been said before (e.g., repeating a comment made by a friend). Text production is a creation of a new text. A new text may be an original text or it may include original text and bits of extant texts, indeed it may be totally made up of bits of extant texts. But its composition as a text is nonetheless new and recognized as new by both the person producing the text (e.g., the student) and the audience (e.g., peers, the teacher).

It is wrong to think of text reproduction and text production as cognitive processes. Although both may involve complex cognitive processes, the cognitive processes involved in, say, text reproduction in one situation may be very different from the cognitive processes involved in text reproduction in another situation. Indeed, the cognitive processes involved in a particular text reproduction activity might be very complex or less so. Rather than thinking of text reproduction and text production as cognitive processes, they are better viewed as sociocultural and linguistic processes. Text reproduction and text production are ways of structuring and signaling social relationships among people through the use of language. In copying from the encyclopedia, the student was doing what he thought was appropriate to his social status as student and to the teacher's social status. He was signaling his role and structuring his relationship to the teacher, who was supposed to review the information he copied and determine if he got the right information on the paper. In addition, he was enacting what he thought he was supposed to do in the lesson, which as we just discussed, can be viewed as a cultural activity. Thus, text reproduction and text production are ways of structuring social relationships and ways of enacting various cultural activities (in this case, cultural activities related to classroom education)

We recognized that too many students were engaging in text reproduction when we were trying to restructure the activity to promote text production. Student text reproduction was evident in numerous and often humorous samples of student writing. For example, a regular weekly assignment for all students was to find a current event of interest in the newspaper and summarize and respond to it in writing. Dave was reading and responding to the students' current events writing the semester that one student, who was from Korea, turned in a current events picture of the Queen of England accompanied by text from an adjacent article about the Rolling Stones rock band.[2] Toby later revised the current events requirement to consist of only an opinion paragraph instead of a summary statement, but it was these glaring examples of text reproduction that helped us evaluate the learning experiences in which her students were engaged.

Promoting text production is not a matter of engaging students in more complex cognitive processes (although that might occur) and it is not a matter of blindly following a whole language dogma. Rather, whole language had provided us with a broader vision of education and the role that reading and writing could play in that broader vision. We wanted to change the social relationships, cultural activities, and intellectual stances that students were implicitly learning because those social relationships, cultural activities, and intellectual stances were incompatible with our views of knowledge, relationship of schools to communities and families, and cultural and linguistic diversity as an educational resource and joy. Becoming more explicit about what we wanted and the various social and cultural issues involved was very helpful in moving forward, in helping us set a direction.

---

[2]The student's juxtaposition of the picture with the text was not related to either language differences or academic skill. The student had good command of both oral and written English.

GOALS OF THE PROJECT

We called the instructional project we developed, "Learning to Write by Writing Ethnography." It had three main goals: (a) legitimize community knowledge; (b) acquire an ethnographic framework with regard to knowledge, learning, and writing, and (c) apply an ethnographic frame to academic writing. When we started the project, we were aware of efforts similar to ours; for example, the Foxfire Projects (Wiggington, 1975), Robinson and Stock (1990), and Heath and Branscombe (1985), among others. But our goals differed from theirs. Although we were interested in students getting to know and understand their communities better, our primary interest was in moving students from text reproduction to text production, in changing the social relationships involved in academic writing in the classroom. Thus, for us, ethnographic study and writing about their own communities was only one step that we hoped would take the class (the students and both of us) beyond text reproduction as the dominant definition of writing and reading in their classroom education.

We began the project in late fall of the second year of the study. We planned for Dave to take over the class for a 2-week period. Although the students knew him, we thought that the students might view the changes we were introducing as more legitimate because he was an outsider and from the university. We also thought that we would get better data and interpretations of student behavior if Toby was the participant observer and researcher as she had better knowledge of the students and their families. After we ran the project the first time, we made some adjustments and ran it again the second semester with another group of students. The second time we stretched out the project and it ran for more than 2 months. The description of the project given here is based on both runs of the project.

At the time, we were concerned about showing whether the project would indeed improve students' academic writing. So with each run of the project we conducted a pretest and a posttest. We know that pretests and posttests are far from perfect, and indeed we are distrustful of them. But at the same time, we knew that despite all the other data we had collected, there are some educators, administrators, and researchers who are more willing to credit results from an imperfect pretest/posttest report than from qualitative analysis of "natural" data. But we want to emphasize that we were less concerned with proving success to others than we were with developing for ourselves and for the students new ways of approaching and defining writing, reading, knowledge, and learning.

About the Students. There were 40 seventh-grade students in Toby's class, about 50% African American, 15% white, and the rest from a broad range of countries including Nigeria, Nicaragua, China, Korea, India, Hong Kong, the Philippines, and others. Most of the students had previously spent at least several years at Midway School; about 50% lived within walking distance. The students came from a broad range of socioeconomic backgrounds: A few students came from middle-class families, whereas most came from working-class families and some came from families having extremely difficult economic circumstances. Family configurations were diverse and included two parent nuclear families, extended families, single-parent families, students living with relatives. In summary, the students were demographically little different from the overall population of the city with the exception that a larger number of students were born outside the United States and did not speak English as their native language.

THE STRUCTURE OF "LEARNING TO WRITE BY WRITING ETHNOGRAPHY"

As previously mentioned, there were three broad goals: (a) legitimize community knowledge in the classroom; (b) have students acquire an ethnographic framework with regard to knowledge, learning, and writing; and (c) apply an ethnographic framework to academic writing. Table 2.1 shows the subgoals we had within each major goal.

The structure of the project generally followed the goals and subgoals as they are laid out in Table 2.1. We began by focusing on Identifying Community, then engaged the students in a series of ethnographic and cross-cultural projects and reports that were intended to help them acquire an ethnographic framework, and then emphasized applying the strategies and insights they had learned to academic (school) writing.

It is important to note that we also borrowed ideas from several other instructional models. From discussions of writing instruction, we borrowed ideas for having students plan their writing, use peers for help in planning and revising, and share their writing with others. We did not require students to transform each rough draft into a final draft but at appropriate points asked them to choose which drafts they wanted to develop into final papers. From the cognitively oriented curriculum developed by teachers in another school in the city (McClendon 1986),[3] we borrowed strategies for students developing plans for their learning activities and for evaluating and reflecting on the success of their plans and

---

[3]The cognitively oriented curriculum developed by Judith McClendon and her colleagues was based on a curriculum model originally developed at the High/Scope Educational Research Foundation (Hsu, 1977).

Table 2.1 Goals and Subgoals.

Goal 1: Legitimize Community Knowledge in the Classroom

    1.1 Identify Community
    1.2 Locate Sources of Knowledge Within the Community
    1.3 Make Explicit Community Knowledge

Goal 2: Acquire an Ethnographic Framework With Regard to Knowledge, Learning, and Writing

    2.1 Dimensions of the Ethnographic Frame We Wanted to Emphasize:
        Emic and Etic Perspectives
        Generic and Particularistic Knowledge
        Commonalties and Differences Within and Across Communities
        Abductive and Analogic Reasoning
        Continuity and Change
    2.2 Types of Writing We Wanted to Emphasize:
        Process/Procedures
        Use of Planning, Drafting, Reflecting, Consulting With Peers and
          Others
        Student Self-Evaluation of Writing Processes
        Genres
        Ethnographic Reports
        Cross-cultural Reports

Goal 3: Apply Ethnographic Framework to Academic Writing

    3.1 Orientation to Academic (School) Topics We Wanted to
        Emphasize:
        Automatic Activation of Ethnographic Framework When Presented
          With an Academic Topic
        Automatic Seeking of Knowledge in One's Community (or in a
          Community to Which One has Access) Related to an Academic
          Topic Being Considered
    3.2 Academic Writing That Includes Analysis of the Academic Topic in
        Terms of Community Knowledge via an Ethnographic Framework

activities. And, from synectics (cf. Gordon, 1961, cited in Joyce & Weil, 1972), we borrowed strategies for incorporating creativity and the use of metaphor in problem solving and in writing.

In the next three sections, we give a brief narrative of what happened with some samples of student writing. The three sections are organized by the goals we had: legitimizing community knowledge, acquiring an ethnographic frame, and applying an ethnographic frame to academic writing. Before we began the project, we told the students a little about what we were going to do. We sent home permission slips so that we could audiotape and videotape the classroom. We gave each student a wire-bound notebook and informed them that we would be keeping the notebooks at the end of the project. We gave them a writing pretest. One group wrote a pretest essay on "pollution," another group on "endangered species." Both topics had been studied in school as part of their science education, and the first topic had special relevance for the students (which is discussed later).

Legitimizing Community Knowledge

We began by discussing the concept of *community*, how it was the same as or differed from concepts like *neighborhood* and *family*. Students were asked to write their own definition of community, share it with a peer who was to write comments on the definition given. We asked the students to draw two "representational maps" of their community. The first was like a traditional map with the places they considered to be in their community. T's map (Figure 2.1) is typical. The second map was a series of concentric circles in which they were to place the people, events, and places they considered more central to their community in the center and to place less important things at appropriate distances from the center. K's map (Figure 2.2) is typical with regard to the types and number of items included. Identifying their community and separating the concept of community from neighborhood and family was a difficult task for almost all the students. We had not anticipated how difficult the task would be and had to spend several days working on it. Of course, the concept of community is a difficult one not only for seventh-grade students but for anthropologists, too. There are many definitions of community, and distinctions among similar terms are sometimes subtle and abstract.

We did not try to force the students into any one definition of community but rather we encouraged them to play with the concept of community and how they defined community and how they defined their own community. The concepts of community suggested by K's and T's maps are not necessarily definitions of community with which scholars would agree, but that was not our intent. K and T, like the other students in the class, were beginning to develop definitions for themselves and to become more explicitly aware of their membership in a community outside of school. Some students had a more difficult time

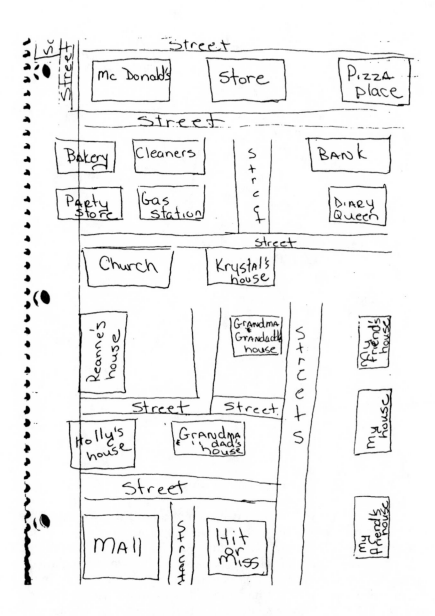

Figure 2.1. T's diagram

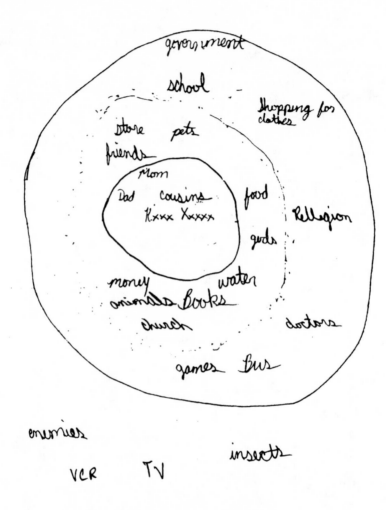

Figure 2.2 K's diagram

than others with the task of identifying community. These were students whose lives were nearly fully circumscribed by school and the house in which they lived. There were some students who, after school would go home and stay inside, in large part because this was their parents' strategy for keeping their children safe from the potential dangers in the area in which they lived. At home they would watch television or do homework. Although these students did participate in a "community,a they did not feel that they did so, said so, and a few became very frustrated with the task.

We asked the students to share their definitions and maps with each other and to comment on each other's work. But the written comments were usually not very insightful or helpful. As in Example 1, students typically commented that their peers' definition was "good" without explaining why they thought so or offering any substantive comment.

Although the comments they wrote in response to each other's work were minimal and minimally helpful, the conversations they had were not. Those conversations were usually lively, sometimes straying to tangential topics but topics nonetheless relevant to the overall goals and purposes of the project. This pattern of minimal written comments on peers' work but lively oral discussion continued throughout the project. Rather than trying to correct this situation, we changed our view of having students make written comments on each other's work. Writing comments became an opportunity for substantive peer conversation.

The next student task was to list cultural events that occurred in their community. They were to choose one event and describe it. We discussed what a community event was, without constraining the students to a single definition. The students listed block parties, festivals, picnics, church events, family events, the mobile pool coming to their neighborhood, teenage parties, fire hydrants being opened as sprinklers, community center events, going to a friend's house, garage sales, among others. D's rough draft of a community event is shown in Example 2. The students shared their lists of cultural events with each other, noting similarities and differences.

Using a planning model described by McClendon (1986), we then had the students write a cultural history of their community. The planning model requires students to write a plan of what they are going to do, to share that plan and get additional suggestions, and then later to evaluate both what happened and how effective their plan was. We had students share their plans as a whole class activity and then later share

---

H's definition of culture:

I think culture is your background or traditions you have in your family. Or your religion or like if you celebrate Christmas or you don't.

K's Comments on H's definition:

I think this definition is very correct I also feel the same way you did very good.

Example 1. Peer comments on a student's definition of culture

---

Roscoe's is a place where you can play video games. When you go in you see more than 40 video games such as Gauntlet, Gauntlet 2, Trojans, Turbo, Space Warrier, etc. When you come in you go to the desk (the manager's name is Roscoe) put your money on the table, the man gives you your tokens, you go to a video game if someone is playing you put your token on the screen if it is one of those games where the more coins you put in the more power you get. In other games you put the token in the machine, and when someone playing is done you have your token and begin to play. On Sunday between 2 o'clock and 6 there is double time where if you gave the man a dollar he would give you four tokens, where on double time if, you gave the man a dollar he would give you eight tokens. Also men bring boys, and women bring girls, men and boys play violent games, and the women and girls play pac-man and other non-violent games. This happens because most women don't like the violence in video games

Example 2. D's rough draft of a community event description

their cultural histories within a small group of peers. The written plans varied in detail, but the conversations about the plans were richer in insight, suggestion, and detail. Because the class was so diverse in student ethnic, linguistic, and cultural backgrounds, the sharing in small groups inherently became a cross-cultural comparison activity. We asked students to note similarities and differences, and to write these in their notebooks. Students became more aware of each other's background and of the fact that others could be used as a source of knowledge, too. The cultural and linguistic diversity of the class was a recognized and manifest asset.

The planning model was especially helpful because it allowed us and the students to focus on sources of knowledge in their community. Most students identified parents and grandparents as sources, but others also identified local community institutions (e.g., a local history society) and nonrelatives. We did not require the students to write a full community history but allowed them to focus on one or two issues or topics. Among the issues chosen were dating, music, schooling, childhood, toys, sports, houses. We had two purposes for having students write cultural histories. First, to locate sources of knowledge in their community and second, to view those sources of knowledge as legitimate sources within the context of schooling.

Acquiring an Ethnographic Framework

At the same time we were writing cultural histories, we began reading Minor's (1975) "Body Ritual Among the Nacirema." It took the students several days before someone figured out that Nacirema was American spelled backward, and then told the class. Before they realized the trick, we had them compare life in America with the Nacirema. Some did not see any similarities, others did. Of course, when they found out that the Nacirema were Americans, they excitedly went through the article identifying all the customs and activities. The article—and especially because the students fell into the trap set by the article—allowed us to explore a range of assumptions and ethnographic principles and goals including cultural relativity and debunking the notion of cultural superiority, making the strange familiar and the familiar strange, whether natives would describe themselves as outsiders might, emic and etic perspectives, among others. Although "Body Ritual Among the Nacirema" was a difficult text for many of the seventh-grade students to read, no one complained.

Later in the project, we had students read Gmelch's (1975) "Baseball Magic," which led to a discussion of taboos, superstitions, and fetishes in our communities. The goal was to emphasize abductive thinking and analysis, seeing similar patterns across various cultural situations and contexts. We also continued emphasizing "making the strange familiar and the familiar strange." One student and her parents objected to reading "Baseball Magic" on religious grounds and she was excused from having to participate in that part of the project.

We began a discussion of folklore. Dave told several folk stories from his community, one traditional folk story and one modern urban folk story. We discussed what made a story a folk story and what kinds of folk stories there were. Again, the emphasis was not on having students learn a standard definition but rather on getting them to play with the concept of folklore and recognize folklore and folk stories in their own communities. They brought into class folk stories from their communities and families. Many of the folk stories were family stories, stories about grandparents or parents handed down through the family. Others were traditional ethnic folk stories. Only a few students brought in modern urban folk stories. We had students share their folk stories in small groups. This activity, like many of the previous ones, emphasized sources of knowledge within their community, family, and among each other. An attempt to get them to compare folk stories did not go well, but that was our fault not the students'. We did not give them enough time, background, or direction—but more importantly, the students were caught up in listening to each other's folk stories and the task of comparison got lost in the enjoyment of listening.

As a final ethnographic report, we had the students do a study of "food gathering" and "food preparation" in their community. They began by listing all the places in their community where people got food. Then, they made observations at two different places and wrote up their findings. We followed the planning model they had used before. There was a great deal of enthusiasm and energy spent on this field project, and the enthusiasm grew as students would return to class and report on what they had done and observed. They drew maps of the stores or markets they studied and analyzed differences in function and social relationships as well as in the foods carried.

The various ethnographic reports helped the students acquire an ethnographic frame. Several lectures by Dave gave the students technical terms—*emic, etic, function, symbol, abductive thinking, taxonomy*—to use in their reports and to guide their thinking. No test was used to check on the students' acquisition of these concepts as it was not necessary for every student to know all of the concepts explicitly. Someone in their group was most likely to remember a needed concept during a peer group discussion or when reviewing a peer's plan or report. And if they could not remember the specific term they nonetheless had a rough sense of the concept.

Applying An Ethnographic Frame To Academic Writing

About two thirds of the way through the project we began to shift the focus from doing and writing ethnographic studies to applying an ethnographic frame to academic writing. Our approach was based on how we defined text production, the creation of original texts. Many scholarly discussions of writing, especially original writing, emphasize personal expression and personal voice. Although our view is not in opposition to that view of writing, we took a different approach. The creation of an original text—text production—does not require a totally original text. Perhaps it is not even possible to have a totally original text. Rather, we saw text production as involving the integration of academic knowledge and texts with community knowledge and texts. By bringing the two together, they inform each other and the tensions between them create original texts. Of course, this is not the only way text production may occur.

At the time, we did not use the term intertextuality, but that term is useful in understanding our approach to emphasizing text production in academic writing. Our efforts involved not just creating links between texts, but between school texts (textbooks, encyclopedias, teacher lectures, etc.) and community texts (cultural events, community history, folklore, community, and family life, etc.), and not just juxtaposing these texts but exploring what the links might mean or be made to mean. The construction of intertextuality was an act of constructing meaning.

With this view of text production in mind, we began various writing exercises, some of which were based on synectics. Students took an academic topic, brainstormed various metaphors, personalized the metaphor and gave it emotions, then explored insights the metaphor might have for a more creative understanding of the academic topic. We explained our intent explicitly. Whenever they were presented with an academic writing task, we wanted them to ask themselves if there was anything in their community that could apply to that academic topic and writing task, were there sources of knowledge in their community that might be used, were there experiences they or their peers had that might be useful. We engaged the students in a number of comparative exercises where students either considered an academic topic in terms of their community or compared a topic across several communities. For example, one student compared the election of George Washington to the election of Ronald Reagan, suggesting that in both elections, people wanted a strong leader but did not necessarily agree with what the leaders did. Another student compared music across communities using his own knowledge, interviewing other students, and using a book from the school library.

E compared slavery in the colonial period with slavery in her community. She wrote five and a half pages of notes and ideas, although her rough draft, which she did not choose to pursue to a final draft, was only a half-page long. Perhaps it was too difficult to make it longer, perhaps she ran out of time, perhaps she found it boring, or perhaps after having made the point she wanted to make she felt no need to pursue it further.

At the end of the project we conducted a posttest. Just as with the pretest, students were given a topic—the same one they had on the pretest—and given several days to write their essay as homework. As we noted at the beginning of this chapter, we were and are suspicious of how much such tests can reveal. But we wanted to know what would happen once the project was over and the students were faced with an

---

Slavery existed in the Colonial Period and still continues today and slavery will always exist. To me slavery isn't just indentured servants with no money. It [is] people who have no control and it's important that we try to stop it for good. But we will probably be without success because there will always be somebody unable to control there own lives. But it's important that we vanish this problem as much as we can.

Example 3. E's rough draft comparing slavery in the colonial period and in her community

academic writing task without instructional support. True, the context was one in which we were the ones giving the writing task and the students might assume we had certain expectations to which they needed to respond that might not exist in other classes. Nonetheless, we wondered what would happen after the project ended.

One of the posttest writing tasks was to write an essay on pollution. This was an especially relevant task. The previous year a truck was caught dumping toxic waste into an open field next to the school and toxic waste was also found in trash dumpsters in an alley next to the school. The dumping of toxic waste had been occurring for a while. Many students crossed the open field going to and from school and all of the students passed through the alley to get to the school's playing fields. The scandal was in the newspapers and many students were tested for PCB poisoning. A number of students had attended the trial of the man responsible for the dumping because Toby had taken her homeroom classes to court for a planned field trip the previous year when the convicted polluter was sentenced. It was reported in the local paper that the fine was increased because of the presence of the students in the courtroom.

On the pretest, only one student mentioned the scandal. Most of the pretest essays were like T's (see Example 4) although not as long.

It is estimated that everyday 175,000,000,000 of sewage and waste put into waterways of the United States. In July 1971 Ohio's Cuyahoga River 6became so filled with oil and debris that it actually caught fire damaging two bridges! The Rhine River in Europe is named the open sewer. One writer named Der Spiegel said, Ulf all of these substances were to transported by rail then you would need more than 3,000 boxcars"—each day. Water can purify itself when not to much pollution is in it. When waste is dumped into a river, the water breaks up and delutes much of the sewage. Then the river "digests" the remaining particles by oxidation and by water bacteria that consumes organic water. This bacteria changes it into harmless, odorless compounds. But today more and more streams are suffering from "indigestion," making them murky, skimmy, and foul smelling. But when lakes or rivers that look pretty good can be dying from eutrophication which means to be over burdened with nutrients. Today farmers use tons of chemical fertilizers rich in nitrates, and house-wives use detergents strong in phosphates which also winds up in the river. The overdose of nutrients feed algae and other small plants that live in the water. When the algae and other small water plants multiplies the sunlight does not penatrate the water as well and in time the water becomes lifeless. In close pollution is getting worse but man can do something about it.

Example 4. T's pretest essay on pollution

They were exercises in text reproduction, either the reproduction of authoritative texts or the reproduction of cliches about pollution (even though they were cliches about which the students might have strong feelings). Not one pretest essay included mention of the PCB pollution at Midway School. T's posttest essay is strikingly different from his pretest. He includes information from academic texts, he even quotes from a dictionary. But he does not stop there. He integrates the experience at Midway School. T's essay is not perfect. It does not need to be. For our purposes, it shows us that T and most of the other students in the class took a different stance toward their academic writing than they had before we began the project.

Subsequent events in the classroom confirmed that community knowledge was legitimized in the classroom and legitimized for use in

---

When I received the assignment on pollution I really didn't know anything about it so I looked in the American Heritage Dictionary and found out the word pollution is contamination of soil, water or the atmosphere by the discharge of noxious substances. I think the word pollution in my own words means dangerous substances that get into the soil, water and the atmosphere.

In my American History book on page 900 I researched and found out that pollution comes from cars, buses, and trucks. The fumes go into the air in large amounts. Pollution also comes from factories that drop chemical waste into rivers and lakes. As I was reading I found out that spray cans cause air pollution. For example, roach cans, odor cans, and oven sprays. These spray cans don't only cause air pollution, it cause damage to the ozone layer too.

I remember when I went to the 36th District Court to witness the sentencing of [Xxxxxx Xxxxxx] for wasting some dangerous chemicals in the back of [Midway]. The chemicals that were wasted in the back of [Midway] was put in a garbage truck and the truck caught on fire. The 10 different chemical caused the truck driver to be hospitalized. I think that people who pollute the air should be punished because, the pollution can kill animals and humans. I think people who pollute the air and water should be fined at least 3,500 and if it harms someone's health pay for that too.

I feel pollution is something that everyone in the world will have to deal with. I hope that we as people can find something to protect the ozone layer that protects the earth from heavy radiation from the sun. I wish there weren't any pollution on earth because pollution kills our fish and people also can die from pollution, too. I think people should do something to stop pollution from spreading to the ozone layer before it is damaged.

Example 5. T's posttest essay on pollution

---

understanding academic topics. Students continued to apply various ethnographic principles they had learned and seemed to enjoy writing. At the end of the project, just before we collected the notebooks, S wrote the following unsolicited comment to her notebook:

> *Dear Notebook,*
>
> *It has been very interesting and enjoyable having you. I like writing now that I've had to do it for different assignments. I've learned you can write in several ways and also that writing brings out sides of people you may not always see. I used to hate writing but I think it's somehow helped me become a better person in expressing myself on paper. Anyway, you are a very nice notebook and I hope they don't lose you (or burn, dump, etc.).*
>
> > *See Ya Later!*
> > *The Editor*

FOLLOW-UP

It is important to note that what changed—who changed—during the project was not just the students. We changed, too. Toby writes:

> Following the project, I explored new ways of integrating the community into the academic curriculum and into the academic writing. For me, the experience of collaborative research with a fellow teacher "anthropologist" impacted on my self-esteem as a teacher and validated my observations as a teacher-researcher. When Dave organized the students into peer conferencing groups as they responded to one another's writing, I was able to experience the reality of the writing workshop classroom. What I had been reading about in books such as Donald Graves' [1983] *Writing: Teachers and Students at Work* became a real option for instruction. The powerful changes I observed in students' voice and text production had a dramatic influence on my practice. I began guiding my students through the research and publication of their family histories. My classroom became organized around the writing workshop. The publication of extensive student anthologies became the norm, and these anthologies frequently included their inquiries about their families and communities. For me, this project was to mark the beginning of my understanding of authentic learning and what it really means to compose curriculum with children.

Dave also writes about how the project changed his view of education and research:

From the very beginning of our work together, I began to incorporate what I observed and learned from Toby into the teacher education courses I was teaching at the university. I encouraged both preservice and inservice teachers to explore ways to connect classroom reading and writing with students' families and communities. As Toby and I built a better understanding for ourselves about how classroom education could move beyond procedural display and text reproduction, I took those reflections directly into the course I was teaching. Eventually, the project helped me move away from a school-centered model of reading and writing education to what might be called a community-centered model.[4] I became less concerned with how family and community life affected students' classroom performance and life; and much more concerned with how what went on in the classroom affected the students' family and community life.

Other educators have built off of the model described in this chapter, changing it as their goals, insights, and the circumstances of their teaching have required (Chapter 12 is one example). We do not recommend that the model we have described here be followed as a formula but rather that it be adapted or used as a prompt for developing other ways of learning to write by having students research the language and culture of their own communities and for thinking about classroom education.

REFERENCES

Bloome, D. (1989). Beyond access: An ethnographic study of reading and writing in a seventh grade classroom. In D. Bloome (Ed.), *Classrooms and literacy* (pp. 53-106). Norwood, NJ: Ablex.

Bloome, D., Puro, P., & Theodorou, E. (1989). Procedural display and classrooms lessons. *Curriculum Inquiry, 19*(3), 265-291.

Gmelch, G. (1975). Baseball magic. In J. Spradley & M. Rynkiewich (Eds.), *The Nacirema: Reading on American culture* (pp. 348-352). Boston: Little Brown.

Gordon, W. (1961). *Synectics* New York: Harper & Row.

Graves, D. (1983). *Writing: Teachers and students at work.* Portsmouth, NH: Heinemann.

Heath, S., & Branscombe, A. (1985). Intelligent writing in an academic community: Teacher, students and researcher. In S. Freedman (Ed.). *The acquisition of written language: Revision and response* (pp. 3-32) Norwood NJ: Ablex.

---

[4]See Willett and Bloome (1993) for a detailed discussion of a community-centered model of classroom reading and writing education.

Hsu, O.B. (1977). *The cognitively oriented curriculum: Writing and reading.* Ypsilanti, MI: High/Scope Educational Research Foundation.

Joyce, B., & Weil, M. (1971). *Models of teaching.* Englewood Cliffs, NJ: Prentice-Hall.

McClendon, J. (1985). Developing writers in an intermediate-grade classroom. *Theory Into Practice, 25*(2), 117-123.

Minor, H. (1975). Body ritual among the Nacirema. In J. Spradley & M. Rynkiewich (Eds.), *The Nacirema: Reading on American culture* (pp. 10-13). Boston: Little Brown.

Robinson, J., & Stock, P. (1990). The politics of literacy. In J. Robinson (Ed.), *Conversations on the written word* (pp. 271-322). Portsmouth, NH: Boynton/Cook-Heinemann.

Wigginton, E. (1975). *Moments; The Foxfire experience.* Washington, DC: IDEAS.

Willett, J., & Bloome, D. (1993). Literacy, language, school, and community: A community-centered view. In A. Carrassquillo & C. Hedley (Eds.), *Whole language and the bilingual learner* (pp. 35-59). Norwood, NJ: Ablex.

3

Celebrations and Letters Home:
Research as an Ongoing Conversation
Among Students, Parents, and Teacher

Marceline Torres
Bronx Public School System

This chapter describes the "celebrations" and "letters home" that were part of a sixth-grade instructional program that emphasized students as researchers. The celebrations and letters home were events that created an ongoing conversation between students and parents that not only supported the students' education but as importantly, allowed the students and parents to see each other, themselves, and the school in new ways.

The students-as-researchers program began as a collaboration between Carmen Mercado from Hunter College and myself, a sixth grade teacher in a New York City middle school. It is difficult to outline a step-by-step procedure for how the students-as-researchers program was and is done. So much depends on the particular questions and issues the students generate, and on the resources and opportunities made available by parents and in the community. At the broadest level, the students decided on themes. We then categorized each theme into research topics. The students then generated questions. Sometimes the students worked in a group, sometimes alone. We discussed interviewing techniques, writing field notes, and other activities needed to pursue their questions. But the students-as-researchers program involves more than a predetermined set of activities; it involves seeing students as young people who have important questions and concerns about the world in which they live, and who are energetic about understanding and addressing that world; it involves seeing curriculum as inquiry and action rather than as a set of discrete skills to be drilled and then forgotten; and it involves seeing parents in new ways, as resources for student inquiry, as support systems for student curiosity and achievement, and as conversational partners as students seek to explore and understand the worlds in which they live. In brief, the students-as researchers program is more than an academic exercise.

Letters home and celebrations were two activities that became central to the students-as-researcher program. After deciding on a research topic and question, I had the students write letters to their parents, telling them about the research topic and why they were interested in it. These were the letters home. They provoked conversations and letters back from parents as well as parent involvement. The celebrations were monthly meetings I arranged that were attended by students and parents. At the celebrations, students presented their research or gave a progress report. In describing the letters home and the celebrations I am also describing much of what occurs during the students-as-researchers program, but more importantly, the letters home and the celebrations help redefine the possibilities of middle-school classroom education. As young people enter the middle-school age early adolescence—parents may feel that their children need them less, teachers seem to focus more on academic curriculum than on student learning and curiosity, schools often seem less hospitable to parents and the community, and the young people themselves often feel less connected to their families, communities, and schools. Yet, it is exactly at this age that young people continue to need their parents' involvement, and that teachers need to place the student as-active-learner and the worlds in which the student lives at the center of the curriculum. It is an age at which young people's connections to families, communities, and schools need to be strengthened rather than strained. The letters home and the celebrations illustrate some possibilities for meeting these challenges.

THE LETTERS HOME

One of the features of the students-as-researchers program was to give students the opportunity to research a topic that interested and concerned them. Somewhat to my surprise, they selected topics of social concern such as drugs, AIDS, cancer, teen pregnancy, and homelessness. We (Mercado and I; see also Chapter 4) encouraged the students to gather data in ways that included using "real people" as sources of data. I had been thinking of using the community agencies that could provide information, but again to our surprise, some students began to find members of their families and friends who were "authentic" sources of data. For example, one student had an uncle in the hospital who was dying of AIDS. I assured the student that the information he obtained from this experience was as valuable or more so than any found in the books he was reading. The research not only made him eager to read more about AIDS and write about it, but it also gave him an opportunity to vent his feelings through a most difficult time.

As students discussed their research topics and began to collect data and report findings, they revealed information about their lives that compelled me to inform the parents about their children's concerns. The students were asking questions that parents and teachers often think are beyond sixth graders. For this reason I had the students write letters to their parents informing them of their research topics. This was the, beginning of the letters home, which became much more than just letters to parents, they became the starting points for ongoing conversations among students, parents, and myself as teacher.

Dear Dad,

My topic is about "AIDS". I want to know about AIDS because a lot of people in this world are dying of it. And I am scared to get it. So I want to know. I also want to know what prevents people to have this disgusting disease. And I want know what are the ways you can not get AIDS so I can learn these ways and not be afraid. This topic is important to me because I do not want to die of something I was not born with, meaning that I want to die normally

Daughter

This father was, of course, very happy that his daughter was enthusiastic about schoolwork. But as he was a hospital employee, an X-ray technician, he was additionally pleased that his daughter was addressing an issue related to his field and that he could contribute to her research. I had his constant cooperation. Not only did the father get involved, but the mother did also (the parents were divorced). She came to the celebrations and brought the siblings.

Many parents and children do not really talk with each other about significant issues that are of concern to students. Parents do not often view their sixth-grade children as mature enough to understand some of the deeply troubling issues that are a part of our world. Through the letters home and the students-as-researchers program, students learned that it was all right to question and that research could lead to discoveries. Talking and writing about their research topics gave children a valid reason for talking with adults, especially parents. Talking eased anxieties, and created ongoing conversations.

Dear Mother:

As you already know, I am researching on the topic peer pressure. You must wonder why Alesia wanted to do research on that topic. The real reason is I want to understand it more. Sometimes I wonder if I am being pressured by my friend. I think you, the parents, should ask your children if they are being pressured into things they don't want to do and explain what they should do in the situation.

Please write back. Thank you.

Dear Alesia:

Children today, are being pressured more, from times when I was growing up. It doesn't have to be that way. Always have something positive in your life and activities like "After School" programs, help others. Volunteer to do things in the community, etc. In life there are always going to be pressures coming from people, be it friends, enemies, etc., but you have to be strong and believe in yourself. And the rest will follow. I'm proud of you Alesia, researching Peer Pressure is the first step of fighting it.

Your Mom

* * * * * * * * * * *

Dear Mom:

My topic of interest is racism. Mrs. Torres says that it is a strong topic. I have been getting data from t.v. about racism even if you say I watch a lot of t.v. Can you believe this unusual story that I heard blue eyed people are smarter than brown eyed people. Isn't that prejudiced? Tell me about it.

Your daughter

Response

Isn't that stupid. Blue eyed people are not smarter than anyone. Everybody is smart about something. It's true, this is a strong topic.

Mom

The children sought answers to their questions on their own. They did not wait for me. For example, the class was invited to the general post office, which was having a big activity that included Olympic stars. The students generated their questions to interview the stars beforehand and at the event they had their pictures taken with the stars. Afterward, they were sitting on the white marble steps that led up to the post office writing up their field notes and taking other notes. A passerby asked if it was a homework assignment that they had to do. "No," I said, "I didn't tell them to write." I didn't have to tell them anymore, they had made it a part of their life. This is part of the beauty of this approach to learning. I no longer had to say, "Now children, this is what you're going to do." They did it on their own.

As far as reading is concerned, the students were often reading college-level texts related to their research topics. These are students that are all working or scored, according to state tests, below average. Of course they read the college-level texts with difficulty, but they had an interest in understanding what it was they were reading. Anything they were able to see pertaining to their topic of interest they gravitated toward regardless of its level of difficulty.

It was not only college-level texts they pursued, but anything that they felt might contribute to their research topic. I was riding the train with some of the students and they saw billboards that addressed the topics of research of some of their classmates. Even though these were not their topics of interest, the students would say, "Oh, Miss Torres, we have to tell H about this billboard. There's a number there and he can call up to find out more information." They were collaborating with each other even when not in school.

I was facilitating their learning, yet not providing direct instruction or controlling it. The school, their homes, and the community all became their classroom. The letters home began ongoing conversations with parents that expanded into conversations with other students and conversations between the parents and myself. The students supported each other's research and shared their findings with each other. Thus all the students were learning about different topics at the same time.

CELEBRATIONS

The celebrations were monthly meetings attended by parents and students at the school. In addition to enjoying food and coffee, tea and soft drinks, students presented their research and the future directions their research was going to take. Parents listened and contributed, asking questions and offering suggestions.

In many ways the students were in charge of the celebrations. Two students were in charge of greeting the parents at the door, two students took their coats and put them away. One student had the parents sign their names in the official guest list, and two students escorted the parents to a seating area, and then offered them coffee or juice. After the parents began arriving, students came in different numbers to interview the parents some more, as it was an opportunity to gather data that was too good to miss. The parents were bombarded with questions, but they seemed to enjoy it. The attending teachers were also bombarded by interviewers, as the students began to learn that teachers were parents and sources of data, too. The students were there with notebook and pen in hand, too. After parents were settled and the interviewing completed, students would report on the progress of their work and what they intended to do next, where they might go to collect data (e.g., by visiting a shelter or a local hospital). Sometimes the parents made suggestions, thus they began to learn about the work other students were doing, too.

It is important that students share their work with other people, not only with their teacher and their classmates. It was a big thrill for the students to have the opportunity to do that and to be taken seriously. The work they were doing was being done for a real purpose and reported to a real audience.

The celebration around Women's History Month was one of the most memorable because parents presented, too The first part of the celebration began with students sharing the work they had done on famous women who are acknowledged throughout the world. The second part was about famous women who personally influenced their lives. Most of the students referred to their mothers. Some referred to their grandmothers. One student who was new to my class was presenting, but her mother wasn't there. As she spoke about her mother, she began to cry. "I honor my mother because she's always been there for us. And she's raised us three girls by herself. And my mother can't be here today but I know that she would want to be here if she could."

Afterward, the parents were sitting around in a circle and the students were sitting in an outer circle. I told the parents "Well all the students have shared with us the woman that they honor this month, who has had a personal effect on their lives. Now we want the parents to do the same thing." As I had the parents presenting, most of them also spoke about their mothers. The first parent who spoke started to cry, too. She was the parent of one of the students who reported on—honored—his grandmother. It seems that there had been some resentment for years because the grandmother had raised him. I didn't understand what was happening at first. She said, "Well, I, too, have to honor my mother. And the reason why my son was living with her was because I had to send him here for a better life from Guyana. And our life situation was very bad there. So in order to give my son a better life, I sent him with his grandmother." She then described how she was having problems with her husband, who was an alcoholic. I hadn't known any of these things. She retold the story of her struggles as a parent and how she was only looking out for her son's best interest when she sent him to live with his grandparents in the United States. Her presentation gave way to other areas, and other people began to speak about their parents, including one woman who spoke about her mother who had died earlier that year.

The students felt the impact of what was happening, the closeness that occurred as a result of the sharing. Many of them wrote letters home about the celebration. It was something that had to be taken back to the home by many students, and parents wrote back. For example, Alicia wrote to her mother who could not attend:

> Today we had a celebration of woman's history month. The room looked very nice and creative from a child-s imagination. When everyone was talking about who they admire, it was a very touching moment for me and parents. I could feel it in the room. I had a great time and if my mother came she would have also. The food was excellent. So were the cakes and snacks. I had a great time.

Alicia's mother wrote back:

> It's very nice to have a month celebrating women. I'm sure if I had come I would have had a great time also. I would have gladly participated in the conversation about the woman I admire. That could only be my mother. My mother is an extraordinary woman indeed. My mother worked from dawn. Even when she put us to bed she was still working. Still we always felt loved. Times were very hard when I was growing up, but it would have been harder without my mother. To not have that comfort, warm, and loving feeling radiating from your mom is very traumatic. That's why no matter what I always try my best to show my children I love them. I think that it's wonderful that your class celebrated woman's history month that way. Keep up the good work.

As part of our research on women, one of the boys in the class got very interested in battered women. When he mentioned this topic to his mother, she was very surprised at his choice. She was eager to provide him with information that would help him do this work, especially because she worked in the local police station and she was very involved with the community. She began to take him to places that held meetings for battered women, and she was able to help find literature for him. Rather than present the research as a straight report, they performed a little play having to do with battered women. It was their idea and they wrote up the script themselves. In addition to researching and learning about a topic, this student and others in the class learned that there are different ways of presenting research findings.

In schools and classrooms in general, it is sometimes difficult for students to understand and feel that learning is taking place and that it is benefiting them, either now or in the future. Some of the students had the opportunity to present their findings at professional education forums; however, because of the cost not all the students could attend. Part of what the celebrations in school did was provide a way for all of the students to display their learning to the public and to each other. They looked forward to it. There was one student who was very angry at me. I found out about this anger through his writing. He wrote that he did not know why he had not been chosen to go to an outside presentation, because he felt he was ready. He was a very quiet student, the type of student who might not get noticed. I began to call him, and other students who might go unnoticed, the "phantom child." He was doing well and I didn't really focus on him as intently as the students who obviously needed my extra help. I had thought that I was able to reach every child, all 40 students of mine in the classroom. I had thought I was doing a good job. But then I read this phantom student's research journal in which he wrote how angry he was because he had not been selected to attend an outside presentation. (During this time celebrations were not part of the program.) I felt very bad when I read that. He wanted to do a presentation. I did not pick him because he was a quiet student and I thought maybe he did not feel ready, comfortable enough to speak up publicly. But he was working very hard and he wanted to share his work, too, even though he was quiet. He felt that his work needed to be shared, and he needed the opportunity to talk about it.

The added dimension of the celebrations provided each student an opportunity to present his or her work as well as a comfortable forum for critique and evaluation to take place.

PARENT HOMEWORK

The celebrations provided the forum for parents to come to school in a different and friendly manner. They felt unthreatened and comfortable in the classroom. They were happy to be there. They were proud of their children. They were willing to be there whenever asked. Now that the parents were involved, I asked myself what they could do at home to further stimulate student performance. I always encouraged students to write about what happened at the monthly celebrations, because everything involves learning. Then we looked back and reflected on exactly what we had learned. On one occasion when I told the students to write about a celebration, one student said, "Miss Torres, if we did the celebration for the parents and they were here, why don't they write?" I thought this was a good idea. Thus, parent homework began. The students went home with the agenda of getting their parents to do writing homework. The parents were open to doing this homework.

To make the parent homework official, I gave each parent his or her own notebook during one of our celebrations. The notebook and the parent homework became a way of documenting parent involvement. I learned that it was very difficult for some parents to take a day off work to attend our celebrations and equally difficult for an employer to understand. The activity of parents writing allowed parents to participate even if they could not come to school. It continued and extended the conversations begun with the letters home and the celebrations. One parent wrote:

> *Personally, I think that this is an idea that is God sent. Most parents truly want to get involved in their children's academics but with the pressures of household responsibilities at times obligations cannot be met. So then if Mohammed can't come to the mountain let's bring a mountain of homework to Mohammed.*

FINAL COMMENTS

Repeatedly, studies make it clear that if students are to develop into self motivated and independent writers and learners, they need authentic writing and learning experiences. Yet, the constraints of imposed curriculum, assessments, and our traditional ways of thinking about education hinder our ability to provide authentic experiences. The students-as-researchers program was intended to give students authentic writing and learning experiences, a real question to explore, a topic important to their lives, and a real audience to address—an audience invested both in the students and in the students' research.

Studies also state that parent involvement is crucial to the academic success of students; yet, despite superficial attempts, parents are discouraged from truly being involved. As children move up in grades, teachers often seem less willing to make time for parents, and less willing to interrupt their lessons. Building procedures and school policies may inadvertently turn parents away. The students-as researchers program was conceived as a way to involve parents in a substantive and meaningful way in their children's education, to lend their expertise and their experiences to their children's inquiry and learning. In so doing, new opportunities were created for parents to interact with their children and with the school.

What drives the students-as-researchers program is not any particular activity or even the combination of activities, but a commitment to all students as active learners, to families and communities as sources of knowledge, to authentic writing and learning opportunities, and to meaningful inquiry as critically important to the development of students as self-motivated and independent learners and thinkers. Everybody—students, parents, and teacher—is a learner and a teacher.

4

When Young People From Marginalized Communities Enter the World of Ethnographic Research: Scribing, Planning, Reflecting and Sharing

Carmen I. Mercado
Arizona State University

For 5 years, I worked closely with a sixth-grade teacher (Marceline Torres, see Chapter 3) to transform the curriculum in reading and language arts in a Chapter One middle school in the Bronx, New York. When I began my visits in the Fall 1989, it was a school where less than 25% of the students were on grade level according to standardized reading tests. As this narrative suggests, it is a statistic that says more about the ways we organize environments for learning than about the abilities and capabilities of students in marginalized communities.

I did not set out to improve the reading scores of the sixth graders in Torres' class, even though that is what occurred. When I asked to be adopted by the class of my former graduate student, my purpose was to demonstrate to students and to others that "underachieving" students are capable of "college work." I shared how I do research as an educational ethnographer to motivate students to engage in academic uses of literacy that go beyond what they normally encounter in school. These forms of academic literacy, which some describe as the literacies of the powerful and the influential (Delpit, 1987) are a reflection of sociohistorical processes. Consequently, they have been known to evince strong emotional reactions on the part of young adolescent students from marginalized communities who associate them with voices and worlds to which they do not belong.

What began by posing a simple, but unexpected, question: "What do you want to learn about?" led to introducing students, first by me and then by Torres, to the ways of thinking and using language of ethnographic researchers. Together we have worked to demystify the research process and to: "Put ethnography into the hands of those who would use it to improve their knowledge of what was happening around them in their learning and their skills in oral and written language" (Heath, 1985, p. 18). Ethnography is a research approach that involves observation and interaction with others about whom and from whom we want to learn—observations and interactions that are captured and preserved, over time, in field notes. It represents a different way of viewing the construction of knowledge and it is a different way of being in the world.

Ethnographic research contrasts sharply to the type of library research typically emphasized in schools. That "knowledge is all around us," and that it is "in people," is significant for students who do not see their world, their experiences, their forms of expression, in the texts they are required to read. Constructing knowledge in this manner requires constant rereading and dialogue to reflect upon the hidden messages that, like a secret code, are embedded in our notes, and to discover the connections between and among ideas over time, their relevance to our work as researchers, and to our lives as members of particular communities. Many of our sessions were devoted to "talk over text" (Wells, 1990), as we confronted, reflected on, and came to new understandings of the representations of our experiences as they accumulate over time. We learned to appreciate the power of the written word and we began to appropriate each other's forms of expression. We also came to understand and value what researchers and theoreticians mean when they say that "learning is an integral and inseparable aspect of social practice" (Lave & Wenger, 1991, p. 31).

Because constructing knowledge in this manner involves a relentless search to understand that which compels, through the eyes of different people, students engage in observations of and conversations with others whom they regard as authorities. Engaging in the practices of ethnographic researchers enables students to relate to their peers, their families, and members of their immediate community, as sources of academic knowledge. Beyond its obvious motivational value, this creates significant opportunities to extend the limiting boundaries of schooling as classwork into other settings and contexts that, in turn, influence what occurs in the classroom. The blurring of these boundaries is essential for creating educational equity among students from marginalized communities.

Students also examined with new interests and new purposes what are considered to be less traditional sources of academic information such as television programs, newspaper articles, and environmental literature. Moreover, the use of traditional reference sources such as library books and encyclopedias provided a contrastive perspective when seen in relation to other sources of information. As they made use of multiple sources of information, students be an to realize the limitations of relying on any one source, which also led to discussions about how knowledge gets legitimized in the books we read in school. In gaining multiple perspectives from multiple sources of data, students learned far more than an essential characteristic of ethnographic research. They raised questions about and developed new appreciations for the roles of writers and researchers in a democratic society. They also came to a new understanding of the responsibilities we all have to affirm our different voices.

The young adolescent students in Torres' class appropriated academic forms of literacy to learn from and to inform others, but also to connect to others and to understand and affirm themselves. They willingly employed familiar genres to communicate with real people, for purposes that grew naturally from inquiry into topics of their choosing. They learned to use forms of literacy that reflect a different way of thinking and learning about the world. The students gave presentations at research conferences (both professional education conferences and conferences within the school, see Torres, Chapter 3). These oral presentations at research conferences constitute significant literacy events as they involved the preparation of transparencies, speeches, and handouts that enabled us to explain ourselves to our audiences and, in the process, to ourselves. Re-presenting what we are doing in dialogue with others helped us to refocus and redirect our work as we gained new insights through interaction. Going beyond their immediate community is a powerful influence on students' perceptions of themselves and their abilities as literate thinkers and as human beings. Because we all define who we are in relation to others, interacting with those who are considered "intelligent" and "successful," demystifies the meaning of these labels and, more importantly, boosts students' self-confidence and self-esteem in academic settings. Moreover, as we interacted with those who were less familiar with our work, we all gained insights into our communicative abilities and our interpretive skills.

When underachieving middle school students engage in ethnographic research, they accomplish far more than acquiring competency in the language arts and learning to use language to become self-directed learners. Young adolescent students gain new understandings of "possible selves"—what they would like to become, could become, or are afraid of becoming—which serve as a link between cognition and motivation.

As students engaged in their research activities, Torres and I engaged in similar practices to understand the influences of these activities on students' uses of academic literacies and to respond to individual and collective needs. We took notes of students' words and actions during our sessions together and occasionally we recorded our conversations or interviews with individual students and with groups of students on audio and videotape. Mostly, however, we reviewed and reflected on—by ourselves, together, and with students the content of students' research journals to uncover or discover what these revealed about students' understandings of and reactions to our activities. Throughout, research, pedagogy, and assessment were intertwined and were mutually influential processes directed at making school learning meaningful to students. Not only does collaborative research play a critical role in creating social arrangements for learning, it also enables students to benefit from observing and engaging in the practices of "real" researchers.

The activity of doing ethnographic research, therefore, gave us a purpose for coming together over an extended period of time in a school setting; provided a common experience from which to engage in collective reflection; and allowed us to benefit from each other's efforts and perspectives. Through our activities in and out of school, we created a community of learners with a shared interest in research, a common concern for one another as human beings, and a commitment to making this a better world. We supported and learned from one another in a manner that allowed each of us the status of learner, teacher, researcher, and expert. Because students excel at different tasks, we prefer to capitalize on unique talents that are discovered, sometimes unexpectedly, as we work together, than to limit students' contributions by adhering to prescribed roles that may reflect preconceptions or misconceptions that we all have. In our community of practice, students determine the roles and responsibilities they want to assume; they "have different interests, make diverse contributions to activity and hold varied viewpoints" (Lave & Wenger, 1991, p. 98).

Torres and I realized that our relationship, which began as that of graduate student and university teacher, has gone through various transformations over time. Recently, we came to the realization that my role was that of *madrina* or godmother of the class, which made her my *comadre*, a relationship that reflects the notion of extended family we both value as Latinas and that our students understand, whether or not they are Latinos. When we do research, we are "like a family," as students observe, and it is this distinctive way of relating that characterizes our community of practice and that is a powerful emotional incentive for students to invest in academic activities, even when these seem to have no end.

Although our approach is similar to what others have done before us (see, e.g., the work of Heath, 1985; Moll & Diaz, 1987; Trueba, 1987), it is distinct in that young adolescent students entered the world of ethnographic research, as fully participating members. They were not just playing at being ethnographers to acquire practice in/with academic literacies, a valuable activity in and of itself. Students were real researchers in that they chronicled our activities over time; they collaborated with us to make sense of what occurred, and participated in sharing our collective work at research conferences. Through their efforts, students taught us about schooling, their families and life in their community, from their perspective, a dimension that is missing in the current discourse on educational reform and performance standards. Through our work together, students also began to understand that literacy and inquiry are inseparable and essential practices that are intended to improve teaching and learning in their classroom, in their school, and in more distant classrooms. Assuming the role of researcher also broadened students' career possibilities at a time when they were beginning to give serious thought to what they wanted to be and what they believed they were capable of becoming.

Although It is evident that the language arts are naturally interwoven in all these activities, writing is central to this type of research. We agree with Van Maanen (1988) that research is the work of writing. Students write to gather data, they write to analyze data and they write to share it with others. The intensity of written activity and the range and quantity of writing that young adolescent learners produce through our activities gives us an unusual opportunity to examine the values, beliefs, competencies, and concerns reflected in their written words.

Torres and I examined students' writings over a 1-year period, and in a few cases over 2- and 3-year periods. The written words of young adolescents shed insights on their experience of the curriculum and enable us to understand the character of their writing as it changes over time. I have organized their words within four activities that characterized our research: scribing, planning, reflecting, and sharing. After describing each of these activities, I briefly discuss some of what we learned about writing and young adolescents and about writing and biliterate students.

SCRIBING

Scribing or "observing and taking notes," is essential to the way ethnographers generate data and students realized that "there is no research without notes." Scribing challenges students to listen closely and attend carefully to details of events. We began "scribing" during our activities together and it became a common experience from which we could support each other, reflect on and become more familiar with careful observation and recording. What we did not anticipate was the value of scribing in preserving students' perspectives of our activities over the duration of the school year.

For example, early in our work together I shared field notes from my visits to the school to contrast the similarities and differences between my ethnographic notes with those students took during class discussions and lectures. I wanted to make public the ways of thinking of ethnographic researchers that are inherent in their uses of oral and written language. I emphasized that, as an educational ethnographer, it is students' actions and words that I find most compelling because of what they teach me about teaching and learning in schools. Eventually, more experienced student researchers shared this responsibility with me, as did the teacher. The following journal entry illustrates how students affirm themselves through scribing:

> At 11:40, Mrs. T. asked me to be a scribe and to observe her class. I am a seventh grader now, last year I was in Mrs. T's class and I knew about scribing. Mrs. T. went to the front of the room. Mrs. T. told the kid or her students. She asked them what is scribing the class happily answer "scribing is observing and writing." Mrs. T. told them about me and how I used to be a scribe in 6th grade . . .

Moreover, this excerpt reveals what students have learned about the need for precision in research: to pay attention to details such as the date and time when observations occur and to note the exact words individuals use when making important points. Quoting, they realized, is essential to minimize misrepresentation, as the following student journal entry shows:

> Quotes are very important to researchers because you may be interviewing somebody and they say something important that you need or you could tell other people about the person you interviewed and tell them about the important quotes that person gave to you and the researchers can find out what that person ment or said.

I also shared my notes to emphasize that ethnographers need to validate and to correct the information they have recorded and I photocopied and distributed copies of students' scribe notes anonymously to dramatize that there are always differences in the way we capture shared experiences. It is important for youngsters who, in academic settings, are insecure about what they know to understand the individual and constructive nature of comprehension. Acknowledging that there is no one right way to represent what occurred when we work in this manner helps to build self-confidence. However, it also teaches students that researchers have the responsibility of sharing their notes with others who have had a common experience to become aware of what they have overlooked and to gain other perspectives on what occurred, as these excerpts from student journals reveal:

> Dr. Mercado gave out copies of students research notes.. . . . She said
> we can learn from someone else's notes
>
> I think everybody should share each other's notes because we can
> get notes that you don't have.

In addition to gaining new appreciation for the value of collaborative research, students learn about the ethics of research and of respecting the desires of informants who wish to remain anonymous, which one student likened to "quoting people and putting it in nicknames."

Although these aspects of scribing get at some of the rigors of qualitative research, scribing also has an empowering effect on students who are now in the position of being subjects, rather than objects, in the teaching and learning process (cf. Freire & Macedo, 1987), as these statements from students suggest:

> When you quote someone it shows that you are listening, it shows
> that what others say is important (and when somebody quotes you,
> it shows that) you are authorities. (Keith, 10/90.
>
> Ms. T said our words are very valuable and Dr. M. wrote it down on
> the board. (Keith, 10/90)
>
> I know you want me to take notes, but I can't. . . . Oh, are you
> quoting me? (Puli, 03/91)

Students take notes of what the adults say and do in much the way that adults take notes of what students say and do. This was sometimes startling to me, as when I encountered this student interpretation of how I reacted after reading students' research journals:

> This is a quote from Dr. Mercado. "Some people don't speak and
> they have wonderfull handwriting in their research notebooks and
> some people speak alot and they don't have wonderful handwriting
> in their research notebook." I think this is a powerful quote.

Students also learn that language differences do not have to be a barrier to scribing, as one student discovered when she was invited to attend the AIDS Conference organized by a social studies class in the bilingual program—an activity that reflects the influence of this project on other teachers:

> Today I got picked to go to a conference, but I don't know any
> Spanish so Mrs. T. is going to translate the speaking so I could take
> notes because I'm very good in taking notes.

We all learned a great deal from students' scribe notes, especially about their changing perceptions of the research process, and their abilities to accomplish challenging academic work. These notes gave us insights into the thoughts and emotions of students who were often quiet during our activities in class. They also gave us reason to question what we are repeatedly told about the capabilities of students from marginalized communities: They "are very basic," they are "poor in writing," they have "problems with reading," and they are "not interested in school work."

PLANNING

From the outset, collaborative planning is a practice that we emphasized once students decided on a direction for their work and had organized themselves into research groups with peers of their choosing. This provided a different experience with literacy than students are accustomed to at this grade level: literacy as a tool to guide and control our actions. Typically, at the end of our regular meetings we prompted students to consider: "What do you plan on doing next?" for which we required a collaboratively written response. We expected that students would benefit from verbalizing their intentions through oral and written language. In a similar manner, these written responses would guide our interactions with students, enabling us to provide timely support. However, it is one thing to formulate plans and quite another to follow them. We all realized that we are sometimes unable to adhere to our plans, as these may need revision to accommodate the unexpected or to be within the realm of the possible. We preferred to assume a flexible attitude toward these plans, viewing value in the dialogue and writing that are part of the act of planning as a means to help us understand the purposes of our actions and to guide future actions. To have insisted on adhering too strictly to the plans we each formulated would have defeated the goals we wanted to accomplish.

In reading their research journals and through conversations with students, we discovered that allowing them to tell us what they planned on doing rather than dictating what they should do, motivated young adolescent students to "take their work seriously" and boosted their self-confidence, as their words suggest:

> Dr. Mercado wants us to plan what we're going to do in our groups
>
> Now we're in groups. Dr. Mercado gave us an activity sheet. It has the group members, recorder, specific questions and ways to learn about our topic.
>
> What I want to know / What I know / How I'm going to find out.
>
> She is treating us like adults.

Although most of these plans were narrative descriptions, student's individuality also became evident in the way they proceeded with this task. For the student who developed the plan that follows, organizing information into chart form was a striking pattern we noticed in all her work (see Document 1). Although this type of planning became routine, it was not until we began submitting proposals for and honoring commitments to participate at conferences where collaborative classroom research is shared that students grew to appreciate the value of and necessity for long-term planning. They were surprised to learn that, as a researcher, I was committed to and had to prepare for activities

---

PLANS

Childrens Sickness
Notes

Where are going	Memorial Sloan Ketering 1275 York Ave
What we have to do	we have to get permission from parent and teacher
to children in hospital	write get well sone (soon) cards and may6e get little present to.
we have to do Maleen	we take pictures if we can
ralena	Ask your mom permission for tape recorded (recorder).

We would like to have the children in the hospital as foster kids

Maleen boy	Ray Ray Girl	Cristina Girl
Lila boy	Jessica Girl	Ask Mr. Franklin about his son

Document 1

---

many months in advance when I made public my travel schedule as a reminder of the dates when I would not be visiting the classroom. However, it was not until we began to make our own conference plans that long-term planning took on added significance. Having an authentic conference activity to look forward to, an exciting event that gave added legitimacy to our activities, proved a powerful incentive for young adolescent students.

Because I became aware, early on in our activities, that students were often oblivious to the passage of time, I provided each student with his or her own Hunter College planner or appointment book. I wanted them to use this indispensible tool to make note of important events, to schedule meetings and trips, to remember the dates of our conference presentations and to gain a concrete sense of how much time remained and was needed to organize these activities, as they drew near. Students enjoyed using their planners to be mindful of our commitments and to pace their activities accordingly, as one student simply wrote: "We got our special project books and we write down our schedule."

These planners enabled students to determine what they would have to do to assure participation at research conferences. We wanted students to know that we were there to support them if they decided they were ready to share their work, but because of our limited budget, it would not be possible for all students to attend every conference. As it turned out, the time planners enabled students to assume responsibility for pacing their work in a manner that was appropriate to each individual and eventually all had the opportunity to present at least once, when they felt prepared and had parental consent to do so. We used agendas to guide our activities during our meetings and to organize conference presentations. I introduced students to this planning tool at our first meeting as a way of giving them a sense of what we were to accomplish that day. I told students that I used agendas to guide my activities with graduate students, which impressed them because of what it suggested about their capabilities to do "college work." With time, students understood that I expected them to share in this responsibility:

> Dr. Mercado is writing the agenda. She says . . . the next time I come I will not write the agenda. I am going to let you write your own agenda. (Jerry, 12/14)

It was significant for students to assume the responsibility of giving direction to our activities, a responsibility that they accepted and took seriously even when the teacher assigned it as homework. Eventually, students prepared agendas for our conference presentations and they delighted in telling their adult collaborators what to do in the same way that we delighted in their accomplishments, as we did when we saw the agenda shown in Document 2, which was prepared by a student as a way of organizing one of our conference presentations. Learning to plan in order to regulate one's own behaviors through the written word has added meaning for middle school students who are sensitive about being regulated and controlled by others through the spoken word. In effect, when students plan, they are telling themselves what to do, taking responsibility for their own learning.

REFLECTING

Although reflection is commonly referred to as a mental process in which past actions are considered in light of current understandings, in ethnographic research reflection is a powerful social, dialogic process that is an essential form of data analysis. In our collaboration reflection, which tends to be a rare occurrence in most school contexts, was a common activity that took a number of different forms. Although we always reflected in action as we engaged in specific activities, it was

---

Persentain (Presentation) Agenda: learing (Learning) about learing Colabaritily (Collaboratively)

2/22/91

1. Introduction
   Angle (Angel) he is going to say our name
   school, the fact that he is from 7 and we are from 6 grade.

2. the project abstract for 6M21 Research project
   Angel, Epi, they have project abstract for class

3. How we got started
   Anthony, Jessica we start talking about when we got started

4. What are the diffrent (different) groups doing.
   Laila will show the trainsparentsi (transparency) with me the I will say how we got the interview with doctor B then make a play back

5. What we are learning about learning

Document 2

---

when we stepped outside of and re-presented our experiences in language that we benefited from the "looking again," that we gained clarity about the meanings of certain behaviors and events and that we were able to better understand what we had accomplished. That is why we emphasized writing to reflect. We wrote reflections of past activities and events, we engaged in discussions about what occurred, and we reflected individually, playing back moments and experiences in our minds. However, it was the practice of collective reflection, whether with individual students, with small groups of students, or with the whole class, that was most characteristic of how we gained insights about ourselves as individuals, about our relationships to one another, and about what we were accomplishing. Engaging in collective reflection was especially significant in understanding and challenging individual perspectives we brought to this collaborative effort. Collective reflection always involved the use of oral and written language (and sometimes visual texts of past experiences) to evoke new thoughts.

Typically, we engaged in reflection during our weekly meetings using textual representations of previous experiences. For example, in preparation for one of our conference presentations, I prepared a project chronology, using quotes from our research notebooks, as a way of synthesizing and re-presenting what I considered to be the highlights of our activities. This enabled students to reconstruct their own understandings of what we had accomplished. Document 3 is an excerpt from this first chronology. Eventually, students shared in the responsibility of preparing project chronologies, gaining even more from the rereadings this required. One student described her experiences attempting this task without the aid of a computer (see Document 4).

As our activities progressed, we broadened the range of texts that were included for this purpose and we began using visual texts such as videotapes and photographs. Although language is a powerful tool for reflection, for young adolescent students the visual images provided an important aid to memory, as one student suggested when she examined a photograph of her first interview questions:

> In this picture I was writing questions for interviews with adults and doctors. My questions are or I consider good questions. My best questions Dr. Mercado said to put a little star next to it. I have really learned alot about interviewing people since I came to this class. And Elza has helped me alot to understand, and take notes when I do interviews. I like interviewing because of people's diffrent appinions and reactions to my questions.

Collective reflective processes in research with young adolescent learners were occasionally problematic for students who are shy or who are easily distracted or preoccupied with other concerns. In addition,

A CHRONOLOGY OF 6M21'S SESSIONS WITH DR. MERCADO
SEPTEMBER-DECEMBER 1990

SEPTEMBER

09/14" Our special project begins today." (Mrs. Torres)
"We were talking about what she looked like and how she was."
"Dr. Mercado talked about where she came from and how she
got there." (Teddy, 09/17) "What is research?...Its just like
searching." (Jezebel)
"We got our special project books and we write down our
schedule." (Anthony)
"I learn about college work." (Asser)

OCTOBER

10/09" Dr. Mercado explained about what did we want to learn about."
(Tyrone) "and made a chart." (Jessica)
"What I want to know/ What I know/ How I'm going to find
out" "We are doing real research like big and grown people."
(Anthony)
"Research is something that makes you curious...Taking notes is
essential to be a good researcher.'" (Jezebel)
We started to talk about collaborative...we are not working by
ourselves, we are working together." (Jessica)
"We should make a group of kids." (Anthony)
"Dr. Mercado brings in (a proposal) abstract for the class."
(Jezebel)
"I think the college teacher is very nice and truthful to us. She
tells us her personal things." (Laila)

10/19" Dr. Mercado was impressed with our notes (Puli)
"She said a researcher takes good notes." (Jessica)
"She said that last year she did not correct spelling but this she
would like to correct us." (Jezebel)
"Dr. Mercado gave us the abstract papers she promised. Dr.
Mercado said she's going to give us notes from other people."
(Anthony)
"She is treating us like adults." (Jerry)
Now we're in groups. Dr. Mercado gave us an activity sheet. It
has the group members, recorder, specific questions and ways to
learn about the topic." (Anthony)
My group and I discussed the questions in the paper." (Puli)

Document 3

How difficult it is to write a chronology

It is hard to write a chronology because you have to write down an event that happened on a certain date. Then that takes a lot of time to do. You have to look up all your notes. From day one you have to start all your events.
Then sometimes you leave a date out and it is hard to resqueeze that event in your chronology. You have to re-write it.

Document 4

---

students sometimes found it difficult to express individual viewpoints, and to control the natural inclination to agree with the viewpoints of others who are held in high regard. Most importantly, reflection involves evoking thinking about past events and behaviors, and students need tools or aids to help them represent what occurred. In our activities, listening closely to students, legitimizing students' words in print, reviewing their work over time with them, viewing photographs and videotapes, and listening to recordings proved most effective in engaging our young collaborators in reflection.

SHARING

Both the nature of the research activities and the sharing of what the students found (through research presentations, report writing, etc.), created real needs for writing in a broad range of familiar and unfamiliar forms, including the writing of letters, interviews, autobiographical sketches, field notes, speeches, and others. Table 4.1 lists some of the different forms of writing. For example, the students wrote self-assessments, creating an awareness of how they could communicate more effectively with the audiences they addressed (see Document 5). They wrote notes to their adult guides to let us know how we could be of help (see Document 6). Even copying from the board presented an opportunity to extend what students know in a way that did not underestimate their abilities to understand and to learn; as Document 7 illustrates. Through their writings in their research notebooks, the students played a key role in documenting our activities. For example, Jezebel transcribed an activity in which Pamela, a graduate student, and students in the class who were part of an Indian Culture group, reflected on their analysis of an Indian legend. The transcription also illustrates how collaborative research becomes a pedagogical act (see Document 8).

Table 4.1. Some Of The Written Texts Produced By The Student-Researchers.

Contents of Students' Research Journal

> Observational Notes (Scribe Notes)
> Explanations for Selecting Their Research Topics
> Research Plans & Agendas
> Notes on Information Obtained From
> > interviews and conversations
> > reading books, magazines, newspapers
> > viewing videos or TV programs
> > conferences or meetings attended
> Self-Assessments and Peer Assessments
> Project Chronologies and Other Data Summaries
> Transcriptions of Interviews and Dialogues

Documents Written/Prepared by Students

> Progress Reports
> Speeches and Presentation Notes
> Handouts and Transparencies for Presentations
> Thank You Notes and Letters
> Project Abstracts
> Autobiographical Sketches

Students Also Recorded Activities in the Date Planner

> What I like about the presentation
> What I didn't like
> How you and others can improve

I liked the conference because everyone listened to each other everyone was a good odiance (audience)I like when Jessica made the flashback of the interview with Mr. B. and when I was Mr. G. and they asked questions. I didn't like (it) when we messed up in the begining I think we can improve by planning what we are going to do because then we forget....I think we should help each other for example if some one gets stuck someone should help the person.

(2/91)

Document 5

May 17, 1991
Dear Dr. Mercado,

I am willing to ask you to help my group. Because we haven't done much in my group. And we just read each others agendas and take notes. I want my group to discover what is happen on the bright side. What I am trying to say is I want my group to do more work. So we can become real researchers.

Sincerely,
Peilian

Document 6

Homework for Research   2/1/91

1) We need to develop an agenda for our next presentation Remember that we will only have an hour and fifteen minutes to tell the conference participants about our project.

2) We need to develop a abstract of our special research project this will be used as a hand out for our next presentation. we can develop this abstract collaboratively. That is, different groups can answer diffrent questions and then we can put all the answers together.

Document 7

After our first year's experiences, I provided students with black-and-white marble composition notebooks to preserve this documentation, which was sometimes lost when notes were kept in loose-leaf binders. Students used these notebooks to take scribe notes in and out of school, for their own purposes. Over time, these research journals became a personal chronicle of each student's entry into the world of ethnographic research (see Document 9). These journals are testimony that students appropriated these literacy practices associated with the work of "real" educational ethnographers, and made them their own, a significant and empowering learning, particularly when their notes served to inform us of what transpired during other classes or when substitutes were assigned to the class.

Regardless of their previous experiences with literacy, young adolescents willingly engaged in a broad range of academic uses of

(We are talking about the story that we had taped along time ago).

P: What did you think about the story?
Epi: It looks as if they made up the story right?
Pam. Uhah
Epi: Because it's funny because there was a fox or a kioty or when he wanted the monster to swallow him. But why would he do that?
Pam: Because he had
Anthony: Because he had magic and he could distroy it
Pam: Does this remind you of any other story you ever heard?
Epi/Anthony/me/Jerry: Nop
Pam: No?
Epi: But sopose his magic back fires?
Anthony: Yea
Epi: I didn't work and he would be swallowed.
Pam: That's true.

Document 8

literacy necessary to pursue advanced academic studies. Our data suggest that when young students do research (a) on topics that represent experiences that are lived rather than studied in textbooks; (b) intensively over the course of one school year; (c) for authentic purposes of their own choosing; and (d) with respected adults who write along with them, they usually have something to say and want to write. Similar findings have been obtained from research with bilingual students at the primary, elementary school (Edelsky, 1986; Moll & Diaz, 1987) and at the high school level (Heath, 1985; Trueba, 1987). Although students sometimes express reluctance or unwillingness to write, generally they are willing participants in this special community of writers where writing is a requirement for membership.

However, our data reveal other important influences on writing. Data from this ethnographic case study with middle school students suggest that peers are a positive influence on motivating writing, as this journal entry by Mario (02/91) revealed to us:

Today Mrs. Torres was talking to Dr. Mercado. Angel was here. He said all of them should be writing so we started writing. It help me a lot because if it wasn't for him I wouldn't write these words right now.

Thank You
Angel

THE CONTENTS OF JESSICA'S RESEARCH NOTEBOOK

1. Pen-Pal Letter (09/27)
2. Research Notes (10/09)
3. Meeting with Research Group (10/10)
4. Research Notes (10/11)
5. Research Group Members (10/11)
6. Rationale for Topic (10/11)
7. 3 drafts of Research Notes (10/19)
8. Activity Sheet (10/19)
9. Research Notes (10/26)
10. How Research Helps (11/09)
11. Research Notes (11/20)
12. Biographical Sketch (11/20)
13. What is Research? Group Notes (01/02)
14. What is Research? Jessica's View (01/03)
15. Copying Notes from Board (undated)
16. Thank You Letter (01/17)
17. Peer/Self Assessment (01/18)
18. 1 am wondering... (01/18)
19. Peer Interview (01/21)
20. Doing Research on Gossip (01/21)
21. The Parents Conference (01/31)
22. Copying Homework from the Board (02/01)
23. 2 Drafts of About my Trip with Mr. G. (undated)
24. What We Have Been Doing: Outline for Boston Presentation
25. Notes on way to Boston
26. Copying notes from the board (undated)
27. What I plan to do in Boston
28. What I plan to say
29. Trip to Boston (02/10)
30. Taking notes at the conference (02/11)
31. Interview of Conference Participant (02/11)
32. Research Notes about trip to Boston (undated)
33. Polio (02/21)
34. Agenda for Presentation (02/22)
35. Response to teacher's questions (02/27)
36. On return from Philadelphia (02/23)
37. Research without Dr. M. (02/26)
38. My data chart (02/27)
39. Meeting with Nutritionist (02/28)

40. Self and Peer Assessments 02/28
41. Interview with Mom (02/28)
42. Agenda for Friday (03/01)
43. Notes on our guest (03/01)
44. Agenda for Monday, March 4th
45. What do Cm and MT talk about? (03/01)
46. Notes for March 15th
47. List for Project (04/12)
48. Talking about people that are pregnant (04/26)
49. Questions
50. Agenda for Thursday

Document 9

Public acknowledgment and sharing of students' work, read by the teacher or shared anonymously with the class appear to be another important influence:

> Dr. Mercado was impressed with our notes. (Puli, 10/19/90)
>
> Dr. M. was impressed with our notes again. (Keith, 10/30/90)
>
> Dr. M started talking about college people look at our paper and are interested in it. (Puli, 10/26/90)

Also important was challenging students, or treating students like adults, as one student expressed it (see earlier quote).

Through their involvement in their research work, students got into writing and, as many stated emphatically, were surprised at what they had discovered about themselves:

> I can't stop taking notes. I love it! (Puli, 10/90)
>
> When I started scribing, it helped me . . . to write more. (Angel, 12/90)
>
> I can't help it. I keep writing! (Epi, 03/91)

In effect, data from this case study suggest that for the sixth graders in our community of literate thinkers, writing quickly transformed itself into a social practice that we all engaged in naturally and for authentic purposes and as a means of establishing membership among a very special community of writers. Students understood the unspoken rule they were responsible for creating: "If you want to belong, you have to write."

WHAT WRITING REVEALS ABOUT
YOUNG ADOLESCENT STUDENTS

In the foreword of Atwell's (1987) classic text on writing, reading, and learning with adolescents, Graves observed:

> For some time now the nation has been preoccupied with student improvement in writing and reading. . . . Some improvement is seen in the elementary years but by the middle school and senior high school years problems are particularly acute. Teachers have less time with their students, and the accumulation of school failure causes still greater problems in student attitude. . . . There remain major problems in text coherence and the ability of students to use information to persuade is severely lacking.

Graves's statement accurately captures the pervasive belief among practitioners that young adolescent students of all backgrounds are "very poor in writing." The perception that the problem is especially acute among racial and linguistic minorities is even more pronounced, especially when attention is paid to aspects such as penmanship, punctuation, spelling, standard English usage, and length.

Although students in this case study were described by some educators and assessments as being "very poor in writing," our data suggest otherwise. We found that students demonstrated sophisticated writing abilities early in the school year; for example Heidi, who was the type of student who spoke through her writing, as her letter below illustrates.

September 27, 1990

Dear Pen Pals;

Hi, my name is Heidi. I have 10 years old and I'm in 6th grade my teachers name is Mrs Torres she is really nice techer although she gives homework every day but just a little bit she is still a nice teacher. I live in the Bronx as you could see on the in-side address above. My culture is from the Dominican Republic but don't worry I like Puerto Ricans all my best friends I have are Puerto Ricans so you don't have to worry about it. Dominicans are just like you guys they just want to be your friends so the world could be together. I kind of like the Puerto Ricans alot so lets just forget about that know lets know talk about me. As I told you above my name is Heidi Genao and I have ten years old so far I've told you that OK so lets start now some of my feelings are when I'm crying I want people to leave me alone my favorite sport that I like to go swiming and when I go swiming I don't want to leave I like to eat alot of arroz con mollejaz those are the things I like to eat, well my little conversation with me and you is finish here something I want to say wright back soon my pen pal.

Yours truly friend
Heidi

There were, of course, tremendous fluctuations in students' willingness to engage themselves meaningfully and authentically in their writing, which suggests other explanations for "not writing" or being very poor in writing, as these statements reveal:

> Today I didn't feel like talking or anything else because I was bored and I didn't feel like doing research today. (06/90)

We agree with Edelsky (1991) that the term *development* may not accurately explain changes in the writings of young adolescent students students who are going through a period of rapid growth and physical development and, as a result, experience dramatic shifts in temperament.

We found that students wanted to write "correctly" and to be corrected. We had assumed the posture of not correcting students as a way of encouraging them to write and of giving them the opportunity to self-correct. However, we learned a great deal from their reactions to these procedures. Rebecca was particularly angry when we shared her work at the Ethnography Conference with what she perceived were mistakes and Nadia was indignant because we did not correct her spelling of "research." The issue of correction is an especially important one among young adolescent students who do not want to be publicly humiliated because their work does not conform to established norms of correctness which they know exist even if not reflected in their writings. Moreover, when given an opportunity to reread their work, students often cited carelessness and writing too fast as explanations for "mistakes" they had made.

It should be evident from the students' writings that have been presented throughout this document that students appropriated the language of researchers as well as the forms of literacy associated with the researcher "subculture," effortlessly and on their own, an important finding that may be explained by the type of relationship we had with the students and the respect and admiration they had for us. Not only did they want to speak like us, as Puli kept insisting, they also wanted to write like us. What is significant is that this appropriation was reciprocal in the sense that we, too, appropriated their words—words that we found to be a powerful means of communicating with the audiences we addressed at gatherings of professionals.

WHAT WRITING REVEALS ABOUT BILITERATE STUDENTS

There is much that we do not know about biliterate development among young adolescents. Data from this case study suggest that even when these Latino students use English to write, their writing reveals their biliteracy in a number of ways: (a) in the way they use Spanish to write English; (b) what they choose to write about; and (c) in affirming the values and beliefs of their cultural heritage.

Using Spanish to Write English

In their journalistic essay, "The Story of English," McCrum, Cran, and MacNeil (1986) document the thesis that just as there are varieties of spoken English, there are varieties of written English that reflect the unique world views and social realities of particular groups of speakers. Hernandez Cruz, a contemporary Latino writer, argued that when Spanish/English bilinguals write English, they are involved in a process of revitalizing the English language.

> As the children of these immigrants, we are at the centre of a world debate; we can speak of the shift from agriculture to industry to technology and the toll it has taken upon the human equilibrium. Let us look at it with clear eyes in our trajectory from one language (Spanish) to another (English). What have we lost or gained? . . . Is there an inner flower which passions its fragrance despite its being clothed in English words? I believe that this is happening in much U.S. Hispanic literature; the syntax of the English is being changed. . . . Of course we must strive for an English that is standard and universal, a language that can be understood by as many people as possible, but why lose the Spanish in the process? We should change the English and give it spice, Hispanic mobility, all this can be done within the framework of understanding, whether the reader is Anglo or Latin. (Hernandez Cruz, 1991, pp. 88-89)

Our data suggest that this revitalization occurs naturally when young adolescent students express themselves through the written word and that neither theories of transference nor interference adequately explain the phenomenon, one of clothing cultural values and beliefs in the clothing of English words, as these examples illustrate.

> My father gives me a good influence because he works hard to buy us food. He tries to do everything he can for us so we can have what we want. This is a good influence for me because in the future I can help my family. And also give the example my father gave me. My mother gives me a good influence because she gives me love and care. And in the future I can love and care alot about my family. (Epi)

> I am very worried because people in the street use crack and kill people and the family of the victim cry alot for the victim and God must be crying even more. (Danny)

> My mother and father are the most precious things that I have
> because they gave me a home and did the best they could do. I am
> very proud of my parents. They are very nice. (Heidi)

Reinventing English enables young adolescent Latino students to add to
their expressive possibilities (Hernandez Cruz, 1991) and to
communicate cultural values and beliefs that are otherwise impossible to
express, among them the importance of the family, caring and
compassion for others, respect, trust, and pride. Many of these cultural
values and beliefs are evident in the previous excerpts.

   The concern for the ill or less fortunate is evident in the plans
recorded by Jessica for the group of five girls interested in doing
research on children's illness (see Document 1). However, this value is
also evident in the writings of male students, as it was when Angel
expressed a renewed compassion for the problems of the homeless.
The theme of respect, both respecting and being respectful of others, was
especially dominant among the writings of the young adolescent
students we examined.

> I don't like to talk too much and I don't like people who talk too
> much. I only have friends that repects so I could respect them too.
> Sometimes I don't like people to talk or joke about me because I take
> it seriously. I respect people and teachers, specially Mrs. T. my
> official teacher. (Mario)

Most importantly, students' writings reveal their desire to excel and
achieve and to make their families and teachers proud, as well as to be
proud of accomplishments obtained through effort and hard work.

> I made a speech of all the things I wrote about my topic drugs. I
> talked about how do drugs effect your your body and what are the
> consequences of the victim using drugs. Of course I was nervous
> because it was the first time I been to a presentation before. But after
> I finish talking, I felt proud of myself. (Danny)

FINAL COMMENTS

By engaging in writing for authentic purposes—by scribing, planning,
sharing, and reflecting—students, teacher, researcher, parents, and other
adults learned a powerful message about the significance that writing
has in our personal lives and of the power of the writing to inform,
reveal, and affirm. Not only did students gain a new perspective on the
importance and utility of writing, but they also began to see themselves
as writers and to understand that writing is social responsibility for
individuals who come from marginalized communities. Especially those

of us who come from marginalized communities, we need to tell our own stories, we need to inform others of our cultural and linguistic heritages, and we need to preserve these treasures, even when there are multiple and competing demands on our time. Our experiences with students as researchers suggest ways to organize learning environments that support learning, environments in which writing is for sharing, for reflecting together and for fashioning new texts—texts of our collective voices, as is this one.

REFERENCES

Atwell, N. (1987). *In the middle. Writing, reading, and learning with adolescents*. Portsmouth, NH: Boynton/Cook Publishers.

Delpit, L. (1990). Language diversity and learning. In S. Hynds & D.L. Rubin (Eds.), *Perspectives on talk and learning*. Urbana, IL: National Council of Teachers of English.

Edelsky, C. (1986). *Writing in a bilingual program. Habia una vez*. Norwood, NJ: Ablex.

Edelsky, C. (1991). *With liberty and justice for all*. Bristol, PA: Falmer Press.

Freire, P., & Macedo, D. (1987). *Literacy. Reading the word and reading the world*. New York: Bergin & Garvey.

Heath, S. (1985). Literacy or literate skills? Considerations for ESL/EFL learners. In P. Larson, E.L. Judd, & L.S. Messerschmidt (Eds.), *On TESOL '84: Brave new world for TESOL*. Washington, DC: TESOL.

Hernandez Cruz, V. (1991). *Red beans*. Minneapolis, MN: Coffee House Press.

Lave, J., & Wenger, E. (1991). *Situated learning: Legitimate peripheral participation*. Cambridge: Cambridge University Press.

McCrum, R., Cran, W., & MacNeil, R. (1986). *The story of English*. New York: Viking Press.

Moll, L.C., & Diaz, S. (1987). Change as the goal of educational research. *Anthropology in Education Quarterly, 18*, 300-311.

Trueba, H.T. (1987). Organizing classroom instruction in specific sociocultural contexts: Teaching Mexican youth to write. In S.R. Goldman & H.T. Trueba (Eds.), *Becoming literate in English as a second language* (pp. 235-252). Norwood, NJ: Ablex.

van Maanen, J. (1988). *Tales of the field: On writing ethnography*. Chicago: University of Chicago Press.

Wells, G. (1990). Creating the conditions to encourage literate thinking. *Educational Leadership, 47*(6),13-17.

5

Life in Elementary School: Children's Ethnographic Reflections

Rosi A. C. Andrade
University of Arizona

How do children experience and perceive their lives?
What are the realities of children's social lives?

Spradley (1979) wrote that "rather than studying people, ethnography means learning from people" (p. 3). This learning process is shared by the researcher and informant alike. For example, Susana (a pseudonym), currently a ninth-grade student and a key informant in my study, is also an ethnographer in the sense that a conscious effort was made on her part to question, reflect, and understand her life in the contexts of home, school, and community, in order to learn not only from her classmates in general and from her reflections in particular, but also to share that retrospective knowledge with me. These efforts were recorded in dialogue journals that Susana and I exchanged, as well as subsequent and ongoing letters, phone conversations, and visits maintained by both of us. I use the combined terms *ethnographic reflections* to describe our efforts because ethnographic reflections denotes a learning and relearning over time, both on Susana's part as well as mine.

It is in this vein that I perceive students as ethnographers; as quintessential participant observers of their own worlds, not as miniature adults setting out to complete the adult tasks of ethnographer. This view of students as ethnographers allows us to see children in a new light, as active creators and participants in their own social worlds. Additionally, and as discussed in this chapter, it entails new forms of adult-child relationships.

My interest in how children experience and perceive their lives and the realities of the social worlds in which they live was prompted by discussions of our previous research called the Community Literacy Project (see Andrade & Moll, 1990). The aim of the project was to document "funds of knowledge," economic and labor resources vital to a family's survival, with pedagogical implications for children's learning in school (Moll, 1992a, 1992b). Although the research successfully accomplished documenting and bringing home knowledge into the school, nowhere were children's funds of knowledge evidenced. Although there were discussions about children, statements and observations were made by parents and teachers not by the children themselves. This led me to focus on the notion 'of children's understandings of their knowledge and experiences (social worlds), which is the focus of this chapter.

I specifically sought to understand the role and extent of Mexican and Mexican-American language minority children's bilingualism and literacy, as perceived and practiced by them. The study was conducted in a community where I not only have familial roots, but where I was also raised. This was accompanied by a critical appraisal, literature review, and preliminary inquiry of research related to children's lives (Andrade, 1993). The study was limited in scope, nonetheless it gives insight into the nature of how children experience and perceive their social worlds as well as provide a definition of students as ethnographers.

Historically in the research literature, education, and research conferences, children have only rarely been acknowledged as having valid knowledge or perspectives about their own social worlds. What is written about them is most often taken from observations of them as subjects in research studies. Similarly, much of the history of childhood has been gleaned from the writings of adults via diaries, biographies, letters, and documentation from respective historical periods (Ariès, 1962; deMause, 1974). Even in this century, with few exceptions (e.g., Coles, 1970, 1986, 1990), children are not allowed to pour out the minutiae of their lives. What is known about children's lives is often an adult interpretation (see Cahan, Mechling, Sutton-Smith, & White, 1993, for a discussion on the "imperial" practices of adults). In a sense, it always will be so, given that the adult will necessarily serve in an intermediary capacity to obtain and disseminate this knowledge. What is significant, however, is the source of that knowledge.

The evolving relationship between my work, research experience, and other research findings has led me to two methodological innovations: the dialogue journal as a document of interaction and the metaphor of researcher as "peer." In the highly personalized dialogue journal, children "speak" in an established interactive relationship. The researcher as "peer" metaphor is based on a reciprocity of actions (e.g., intellectual, emotional). This mutuality has by children's accounts made me a friend, peer, confidante.

In the next section, I place the study and the questions that began this chapter (How do children experience and perceive their lives? What are the realities of children's social lives?) in several related contexts: the problems that affect contemporary schooling, the treatment of children's experience and social worlds in educational research, and the specific situation of the students in the study. Then, I discuss the study focusing on students as ethnographers because it is this concept that provides the means for addressing the key questions that began this chapter and that are recurrent throughout the chapter.

FOCUSING ON CHILDREN'S EXPERIENCES AND SOCIAL WORLDS

The United States and other western nations are undergoing serious woes regarding their youth populations. Increasingly, the media are bringing into our homes the daily violence and despair that children are contributing to or are facing. The media have also pointed out that academic achievement in many school districts is appallingly low. These problems are not limited to the inner city, but also affect suburban and rural communities. Nor are they problems of the lower socioeconomic classes alone.

Part of the response in the United States has been a series of intervention programs initiated in schools and communities, programs that revolve on notions of "drug-free zones," "gun-free zones," "building self-esteem," and "peer mediation." Although these programs and others are socially responsive educational measures, there is a marked difference between what these programs strive for and what they pedagogically dictate. These programs are based on telling children what to do and how to conduct themselves, not on what it is children do and why.

How is it that countries rich in so many advances and technologies fail so many of their children?

The answer is complicated, but I suggest a few questions that may help serve as a beginning. What do we really know about children? What is the nature of children's presence in home, school, and community? What is the nature of adult-child experiences and relationships?

The analysis of children's social worlds within home, community, and school is somewhat novel (e.g., D'Amato, 1986, 1993) and is still evolving. For example, although Moll, Vélez-Ibáñez, and Greenberg (1989) focused on home, community, and school experiences of children, their study was not based on the children's social worlds, but the adults', parents' and teachers'. Goodnow and Burns (1985) and Cullingford (1991) looked solely to home and school as the extent of children's worlds, and did not intentionally delve into other aspects of those worlds. In Taylor's (1990) study we do not see children beyond what teachers describe in the classroom, and a few writing samples. In terms of bringing forth children's lives and knowledge, these studies fall short. Nevertheless, they remain important for two reasons. For one, they serve to reinforce the importance of understanding the child from an "emic" point of view. My definition of *emic* is one that seeks to capture children's perspectives and understandings of their worlds (Andrade & Moll, 1993). Second, they emphasize the scarcity of theory and methods and point to problems in researching children's experiences and social worlds (see also Erickson & Shultz, 1992). As adult-child relations currently seem to be understood in educational research and programs, they are tainted by adult-centric views. We see primarily the adult in those relations, as the adult fashions him or herself and as he or she fashions the child as an approximation of the adult (Cahan et al., 1993; Jenks, 1982).

In order to bring a wholeness to the discussion and description of children's social lives in my study, I developed a theoretical and methodological framework based on four interdisciplinary "steps" or "directions." First, given the population focus of this work, predominantly Mexican and Mexican-American children of the community of South Tucson, an initial step was to gain a better understanding of the history of childhood within the confines of South Tucson, a 1.2 square mile city incorporated in 1938. How has childhood been created and perceived, and how has it evolved over time? Interestingly, historians have had to rely heavily on literature to document histories of childhood, because no explicit documentation has ever been made (Ariès, 1962; deMause, 1974; Hawes & Hiner, 1991). Therefore, given the special characteristics of the population under study, I examined the bilingual "poetics" to gain greater insight into the bilingual experience of the children.

A second step was to acknowledge that children's interpretations and experiences are valid in and of themselves, which called for a phenomenological approach to the child's construction of reality, especially those phenomenological approaches exemplified in ethnographic lines of research.

Third, I sought to examine children's lives in the various social realms that envelop them, such as home, school, and community. This called for an ecological or sociocultural approach to human development. This ecological approach allows us to understand children's actions within their social contexts.

And fourth, when children's social worlds begin to materialize in the adult eye, socializing institutions such as the school, for example, can be seen as artificial constructs. We must, therefore, question their validity and effectiveness with respect to how they define childhood experiences.

STUDENTS AS ETHNOGRAPHERS

As mentioned earlier, I have been involved in the Community Literacy Project study that for several years has been studying households, classrooms, and after-school settings to advance understanding of home and school dynamics. The Community Literacy Project study involves participant observations, collecting writing samples, conducting interviews and administering questionnaires. Within this design, however, I have been developing a novel methodology that will allow me to interact more frequently and fruitfully in children's lives; a methodology that allows for the active inclusion of the child and her or his social world (see Andrade, 1993; Andrade & Moll, 1993). In my research I have used dialogue journals and found that they complement and facilitate the goals and findings of that research, as well as maintain the integrity of the child (as opposed to recreating the child in the image of the adult-researcher).

Dialogue Journals

> It is hard, despite what all sorts of doctors and social scientists have discovered, it is hard to accept the fact that young boys and girls can be so awfully, brutally, precisely clear about themselves, their present and their future—about the kind of lives they now live and the kind of lives they expect to live. (Coles, 1970, p. 29)

I have been using interactive dialogue journals to obtain children's perspectives on themselves and their social worlds. The dialogue journal falls into four central themes, similar to those originally outlined by Staton (1988): (a) the development of a mutual understanding among the participants, (b) the value of functional contexts for writing, (c) the cognitive demands of the dialogue on students' thinking, and (d) the way in which the dialogue personalizes education. These four themes allow access to children's social worlds, and have become central to my methodology (see Andrade, 1993, for a fuller discussion of the dialogue interaction). The dialogue journals in my study are further complemented by conversations with the children (individually, as well as in groups) and participant observations of the children within and outside the classroom, in the community, and in the home.

The type of dialogue journal that I have maintained with the children, I believe, goes beyond current applications. Staton's (1988), and Staton and Kreeft Peyton's (1988) use of the dialogue journal focused predominantly on promoting writing as authentic. However, the dialogue of the children is not only authentic writing but also an authentic representation of the children themselves, as each child represents her or himself through feelings, experiences, beliefs, and knowledge. In essence, the dialogue journal is presented as a forum in which the children can openly discuss any topic. For the children, the journal becomes a vehicle by which to define their actions and their surroundings.

In reading and responding to journal entries, I respect the privacy of the interactants and their respective journals as well. Confidentiality from fellow students, as well as from the classroom teacher, is crucial. My responses are a continuation of each child's previous entry. I can question and follow specific interests that I have, but this is only possible if the child permits it. The termination of content is a viable option, and is evidenced when the child chooses to change the subject altogether. During the course of the research, each child controls the course and direction of her or his dialogue (see also Fine & Sandstrom, 1988).

Susana as Ethnographer. The following information is the product of dialogue journal entries, taken from Susana's fifth- and sixth-grade journals, observations, and focused interviews regarding biliteracy conducted during the sixth-grade school year, as well as countless follow-up discussions with Susana during the past few years. When discussing her reflections on the nature of her biliteracy, Susana provides her respective experiences. What follows is first a description of Susana and the community in which she lives, and then a description of what school and classroom life have been like for Susana and other children in relation to their biliteracy.

Susana was born in Magdalena de Kino, Sonora, México, a relatively small town, just 110 miles north of Hermosillo, Sonora, and 50 miles south of Nogales, Arizona. The local economy of Magdalena relies on cattle and agricultural crops such as wheat, fruit, and chickpeas. The town is also renowned for being the burial place of Father Eusebio Francisco Kino, who came to the area in the late 1690s. Father Kino is well known for his teachings and contributions to the area. His fame not only extends westward into Arizona but internationally as well. Because Magdalena is a few hours driving distance from Tucson, it is not an uncommon trip for Susana and her family to make, especially during holidays and summer vacations.

Susana celebrated her 14th birthday in June 1993, and is the oldest of three children (two girls and a boy). She has a 13-year-old sister, and an 8-year-old brother. Susana and her family have been living in South Tucson since 1986. Susana's father works as a gardener for the University of Arizona, and her mother is a homemaker who also provides day care and ironing out of the home, and frequently helps her husband on weekend gardening jobs. Her father, however, has lived and worked in Tucson long before 1986, at which time he brought his family to live in South Tucson. Home for Susana and her family consists of a small, outdated trailer that the family rents for $100 a month. The home is crowded and modestly furnished, but clean by any standard.

Susana is Spanish/English bilingual, but prefers to speak Spanish; her mother is Spanish monolingual; her father is learning English, but at home he speaks Spanish exclusively; her sister is bilingual, but prefers to speak English; and her brother began learning English in first grade. The variety in language abilities found in this family is not uncommon for Mexican families in the Southwest. Even in families who have resided in the United States for a number of generations, there may be family members who remain Spanish monolingual, while the young begin to learn English upon entering school.

The city where Susana has lived since her arrival in the United States, is South Tucson, a predominantly Mexican and Mexican American enclave. It is more accurately, a 1.2 square mile city within the city of Tucson, incorporated in 1938. South Tucson has gone the route of many inner cities in the last few decades. The original luster of the city is long gone and has been tarnished by the economic and social depression of its dwellers (see Kotlowitz, 1991; Kozol, 1991). Amenities often taken for granted by other communities in the United States, or in Tucson for that matter, such as clean and well stocked grocery stores, manicured parks, and flourishing businesses, have long been absent from this community. Restaurants and bars do prevail and thrive, but they serve mainly as a tourist haven for authentic Mexican food, and a getaway from the larger Tucson community that surrounds it. Although these restaurants sit at the edge of the city and are generally overflowing with patrons, they are but a stone's throw away from the local bar strip, and bordered by abandoned homes and businesses. These are abandoned structures frequently used as drug houses or makeshift homes for homeless boys and men, as well as sites where acts of prostitution take place.

The elementary school that Susana attended was built in 1923, 15 years before the actual incorporation of South Tucson. Surprisingly, like South Tucson's other elementary school, it is run by the Tucson Unified School District. This is a surprise for several reasons. First, the purpose of South Tucson's incorporation was to maintain autonomy. Mexican culture and the Spanish language were part and parcel of that self-contained body. And South Tucson moved toward autonomy by nominating its own mayor and city council, appointing its own police chief, hiring its own police force and firefighters, and running its own sanitation department and jail compound. Yet when it came to the education of its children, South Tucson stepped back and left the instruction of its children to the outside experts. Second, in a community that valued its Mexican heritage and Spanish language, formal education was a cruel and humbling experience (see Sheridan, 1986). In great part due to the sociopolitical climate in the United States toward minorities and their native languages, many Mexican and Mexican-American children suffered the brunt of our society's dislike of, or distrust toward their language and culture.

In South Tucson, language-minority children entering school during the decades of the 1930s, 1940s, 1950s, and 1960s, were not allowed to speak Spanish. They were penalized if they were caught speaking Spanish, by means of corporal punishment, if not ridicule. Those children speaking Spanish or speaking English with an accent were considered slow learners or worse yet, mentally retarded (for discussions on these practices see Bogdan & Taylor, 1982; Camarillo, 1990; Carrasquillo, 1991). One adult, now in his mid-50s, who attended the same elementary school as Susana, explained:

> They would flunk everyone in the second grade, and say that we were slow. They would send us to another [elementary school], to the Special Room. But at that school, they would say there was nothing wrong with us and send us back. We didn't know any better. We had never experienced or seen anything out of South Tucson. We thought that was the way it was. Not until I joined the army, did I understand what was going on. Our parents trusted the schools. They weren't going to argue with them. (M. Villegas, Summer, 1991)

This seeming complacency on the parents' part, often interpreted by the school as lack of interest, was far from that, but rather it was a respect for the educational institution and the teaching profession.

A common reaction to Mr. Villegas's experience is one of disbelief and anger at the injustice and inhumanity imposed upon unsuspecting children. The "Special Room" was after all but a metaphor for the holding pen that housed those children discriminately labeled "mentally retarded." Yet Mr. Villegas seems quite accepting of the past. Through this disparity in our respective reaction and attitude towards an infraction of human rights, a decisive generational difference is laid open. As Mannheim (1927/1982) wrote, such a discrepancy in reactions is important, in that, "it is one of the indispensable guides to an understanding of the structure of social and intellectual movements" (p. 256). Outrage and anger were not an option to be considered for much of Mr. Villegas's generation, a generation taught to defer to the experts, be they teachers, physicians, clergy, or other professionals. The deference can best be described as a blind trust and unquestioning acceptance. Generations later, the ability to demonstrate anger and outrage at such injustice cannot yet be characterized as an inalienable right, for it is still an option to be expressed, as it was in Mr. Villegas's youth. And as Mannheim's observation suggests, understanding discrepancies between generations may aid in our understandings of a new generation of children by stirring critical questions: How does the present generation of children react to their experiences? Where do these children fit in? Which doors are open (or shut) to them? Such questions help frame an understanding of Susana's dialogue journal interaction.

In the entries that follow, Susana's own words convey some of her feelings, beliefs, and experiences in order to give the reader an understanding of who this child is before going into the discussion of biliteracy. English translations are on the right, Spanish originals are provided to the left (no grammatical corrections are made to the children's writing).

Yo me llamo Susana, mi apellido es O__igual que la escuela. Toda la gente que no me conoce escribe mi nombre mal. Unos lo escriben con Z otras personas lo escriben con dos n. Ami me enfada cuando escriben o docen mi nombre mal. Yo tengo diez años de edad, yo cumplo los once años de edad en Julio 16. Casi todo el tiempo me hacen fiesta en mi casa. Hace poco hybo un concurso de ortografía aquí en la escuela. Yo participe en ese concurso de ortografía. Yo gane en ese concurso de ortografía. En abril 21 tengo que ir para el Community Center para participar con las demás escuelas de Arizona. De cada escuela de Arizona van a ir dos niñas o niños. Tengo que estudiar mucho las palabras para participar en ese concurso de ortografía. Cuando gane el concurso de ortografía me dieron dos certificados. El año pasado también participe pero no gane

My name is Susana, my last name is O__, the same as the school. Those that don't know me misspell my name. Some write it with a Z others with 2 Ns. It upsets me when they misspell or mispronounce my name. I am ten years of age, I will be eleven years of age on July 16. They almost always make me a party at home. Not too long ago there was a spelling contest here at school. I participated in that context, I won in that contest. On April 21 I have to go to the Community Center to participate with the other schools in Arizona. Two girls or boys are going from each school in Arizona. I must study the words a lot to participate in that spelling contest. When I won the spelling contest they gave me two certificates. Last year I also participated but I did not win because I made a mistake in 'excitados' I forgot the 'c'. But that time I was a little nervous. My

porque me equivoque en excitados me falto la c. Pero esa vez estaba un poco nerviosa. Mi comida favorita es la sopa Campbell's de gallina. También me gusta mucho la nieve y las paletas heladas. Cuando llego a casa me pongo a ver calicaturas o hacer tarea. También me pongo a jugar. Primero saludo a la gente y luego le doy un beso a mi mamá y a mi nana. A las cuatro llega mi papá del trabajo. Mi mamá cuida un niño el niño se llama Arturo pero de sobrenombre le decimos magu. Yo quiro mucho al magu. El magu es jugueton, bueno, curioso, bonito y además come de todo y no es chillón. Ahora Rosi te quiero preguntar algunas preguntas. ¿Como te llamas? ¿Cuantos años tienes? Tu eres muy bonita, buena se te nota mucho. Tu eres como una estrella que esta en el cielo azul. Eres como una flor que esta planta en la tierra fértil. Es todo gracias.
(Susana, 5th grade, 3/23/90)

favorite soup is Campbell's chicken soup. Also I really like ice cream and frozen popsicles. When I get home I watch cartoons or do my homework. Also, I play. First I say hello to the people and then I give my mother and my nana a kiss. My father arrives from work at four. My mother takes care of a little boy, the little boy's name is Arturo but we have nicknames him Magu. I love Magu very much. Magu is playful, good, cut and pretty and furthermore he eats everything and he is not a crybaby. Now Rosi I would like to ask you some questions. What is your name? How old are you? You are pretty, nice you can really tell. You are like a star which is in the blue sky. You are like a flower that is planted in the fertile ground. That is all thank you.
(Susana, 5th grade, 3/23/90)

DESDE SEGUNDO GRADO ESTOY EN ESTA ESCUELA. YA TODOS ME TIENEN BIEN ENFADADA TODOS. ME TIENEN BIEN ENFADADA PORQUE YO NO VENGO A LA ESCUELA PARA QUE ME INSULTEN YO VENGO A LA ESCUELA PARA ESTUDIAR, TANPOCO VENGO PARA QUE ME ESTEN PIDENDO LAS RESPUESTAS. PARECE QUE CREN QUE SOY CALCULADORA. ELLOS DEBEN PONER ATENCION PARA QUE NO ME ESTEN PIDIENDO LAS RESPUESTAS.

I have been at this school since the second grade. I am fed-up with everyone [fellow students] here. I am fed-up because I don't come to school to be insulted I come to school to study, nor do I come to school so that they can be asking me for answers. It seems that they think I am a calculator. They should pay attention so that they don't have to ask me for answers and also so that they don't have to copy me [my work]. When I am distracted they take my paper and

PARECE QUE CREN QUE SOY CALCULADORA. ELLOS DEBEN PONER ATENCION PARA QUE NO ME ESTEN PIDIENDO LAS RESPUESTAS Y TAMBIEN PARA QUE NO ME ESTEN COPIANDO. CUANDO ME DESCUIDO ME AGARRAN EL PAPEL Y ME COPEAN LAS RESPUESTAS. CUANDO VOY A TOMAR AGUA, A SACARLE PUNTA AL LAPIZ Y CUANDO ME LEVANTO A AGARRAR UNA COSA QUE SE ME CAYO. TAMBIEN CADA RATO ME AGARRAN LOS LAPICES, Y OTRAS COSAS MAS.
(Susana, 5th grade, 5/8/90)

copy the answers—when I go to drink water, sharpen my pencil and when I go to pick up something that I've dropped. Also, they are always taking my pencils, and many other things.
(Susana, 5th grade, 5/8/90)

Para mi aprender inglés es estar aprendiendo más. Así entiendo más. Aprendo más. Habló más inglés. I tambien le entiendo mas a la gente que me haabla inglés....YO SI SEQUIRE CON EL ESPANOL PORQUE ES MI IDIOMA Y NADIE ME HACER QUE HABLE OTRO IDIOMA. YO VOY A HABLAR OTRO IDIOMA CUANDO ME DE MI GANA. PERDONAME PERO ES CIERTO A TI NO TE DIGO ESO PORQUE ERES ADULTO.
(Susana, 5th grade, 5/17/90)

For me learning English is to be learning more. That way I understand more. I learn more. I speak more English. And I also better understand the people who speak to me in English. . . . I will continue with the Spanish because it is my language and no one will make me speak another language. I will speak another language when I please. Forgive me but it is true I don't tell you that because you are an adult.
(Susana, 5th grade, 5/17/90)

MI PAPA TRABAJA EN LA UNIVERSIDAD DE ARIZONA DE JARDINERO. MI PAPA SABE MUCHO DE PLANTAS DE ARBOLES DE FLORES Y MUCHAS COSAS MAS. MI PAPA ES MUY INTELIGENTE. NOS A TRAIDO A LA CASA DIFERENTES ANIMALES. ESTOS SON LOS ANIMALES QUE NOS A TRAIDO MI PAPA

My father works at the University of Arizona as a gardener. My father knows a lot about plants about trees about flowers and many more things. My father is very intelligent. He has brought us home different animals. These are the animals my father has brought us—snakes, recently hatched birds, turtles, small rabbits and large rabbits, cats of all

VIBORAS, PAJARITOS RECIEN NACIDOS, TORTUGAS, CONEJOS CHIQUITOS Y CONEJOS GRANDES, GATOS DE TODOS TAMANOS Y TAMBIEN PERROS DE TODOS TAMANOS. SE ME HACE QUE SI LES GUSTA TUCSON. A MI NO ME GUSTA TUCSON PORQUE LOS GRINGOS SE CREEN MUCHO Y A LOS MEXICANOS LOS TRANTAN COMO ANIMALES. LOS GRINGOS SE CREEN LOS REYES DE TODOS LOS MEXICANOS. YO NO SE PORQUE MI FAMILIA SE QUISO VENIR A LOS ESTADOS UNIDOS. SOLAMENTE QUE LES PREGUNTE.
(Susana, 5th grade, 5/25/90)

sizes and also dogs of all sizes. I think they [my parents] like Tucson. I don't like Tucson. I don't feel comfortable being there with the 'Gringos' [Anglos or anglicized people] and not with my people from over there in Mexico. I would like to go to Mexico with my own people. . . I am not comfortable in foreign lands like for example the United States. Where I am comfortable is in my beautiful land of Mexico. And only in my land of Mexico will I always feel comfortable. Because the Gringos are full of themselves and they treat Mexicans like animals. The Gringos think they are the kings of all the Mexicans. Because they think they can go around bossing Mexicans. They have no right to mistreat in that way. They [Gringos] only take advantage of them [Mexicans] to make them suffer. I don't know why my family decided to come to the United States. Unless I ask them.
(Susana, 5th Grade, 5/25/90)

Just these few dialogue journal entries make it apparent that even young children have legitimate experiences that begin to form their interests and outlook in life. Susana is very much concerned with race relations and language matters. These concerns influence her character and how she chooses to portray herself; for example, although she is a fluent bilingual Susana refuses to be forced into English. In school, Susana does well. She completes the tasks assigned, yet she is not the socially and politically conscious Susana we come to know in the dialogue journal.

With respect to school activity, children like Susana and her classmates have become disconnected from their own knowledge and experiences. They act in ways that are expected, even if they do not consider it appropriate. They don't readily share their day to day concerns, nor their deepest ponderings. The school gives them at best a facade; at worst, rejection. A traditional research view of these children would yield inadequate and misleading conclusions.

Studying biliteracy. In attempting to understand children's biliteracy, it became increasingly clear that it would require gaining an understanding of children's lives and how their lives flow back and forth into the realms of home, school, and community. This required recognition that the most important aspects of literacy learning may take place outside the classroom. In fact, it entailed acknowledging that what is often taken for literacy in the classroom may be the more stagnant forms its existence can take. A major purpose of the biliteracy study, therefore, was to take a critical look at literacy; a view that affirmed the importance of children's social lives outside of the classroom.

In addition to dialogue journal interaction and participant observations, children were also interviewed. They were asked to reflect on several written questions; for example, when did they first perceive themselves as becoming bilingual? How did they feel about their reading and writing in both languages? Which language did they prefer to speak? Why? Did they plan to continue speaking their mother tongue? Why? During the process of the interview, the children wrote their responses with ease and were given no time limit. This was facilitated and made possible by the teacher's cooperation and absence for the duration of the morning session, as well as my already established presence in the classroom as both a dialogue journal interactant, and as an occasional substitute teacher. The activity took between 1 1/2 to 2 hours. After reviewing the children's responses a follow-up interview was conducted away from the classroom. The fact that I had already established a rapport with these children through the Community Literacy Project and there was a mutual understanding as to my goals and their lives, and established *confianza*[1] between us facilitated the biliteracy study.

One goal of the biliteracy study was to develop a more accurate portrait of children's uses of literacy in two languages: in their day to day activities, and in the various social contexts that encompass their lives (home, school, and community). Although all the children in this study are equally important, in this chapter I focus my discussion on Susana with a few exceptions.

Home. Mothers of bilingual children may not be bilingual, which is very likely a consequence of the restrictive nature of their child-care and household duties. Although some mothers take in additional work, such as outside child-care responsibilities, ironing, and making and selling flour tortillas, they do not have much opportunity to learn English. In general, the same can be said for fathers. For example,

[1]*Confianza* is a Spanish word not easily translated to English, meaning a spirit of mind, and developed not through verbal exchange, as in "I trust you," or "You can trust me," but through actual example and deed.

Susana's father is taking English as a Second Language (ESL) courses at the university; yet he depends on Susana for help in completing his lessons. Although Susana's father works as a groundskeeper at the university, he is not exposed to opportunities to learn English, as would be expected, so he takes the ESL courses during his free time.

Also not mentioned as bilingual are younger siblings and older family members, often restricted to the home by household and childcare duties, as well as age. Susana's younger brother did not begin learning English until entering the first grade.

What occurs in the home for bilingual children therefore, is that they become language and/or cultural brokers to family members (see Hawes, Schulz, & Hiner, 1991). When notes come home from the school, it is the child who translates them to the parents. It is also the child who must first deal with any and all incoming requests as well as any outgoing correspondence from the home. Parents may often pause in a conversation, to ask a child to interpret or confirm what they have understood. If not completely entrusted with the task of communication, bilingual children are at least expected to review the family's outgoing correspondence. The following vignette serves to make this point.

Not so long ago, Susana's father, Mr. O, engaged her assistance in writing a letter to the recently appointed president of the University of Arizona. During the previous winter, Mr. O had mentioned to me, while on a visit to their home, that he felt he worked many long hours, did hard work, and had been with the university as a groundskeeper for a very long time. Yet he had not received an increase in pay; others, who did less and were newer, were surpassing him in pay scale. Ongoing budget cuts had eliminated several groundskeeper positions, yet the workload, which had not diminished, had been relegated to Mr. O and his remaining coworkers. Furthermore, he felt that his wages were meager support, in this day and age, for a family of five. Mr. O told me that he had been thinking of writing a letter to the new university president, in light of so many other university personnel taking th opportunity to do the same. Mr. O then asked me if I approved. My response was that if he felt that strongly and was justified in his cause, I could only encourage him to do so. Mr. O then asked me if I could help him with the English. I told him I could, adding that as soon as he wrote the letter in Spanish, I would translate it to English, and type it for him. Mr. O nodded and said he would probably write the letter. Three to 4 months passed with no further word on the progress of the letter. Susana would later tell me that her father had sent the letter to the president of the university, and gotten a positive response from the university. As a direct result of the letter, Mr. O would receive an upgrade in both pay scale and job title, beginning on July 1 (the new fiscal year). I told Susana that I was very happy to hear about this and asked her for details. Our conversation went as follows:

Rosi: Did your father write the letter in Spanish, or English?

Susana: No, he wrote it in English.

Rosi: What do you mean? Who wrote it?

Susana: Well, I wrote it. My father would tell me in Spanish what he wanted to say, and I would find the best way to say it in English, and write it.

It is in instances like this, where we realize the importance of children's biliteracy skills to the well being of the family as a whole, how those skills are utilized by the parents, and further how unremarkably common are children's contributions to the home.

School

> The desire to learn and to understand begins so early that it must be considered natural, but this desire does not last undiminished through the years of schooling. This, in itself, should give pause for thought. (Cullingford, 1991, p. 1)

As of the sixth grade, Susana had spent the last 5 years residing in the United States. She began attending schools in the United States during the second grade, and had attended the same elementary school for Grades 2 through 6.

Susana explained that she began the study of her second language (English) in the fourth grade, but did not feel she became bilingual until the sixth grade. As to her expressed competencies, when she feels she became bilingual and her degrees of bilingualism, Susana considers herself to be "good" at reading and writing in both English and Spanish.

When asked why she felt it was in the sixth grade that she became bilingual, Susana responded, "Because um, in sixth grade I speak more English and started more English than Spanish." In essence, she feels she is now bilingual because she can communicate more fluently, can understand English speakers more clearly, and is able to read books that interest her personally.

In the classroom, Susana was considered by the teacher to be more of a bilingual, that is, she was considered to have greater command of her second language than other classmates. Subsequently, she was given far greater opportunities to learn and practice English within the school environment. For the major part of the sixth-grade school year, Susana spent afternoons in the monolingual English classroom, in order to receive her social studies and math lessons in

English. In her own classroom, she was encouraged to write and read in English, as well. Although the same textbooks were used in the classroom, some of the children, like Susana, were assigned English text versions, whereas others were assigned Spanish text versions.

Overall, children interviewed voiced discomfort with reading in their second language. Their concerns bordered closely on fears of harassment and the ensuing embarrassment of being singled out. The fear was not that they were incapable of reading in English, but fear that others would make fun of their pronunciation. For children, these concerns interfere with academic learning, for the focus of children's energies is more readily directed towards adapting to this type of stressful situation (Romero, 1973). Susana, for example, explained:

> Like if I, if I don't say the word good, or well or something, I don't say it that good, they start telling that, "you know, you have to tell that, you have to put the tongue out," I don't know, you have to pronounce with more I don't know. . . . Um, some things I don't know how to pronounce and then when you know them wrong, they start telling you funny things, well like you don't know how to read well, you know? . . . I like to read my second language to myself, because if I make a mistake I know it, and not other people. (Susana, Biliteracy Interviews, 1991)

A common reaction for children like Susana and her classmates is to avoid oral reading, which may be interpreted by the teacher as yet another sign of the children's inability to "read" in English. And inherent in this conception of reading is the ability to understand and speak English.

It is unfortunate that so much emphasis continues to be placed on oral pronunciation because it has become a sanctioned act of violence: Children literally pounce upon classmates during any English oral language activity. The children, in this case, are internalizing a concept of oral reading ability based on a pronunciation void of other language inflections. Based on these criteria of reading, children are projecting their own shortcomings unto other children, compounding everyone's fears even further. Clearly, the message relayed to these children is that there is one pronunciation and if one does not hold that, then she or he is unable to read. Further ramifications of such an ideology dictate that those same children are not ready to study other content areas in English, or go beyond basic English.

Rare were the occasions in which some of the children were heard speaking English in school. In fact, they were quite reserved about their intended audience. Only when they felt comfortable with their audience would they speak in English. In the dialogue journal, for example, some children tested its utility for language experience.

Alberto (a pseudonym) is one such child. Here he is writing in English for the second time:

> Hay rosy I hope that you have a new year and we gona see you in January doing the dialog journals . . . thank you for saying that my English writting is very good and I'm gona keep traing to do my best I could in mi English writting. (Alberto, 6th grade, 12/20/90)

Outside of these journal entries in English, Alberto did not practice his oral or written English abilities in the classroom.

During the school year, it was not unusual to witness monolingual teachers approaching the bilingual children, directly aiming a barrage of questions like "Is your teacher in the classroom?" "Where did he go?" "When is he coming back?" "Is he taking your classroom to the party?" and demanding that the children answer immediately. Not only did the children not know where the teacher had gone, when he would return, nor whether they would be permitted to attend the party in question, they were also coy about speaking in English. The children, still in thought, would not answer, and the teacher would have the final word with yet another series of questions "Don't you understand?" "Don't you know English yet?"—and walk away. Meanwhile, the children, still standing in the same position, would continue to gaze at the teacher, shrug their shoulders and return to their activity; occasionally one would say, "she doesn't have to be so rude," to which the others would give a coalescing nod. It was on occasions such as these, that I, as an adult, felt the demeaning nature of schooling, and how very unfair it is for children in general, and minority children in particular. My reaction was to turn inward in disgust, and reflect on the significance to children of such experiences, and in turn their varying reactions, ranging from rebellion to submission. Unlike Taylor's (1990) suggestion that one "imagine" children's lives, I reflected on what I had seen and heard, in order to appreciate what children were saying and doing in their material lives. Cullingford (1991) made a pertinent point regarding these situations of embarrassment or threat when he wrote:

> Many of the pleasures of school, however, are not spectacular events that give an occasional contrast to the routine, but certain times of the day when the routine itself is peaceful. *Children appreciate those quiet moments when they are not under threat, whether from the humiliation they receive from teachers or from the bullying of other children.* (p. 54; emphasis added)

Interestingly, as Cullingford (1991) explained, while other children may bully, teachers have the uncanny ability to humiliate. Given this type of treatment within the school environment, one can understand children's coyness with anything related to second language speech. Yet, as discussed in the next section, whether it was legitimized or not, these children engaged their biliteracy when the situation necessitated it.

Community. Within their community, children maintain active profiles, visiting friends, neighbors, and relatives, shopping at the corner market for parents or with parents, accompanying parents to doctor and (social) institutional appointments, going to the library and to the local youth center, as well as attending religious classes and trips. Thus, with every venture they find people who are either bilingual as they are, monolingual English or Spanish speakers, and even Chinese/English bilingual store keepers (commonly found throughout the neighborhood). In their dealings with these individuals, they take communication for granted when they relay messages, obtain pertinent information, make requests, haggle over prices, and so on. Their bilingualism is an integral part of their daily existence.

In spite of discouraging school experiences, some more overt than others, children continue to read English language books to themselves. Romero, one of Susana's classmates, is highly interested in psychokinesis and parapsychology. It is customary for him and his brother, who is a year older than him, to go to the local or main public library branches on a weekly basis. More often than not, the books related to their personal interests are in English. Romero attempts to read them but is frustrated when there are words he does not know; as he explains, "The bad part is that I don't understand one or another word well. That is why I sometimes get ticked off, because I don't know too well."

Those words that Romero does not know, may not be the words themselves, but the highly technical concepts he is attempting to grasp (i.e., psychokinesis, parapsychology). Discussing his reading in both languages, Romero explains, "they are so many the books which I like to read in English and in Spanish I don't think I would be able to finish telling you which books I read" (Romero, Biliteracy Interviews, 1991).

But he does write about a few, among them *The Power Of Your Subconcince Mind* [sic], in English, and in Spanish: *Extrasensory Perception,The Magic of the Psychic*, and *How to Develop and Augment Your Psychic Powers*. Other English-language books these children read include romance novels, youth literature, science fiction, terror stories, as well as nonfiction. Yet in the school, like many of his classmates, Romero epitomized the nonreading, unmotivated student.

It is important not to equate the impetus to learn the second language with a desire to forego a first language. Quite the contrary, the children are adamant about maintaining their first language, the importance they relegate to it is visible in their oral and written language practices. Unless they are communicating with a monolingual

English speaker, showing off their second language prowess, or simply rebuking a remark made in English, there is an unspoken preference to speak and write in Spanish. Following are some explicit entries regarding language taken from Susana's fifth-grade dialogue journal:

> For me learning English is to be learning more. I learn more. . . . And I can also better understand the people who speak to me in English.I will continue with the Spanish because it is my language and nobody can make me speak another language. Forgive me but it is true I don't tell you that because you are an adult. (Susana, 5/17/90)

Susana wants to learn English, but not be forced to do so, and certainly not at the cost of losing her mother tongue. These are her views and sentiments, yet they are shared by many other students, as suggested by my observations of their daily language practices, and what the children themselves have written in their journals, regarding language issues. From the dialogue journal, we come to know children who visit the public library weekly, searching, for example, for books dealing with the supernatural, children who are prolific story writers and avid pursuers of knowledge. Yet in the classroom, these same children do not voice strong sentiments nor opinions, nor do they do very much reading or writing in English or Spanish. Such a discrepancy between school and nonschool settings may be because "what social reinforcement such a child does receive in school is likely to be more contingent upon his label 'as disadvantaged' than upon his actual behavior" (Bronfenbrenner, 1981, p. 138). And yet, children are fast becoming bilingual and literate with or without the classroom. Those becoming bilingual in spite of classroom practices that limit their second language experiences, are doing so of their own accord. Unfortunately, in the case of literacy development, what we find is that imposed classroom limitations obstruct opportunities to speak and write in English, waste opportunities to capitalize on children's interests and motivations, and often place the burden to learn both English and Spanish on the children and what home and peer resources they can access.

FINAL COMMENTS

The premise of this work has been built on the belief that often what is not visible is as consequential as what is; that for the researcher the perceived be "viewed as more important than the actual" (Bronfenbrenner, 1977, p. 202). In studying children, this has translated into the realization that children are a human entity all their own, and that even the most rigid and controlling of environments cannot undermine the existence of their social worlds (intellectual and physical). In my work, I have striven to keep each child the pinnacle of information, respecting children's knowledge and experience as it is real for them. I see methodologies such as participant observation (researcher as "peer") and dialogue journals, accompanied by changes in theoretical orientations toward children, their needs and interests, and the inclusion of other disciplines, not only as vital to the goals of research claiming to represent children's social worlds but also to educational policy, programs and practice.

From a theoretical standpoint, *we cannot understand adult-child relationships within the home, school, and community without understanding the children's community*. A community that, although separate from that of adults, mediates adult child relations, personal as well as institutional (El'konin, 1980; Venger, Slobodchikov, & El'konin, 1990). Such a view allows the adult to see the child in a new light, as an active agent in the creation of her or his social world and it provides for a fundamentally new way of understanding our own adult activity as well.

REFERENCES

Andrade, R. (1993). *Children's social words: Critical appraisal, literature review, and preliminary inquiry.* Unpublished manuscript, The University of Arizona, Tucson.

Andrade, R., & Moll, L. C. (1990). *Children's domains of knowledge.* Unpublished manuscript, The University of Arizona, Tucson.

Andrade, R., & Moll, L. C. (1993). The social worlds of children: An emic view. *Journal of the Society for Accelerative Learning and Teaching, 18*(1,2), 81-125.

Aries, P. (1962). *Centuries of childhood: A social history of family life.* New York: Knopf.

Bogdan, R., & Taylor, S. J. (1982). Inside out: *The social meaning of mental retardation.* Toronto: University of Toronto Press.

Bronfenbrenner, U. (1977). Lewinian space and ecological substance. *Journal of Social Issues, 33*(4), 199-212.

Bronfenbrenner, U. (1981, January/February). Children and Families: 1984. *Society,* 38-41.

Cahan, E., Mechling, J., Sutton-Smith, B., & White, S. B. (1993). The elusive historical child: Ways of knowing the child of history and psychology. In G. H. Elder, Jr., J. Modell, & R. D. Parke (Eds.), *Children in time and place: Developmental and historical insights* (pp. 192-223). New York: Cambridge University Press.

Camarillo, A. (1990). Mexicans and Europeans in American cities: Some comparative perspectives. In V. G. Lerda (Ed.), *From "melting pot" to multiculturalism: The evolution of ethnic relations in the United States and Canada* (pp. 237-262). Italy: Bulzoni Editore.

Carrasquillo, A. L. (1991). *Hispanic children & youth in the United States : A resource guide.* New York: Garland.

Coles, R. (1970). *Teachers and the children of poverty.* Washington, DC: The Potomac Institute.

Coles, R. (1986). *The political life of children.* Boston: Atlantic Monthly Press.

Coles, R. (1990). *The spiritual life of children.* Boston: Houghton Mifflin.

Cullingford, D. (1991). *The inner world of the school: Children's ideas about schools.* London: Cassell Educational Limited.

D'Amato, J. J. (1986). *"We cool, that's why": A study of personhood and place in a class of Hawaiian second graders.* Unpublished doctoral dissertation, University of Hawaii.

D'Amato, J. J. (1993). Resistance and compliance in minority classrooms. In E. Jacob & C. Jordan (Eds.), *Minority education, anthropological perspectives* (pp. 181-207). Norwood, NJ: Ablex.

deMause, L. (1974). The evolution of childhood. In L. deMause (Ed.), *The history of childhood* (pp. 1-73). New York: The Psychohistory Press.

El'konin, D. B. (1980). *Psicologfa del juego* [The psychology of play]. Madrid: Visor Libros.

Erickson, F., & Shultz, J. (1992). Students' experience of the curriculum. In P. W. Jackson (Ed.), *Handbook of research on curriculum* (pp. 465-485). New York: Macmillan.

Fine, G. A., & Sandstrom, K. L. (1988). *Knowing children: Participant observation with minors* (Sage University Papers Series on Qualitative Research Methods, Vol.15). Beverly Hills, CA: Sage.

Goodnow, J., & Burns, A. (1985). *Home and school: A child's-eye view.* Sydney, Australia: Allen & Urwin.

Hawes, J. M., & Hiner, N. R. (1991). *Children in historical and comparative perspective: An international handbook and research guide.* New York: Greenwood Press.

Hawes, J. M., Schulz, C. B., & Hiner, N. R. (1991). The United States. In J. M. Hawes & N. R. Hiner (Eds.), *Children in historical and comparative perspective: An international handbook and research guide* (pp. 491-522) New York: Greenwood Press.

Jenks, C. (1982). Introduction: Constituting the child. In C. Jenks (Ed.), *The sociology of childhood: Essential readings* (pp. 9-24). Great Britain: Billing & Son Ltd.

Kotlowitz, A. (1991). *There are no children here.* New York: Doubleday.

Kozol, J. (1991). *Savage inequalities: Children in America's schools.* New York: Crown.

Mannheim, K. (1982). The problem of generations. In C. Jenks (Ed.), *The sociology of childhood: Essential readings* (pp. 256-269). Great Britain: Billing & Son Ltd. (Original work published 1927)

Moll, L. C. (1992a). Bilingual classroom studies and community analysis. *Educational Researcher, 21*(2), 20-24.

Moll, L. C. (1992b). Literacy research in community and classrooms: A sociocultural approach. In R. Beach, J. L. Green, M. L. Kamil, & T. Shanahan (Eds.), *Multidisciplinary perspectives on literacy research* (pp. 211-244). Urbana, IL: NCRE/NCTE

Moll, L. C., Velez-lbanez, C., & Greenberg, J. (1989). *Year one progress report: Community knowledge and classroom practice: Combining resources for literacy instruction* (IARP Subcontract No. L-10). Washington, DC: Development Associates.

Romero, A. (1973) The Mexican-American child: A socioecological approach to research. In G. J. Powell (Ed.), *The psychosocial development of minority children* (pp. 538-572). New York: Brunner/Mazel.

Sheridan, T. E. (1986). *Los Tucsonenses: The Mexican community in Tucson, 1854-1941.* Tucson: The University of Arizona Press.

Spradley, J. P. (1979). *The ethnographic interview.* Fort Worth: Holt, Rinehart and Winston.

Staton, J. (1988). Contributions of the dialogue journal research to communicating, thinking, and learning. In J. Staton, R. W. Shuy, J. K. Peyton, & L. Reed (Eds.), *Dialogue journal communication: Classroom, linguistic, social and cognitive views* (pp. 312-321). Norwood, NJ: Ablex.

Staton, J., & Kreeft Peyton, J. (1988). Topics: A window on the construction of knowledge. In J. Staton, R. W. Shuy, J. K. Peyton, & L. Reed (Eds.), *Dialogue journal communication: Classroom, linguistic, social and cognitive views* (pp. 245-276). Norwood, NJ: Ablex.

Taylor, D. (1990). Teaching without testing: Assessing the complexity of children's literacy learning. *English Education. 22*(1).

Venger, A. L., Slobodchikov, V. L., & El'konin, B. D. (1990). Problems of child psychology in the scientific works of D. B. El'konin. *Soviet Psychology, 28*(3), 23-41.

6
Learning to See Learning in the Classroom: Developing an Ethnographic Perspective

Beth Yeager
McKinley Elementary School
Ana Floriani
Judith Green
University of California, Santa Barbara

In this chapter, we examine how ethnography was taken up by Beth Yeager and her fifth-and sixth-grade students to construct an inquiry oriented classroom community. By describing activities and written artifacts from her classes, we illustrate the ways in which Beth helped her students develop an ethnographic perspective and learn how to use ethnographic tools in becoming ethnographers of their own learning across discipline areas. To illustrate this process, we show how they used the ethnographic perspective and tools to compare their own processes and practices with those used by members of the disciplines—historians, artists, mathematicians, scientists, readers, and writers—and how, through- this process, they constructed discipline-based knowledge.

FRAMING BETH'S GOALS FOR ETHNOGRAPHY IN THE CLASSROOM

Beth teaches in a small, linguistically diverse city in southern California. Her students come from different ethnic backgrounds and speak English, Spanish, and Vietnamese. Many are bilingual. Her educational philosophy focuses on getting her students to take a different stance toward knowledge than is traditionally found in classrooms. She emphasizes that knowledge is constructed, rather than given, and that learning is primarily a matter of inquiry and interpretation rather than memorization or reproduction of known facts. Beth believes that inquiry is essential for the children in their roles as students and learners as well as for her, in her role as teacher and learner.

Beth

My goal is to help students develop strategies for learning that they can use both in and out of school. From my first year as a preschool teacher (1970), I have wanted all students to be able to inquire into their thinking, to examine their procedures and processes for learning, and to be able to understand the ways in which the class community was being constructed through the ways they interacted with others.

As I have moved across grade levels, I have become concerned with helping my students acquire discipline-based knowledge. I want my students to understand how discipline knowledge is the product of actions of people and how they can "take up" the actions associated with particular disciplines. I want them to be able to "envision" themselves as anthropologists, artists, readers, historians, writers, scientists, and mathematicians

To put my goals into practice, I create opportunities to explore how people in each discipline go about their work. We explore the ways artists work by entering their lives through their words and creations. For example, we enter the life of Faith Ringgold by reading Tar Beach (1990) and talking about her story quilts. We use what we learn about her as an artist to explore our own writing and painting. As we work as artists, we look back on her process and see how our process is similar to and different from hers. We record our observations and ideas in our writer's notebooks (Calkins, 1986) and our learning logs.

The processes of inquiry and our ways of exploring the work of people within the disciplines for ourselves enable us to create a common language for learning. It also makes visible the processes and practices of those disciplines so that students can take up these practices and can see relationships across disciplines. I also try to communicate this approach to parents so that we, the parents and I can build a support for student inquiry and exploration. This is especially important since some of the projects involve parents.

Since 1991, Beth and her students have been part of the Santa Barbara Classroom Discourse Group. The group includes researchers from the University of California at Santa Barbara and teacher researchers from the South Coast Writing Project. One interesting and unexpected consequence of this collaborative work is that Beth and the other teacher-researchers are using ethnographic processes and practices as a means of constructing knowledge in the academic curriculum and as a way of reflecting on their own learning. Ethnography, therefore, has become more than a research process for describing life in these classrooms, it has also become a resource for learning used by both teachers and students. This process is visible in the following excerpt from an interview with Beth and from a Community Essay written by Maggie, a sixth-grade student.

Beth

What the ethnographic study has contributed to this process is a language to describe what it is I do and how we, the students and I, construct a common language for looking at learning and for exploring how others engage in similar processes in all aspects of everyday life.

Tower Community by Maggie Monroy (May 25, 1993)

In the beginning of the year we got to know each other by bringing things that represented our hobbies. We also got to know more about ourselves by writing down how we are as mathematicians. We put that in our portfolios.

Pretty soon, we started to work as a class or a community. For example, way in the beginning, we did a problem with watermelons. From what I remember, we had to figure out how much Ms. Yeager had spent on all six watermelons. First we had to see how much the watermelon weighed. Then we had to guess how much it was per pound, then we had to multiply it by something and something and somehow each table got a price.

But the point is that we all did it as a class, like when someone said an answer or question in either language [English or Spanish] and Ms. Yeager would translate it so we could understand each other and would know what was going on.

Another time was when we were studying on the "Tropical Rain Forest" with Mrs. Pattenaude. Each table had to work together on one layer of the rain forest; some would study on the animals of the layer and others would study trees and plants. We took notes from rain forest books. We also had to do a painting about the layer. Then we presented it and talked about it in both languages. Again, we understood what was going on. We had to take notes, meanwhile, for each presentation for a "Rain Forest" report.

Another thing I am saying is that we work in groups, no matter the language, because at each table there is at least one facilitator. So it doesn't matter with whom we work as long as we are a community. That is probably a way we function as learners.

I guess the way we really function together as learners is that when someone says something, depending on what we are talking about and what the classmate says, we will either agree or say what our point of view is, but from what I know, no one has put someone else down for what they said That's the way I see it.

The way that we, the Tower community, form a community is probably the way we treat each other, with respect, and how we get along, the way we work together and the good times we have together with not a lot of trouble. It's just the way we treat, work and respect each other. That's how I think we make a community.

In her essay, Maggie wrote about the patterns of everyday life and illustrated how community was formed, how it functioned, and how it was sustained across the school year. Maggie's essay illustrates one way Beth helped students develop the tools and processes for self-study (e.g., what was involved in doing the watermelon project), the study of others (e.g., history, science, artists, and writers) and the study of their communities (e.g., home and classroom).

The community essays were initiated in the first year of the classroom ethnography (1991-1992) by a student who elected to write · about her classroom as a free writing activity. In reading it to the other students, she inspired them to write their own accounts of classroom life. These accounts were then videotaped and bits of classroom life were incorporated to provide a collective record of Life in Sixth Grade that was given to students. The success of this student-initiated writing project became part of ongoing life in subsequent years and has become one of the ways of helping students examine what and how they have learned across the year.

CONSTRUCTING AN ETHNOGRAPHIC PERSPECTIVE IN THE CLASSROOM

At the beginning of this project, Ana and Judith entered the classroom with the idea that they would engage in a traditional topic-oriented (Green, 1983; Hymes, 1982) classroom ethnography. Their goal was to examine the patterns of classroom life in order to identify how the teacher established a community of writers with her students and to describe what counted as literate actions (Santa Barbara Classroom Discourse Group, 1992). Like more traditional ethnographers, their goal was to study the patterns of life of a social group, in this instance, the class. By entering the classroom before school started and observing over three school years, Ana and Judith sought to capture the ways in which the teacher, students, and other class participants (e.g., parents, aide, student teachers, administrator, other teachers) worked together to shape the patterns of social and academic life in the classroom (Collins & Green, 1992). As ethnographers, they were concerned with understanding and describing what members needed to know, understand, produce, interpret, and predict in order to participate in and contribute to everyday life within this classroom.

Ana and Judith brought with them the tools of the ethnographer: participant observation, interviewing, and artifact analysis. They planned to use these tools to make visible what students needed to know as members of this class and how such knowledge was constructed. They also brought with them an orienting theory drawn from cognitive anthropology (e.g., Spradley, 1980) to help identify ways people (a) constructed patterned ways of interacting, participating, and interpreting what is occurring; (b) established roles and relationships through the interactions occurring in times and spaces, and serving particular purposes, (c) negotiated what counts as knowledge, action, task, and membership through the patterns of interaction among members, and (d) constructed a language of the classroom. These theoretical principles asked them to consider: Who can do or say what? When? Where? Under what conditions? For what purposes? And with what outcomes? The theory framed a general orientation but did not provide an a priori view of classroom life. This orienting theory became the basis for a "language about life in this group" that Beth and her students used to reflect on their own learning and practices. This theory was also used as a means of understanding what members of a group or a discipline needed to know and do.

Ana and Judith's original plan to be traditional ethnographers became modified and reshaped through interactions with Beth and her students during the initial phase of entry and access.

Shaping Direction: Beth 's Perspective

I set the conditions for Ana and Judith's entry to afford students an opportunity to become co-researchers in the ethnography and to establish a particular relationship between Ana and Judith as researchers and those of us in the classroom—"I would like you to be members of the community and to participate in and contribute to the life of this group. "For example, as we constructed opening events that helped shape the community— shared family stories artifacts from our lives and personal experiences—I expected them to participate in the sharing. I also made visible to students the nature of the research project, shared ways they would contribute to the project, and described some of the opportunities they would have to participate as co-researchers of life in sixth grade.

Additionally, I asked Ana and Judith to share their field notes and purposes for doing ethnography with the students. I used this sharing to help shape and define what anthropologists do and to set the stage for students to take up the roles and language of anthropologists as we began the study of history as a social science.

What Ana and Judith did not know or anticipate was the degree to which their approach to ethnography matched Beth's goals for students and would support the inquiry approach being shaped. Thus, they could not anticipate how their research theories and processes would become an integral part of classroom practices. Additionally, Beth's goals for students were not visible to Ana and Judith in the initial negotiation for entry. These goals became visible only as they participated in the class and as students sought ways of interacting with them and participating in the processes of data collection.

Negotiating and Reshaping the Ethnographic Process:
Ana and Judith's Perspective

From the first day, students were able to talk informally with us, act as camera persons, and assist in collecting and gathering data. We were continually negotiating our roles, when students could participate, how they would participate, when we could talk with Beth, and how she wanted us to participate.

We entered intending to be observer participants, not participant observers, and were concerned with not disrupting the flow of everyday life. However, because of the ways in which Beth introduced us, her expectation that we become members of the community, and the interest of the students in our work, the relationship between the ethnographic process and classroom practices was reshaped.

For example, on the day we had planned to exit the first phase of the ethnography, Beth asked us to share what an anthropologist did by presenting our field notes. She wanted each of us to read our notes so that the students would be able to see how the same event was observed differently. She also asked us to talk about why we were doing the research and why we needed their help in understanding what happened while we were not present in the next few weeks.

Students agreed to be our "eyes and ears" so that we would be able to understand what we had missed. To help us, they agreed to record daily life for us in a notebook on a special sheet and to give that information to one person at their table group. This person used the information to write a letter (in English or Spanish) describing what had occurred during the week, and Ana answered in Spanish or English. They also agreed that one table group member each week would participate in an interview during lunch on Fridays. In this way, we were able to maintain membership in the community, to re~enter later in the year with "insider" knowledge and to support ongoing student participation in the inquiry process.

What neither Beth nor we anticipated were the ways in which the students' roles would grow over the school year, and how their actions and interactions would shape the direction of both the classroom and the research. We never anticipated how the research process, itself, would become part of the students' repertoires for inquiry in this classroom. Additionally, we could not envision the degree to which Beth would adopt and adapt the language and practices of ethnography to construct a common way of talking about the content and processes of the classroom with students and others (e.g., other teachers, administrators, parents).

Over the 3 years of this collaborative ethnography, the orienting theory has become a common language that teacher, students, and researchers use to talk about everyday life. This language has become part of the everyday practices of members. The ways in which the language has been used by Beth as a means of communicating about life in the classroom can be seen in the following map of learning processes she constructed to share with parents at a back-to-school night (1992).

What is evident in Figure 6.1 is that the processes and practices represented parallel the processes of inquiry used in ethnography. In other words, just as an ethnographer seeks to understand what members of a group can say or do, with whom, when, where, under what conditions, for what purposes, and with what outcomes, Beth's students were asked to engage in similar processes (shown in the circles at the top and bottom of the figure) applied across discipline areas (shown in the rectangles in the center of the figure). These processes ask students to consider and explore what scientists, artists, mathematicians, social scientists, readers, and writers do, how they do it, and why they engage in such processes. Students take on an ethnographic perspective in order to examine what counts as membership within and across disciplinary boundaries. In this way, students have the opportunity to see and understand discipline knowledge as the outcome of the actions of people in the role of artist, mathematician, scientist, social scientist, reader, and writer.

Through such explorations, students learn that knowledge is not an abstract or transmitted body of information. Rather, it is constructed by members of a social group or discipline through their actions and interactions, individually and collectively. Additionally, they come to understand and develop a language for talking about this process. That is, they learn the following:

1. Questions are formulated and reformulated throughout the inquiry process;
2. Data are constructed not found;
3. Observation is a selective process guided by personal as well as formal frames of reference;
4. Observation and data construction require a descriptive language;
5. Interpretation is based on evidence and point of view, not merely personal opinion;
6. Within a group, multiple interpretations of a text (visual, oral, aural, written) are possible and probable; and
7. Multiple ways of presenting information exist.

Thus, students become scientists, not merely engage in doing science. They also become mathematicians, artists, social scientists, readers, and writers, not just "kids" reproducing known bodies of knowledge. Finally, by engaging in these processes and in helping students see that knowledge is both a social (group) accomplishment and an individual accomplishment within a social context, Beth helps students reflect on their own practices as well as those of others.

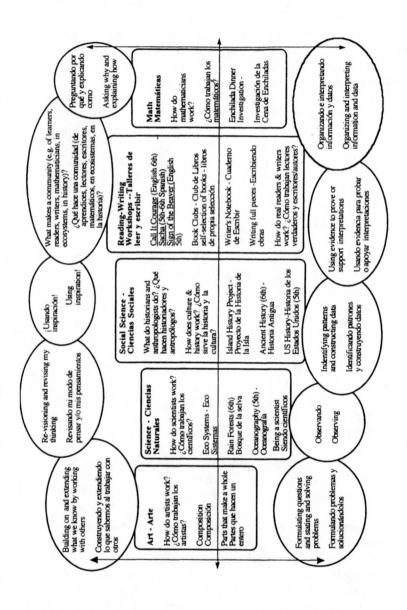

Figure 6.1. Inquiry as a basis for building community
Investigar Es La Base Para Construir La Comunidad

That students understand this perspective and see its value is illustrated in the following excerpts from essays by three students in two different years in sixth grade (1991-1992; 1992-1993). The excerpts are drawn from two types of reflective essays written by students as part of their membership in this class: Community essays and essays in which students reflect on themselves as learners, both written in spring of the school year.

Giselle: What We Do (1993)

(Original in Spanish)	(Translation)
Investigamos juntos. Participamos en trabajos como la investigación de la isla, la cena de enchiladas, e Egipto. . . . investigation, the enchilada dineer, Aprendemos por tener evidencia, por nuestra imaginacion, y por arte.	We investigate together. We participate in work like the Island and Egypt. . . . We learn through having evidence, through our imagination and through art.

Brad: How We Do It (1992)

I think how we learn in our class is to think about how we do our questions instead of just going the easy way and writing down the answer. What I mean by this is, say y we had a fraction, we wouldn't just multiply the two and say we're finished. We would say how we thought about it and how we came up with that answer. Basically we go through the process.

Tony: Myself As A Learner (1992)

I as a learner have matured in my studies, for instance in writing. I was just a fiction crazy writer. I couldn't write like I do now. I would write just whatever I could think of, but now I know to base my story on something. Same in math—instead of one way through a problem, I learned other ways, easier ways.

I have also learned how to be a historian. Before I only knew how to look at maps and read about history, but this year I learned how to make up and write a history and how to have supporting evidence.

This year I am convinced that I did learn a lot and I was ready to.

The voices of Beth and the students indicate that they have constructed a shared valuing of and disposition toward inquiry across disciplines. Given this orientation, the integration of ethnographic processes was a "logical" extension of the processes already in place. The ethnographic process and the orienting theory were resources for engaging in the events of everyday life. These resources helped members of the classroom community make visible to themselves and to others what they needed to do or say as well as who could interact with whom, in what ways, for what purposes, when and where, and with what expected outcomes.

LEARNING TO INQUIRE: ETHNOGRAPHY AS A TOOL FOR THE STUDY OF SOCIAL SCIENCE

The process of becoming social scientists began in the first moments of the first day of school. This process is reflected in the ordinary and marked ways that Beth helped students establish and shape a common language of the classroom (described in detail in Lin, 1993) and construct patterned ways of acting and interacting across disciplines (described in detail in Santa Barbara Classroom Discourse Group (1992, 1995). For example, on Day 1 through an event called the Watermelon Problem, Beth initiated a sequence of practices and processes that students would use throughout the year to engage in learning across disciplines.

Day 1 began a cycle of activity that focused on what it means to be a mathematician. This cycle of activity took 4 days to complete. Across days, students engaged in gathering data (i.e., observing, estimating and recording observations), comparing different interpretations of data, representing and reporting on their processes and observations, and writing about their processes. Through these activities, they began to understand that people called mathematicians have particular processes and practices in which they engage (for further discussion see Brilliant-Mills, 1993).

On subsequent days, the processes begun in mathematics were extended to art, writing, literature, natural science, and social science as well as to the ways of participating in all aspects of classroom life (as shown in Figure 6.1). Through these actions, Beth helped students initiate a process of constructing particular ways of being a student and of engaging in actions that counted as *studenting* in this classroom (for further discussion on becoming students see Fernie, Davies, Kantor, & McMurray, 1993; Santa Barbara Classroom Discourse Group, 1992)

Therefore, the patterns of life preceding the Island History Project provided a historical context for the beginning of the study of history and social science. For example, before the Island History Project began, students were introduced to a series of related and ongoing processes that became resources for students during the Island History Project:

Writing their history as readers (Week 1);
Writing their history as mathematicians (Week 1);
Sharing personal memories, stories, and artifacts (ongoing from Week 1);
Recording their thought processes in Learning Logs (ongoing from Week 1);
Developing a life history timeline (Week 2);

Using personal stories or memories in a writer's notebook
(ongoing from Week 2);
Recording responses to their readings in Literature Logs
(ongoing from Week 2).

These seemingly differentiated tasks are grounded in a common set of
practices involving students, on a daily basis, in gathering data,
observing their own actions and thoughts, examining the world of the
classroom, and making links between the classroom and larger social
world. Thus, social science, in all of its forms, was part of an ongoing
web of activity. One way of viewing this web is that it shaped what
counted as learning, being a student, and discipline-based knowledge in
this classroom.

In providing opportunities for students to take up the actions
and language of historians and anthropologists, Beth helped them apply
knowledge gained in one area to the study of other areas. She helped
students see that members of each discipline observe for different
purposes, adopt particular perspectives, exchange information in
particular ways, and represent their observations in ways that members
of the discipline expect and value.

To illustrate how Beth helped students become historians and
anthropologists, we discuss five events that helped frame the
ethnographic study of social science. The first four form a foundation for
the final event, The Island History Project. The first event, The Three Pigs,
helped students explore the ways data are influenced by point of view
and perspective. The second event, Maps as Sources of Data, involved
students in comparing and contrasting ways of representing the world.
The third event, The Detective Story, provided opportunities for students
to understand what counts as evidence and how evidence can be
interpreted to form hypotheses and theories about what they observed.
The fourth event, the PBS Videotape entitled "The Ice Man," showed
students how scientists representing different fields work collaboratively
and how each field provides particular perspectives and contributions to
theory construction. The final event was The Island History Project in
which students had to draw on personal and group knowledge, consider
point of view, and construct and interpret evidence in order to write a
history or ethnography of the island as an historian or an anthropologist
(for a detailed discussion see Floriani, 1993; Heras, 1993).

The Three Pigs: Point of View, Notetaking and Notemaking

The Three Pigs cycle of activity was used to introduce the idea that the
same data may be perceived and interpreted in a variety of ways. The
cycle of activity was comprised of four events: a group tangram activity,

a saturation observation activity, a text observation activity, and a reconstruction of the Three Pigs text. Each event in this cycle involved students in examining how point of view, purpose, and ways of representing data influenced their interpretation of the data.

This cycle began with an activity to introduce the difference between notetaking (i.e., recording descriptive field notes) and notemaking (i.e., hypothesizing and/or making interpretations based on the data recorded). To help frame this activity, Beth invited Judith and Ana to share their field notes of life on that day. Ana shared her notes from an insider's perspective because she had been a member of the group on a continuing basis from the first day of school, whereas Judith was an occasional member. Thus, Judith's notes were from a more distant position than Ana's.

In reading their notes to the students, they emphasized the similarities and discussed why the notes were different. Judith also asked them to help her understand the meaning of what she had observed. For example, she asked questions about this year's seating patterns since they differed from the previous 2 years in which she had been a member on an ongoing basis. She also asked questions about the objects on the bulletin boards and about the ways in which the students worked together. With Ana and Judith, students explored the types of information that ethnographers record when they take notes during observation and examined the types of questions that ethnographers ask—Who can do or say what? To or with whom? When? Where? For what purposes? Under what conditions? With what outcomes?

After examining Ana and Judith's fieldnotes, students were given an opportunity to become notetakers and notemakers. Four students, two Spanish-dominant and two English-dominant, volunteered to participate in a tangram activity and were asked to come to the center of the circle in the library area. The other students were asked to take out their learning logs and to turn to a notetaking/notemaking sheet (a sheet divided in two parts, one headed notetaking and the other notemaking). The student volunteers were then given a random set of pieces from a tangram set. They were told that they had to make a square and that each square would have the same Five pieces. They were also told that they had to negotiate nonverbally with others in order to get the pieces each needed to complete her or his own square. The remaining students were to record the sequence of actions among the square builders on the notetaking side of their observation sheets.

During the activity, Judith provided clues for students to help them accomplish the task. Once a student completed the square, he or she was encouraged to help the others. After the squares were completed, students were asked to read their notetaking, to add information and to begin recording interpretations under notemaking. Students were then provided with an opportunity to read their notes to the group in English or Spanish and to compare the ways that people recorded what occurred.

Some of those involved in the tangram part of this event responded to their observations from their point of view as "square makers." In one instance, the notes of one observer were challenged by a square maker. This student indicated that the notetaker had not recorded what she did but rather had written an interpretation of her actions. In recording his observations, the notetaker indicated that her actions showed that she was asking for help in completing the task. In responding, she indicated that she was reaching for a piece she needed, not asking for help. This difference in point of view was used as a basis for further discussion on how the same event "looks" different or is "recorded" differently depending on the role, position, and perspective of the observer.

The tangram task set the framework for a homework assignment in writing that asked students to become observers of life in their homes. This activity was called a saturation observation because the students were asked to "saturate" themselves with the sounds, actions, smells, and other sensory data within a particular setting. They were to observe for 15 minutes and to record, as much as possible, what they observed, visually and aurally. These records were written in their writer's notebooks and were to be used as a foundation for writing a narrative description in class on the following day. One of the goals for this activity was to help students see how observation could be used as a basis for writing about life.

Once this activity was completed, the nature of observation for the purpose of writing was compared with the purpose of observations in other disciplines—art, social science, natural science, and the reading of literature. These activities occurred on different days in different disciplines (social science and writing), yet served to frame a common understanding about the relationships among observing, interpreting, and recording data

Two additional activities were used to extend and refine students' understandings of this relationship. The first occurred in the late morning of the second day of this cycle of activity. Just before lunch, Beth told a commonly accepted version of the story of the Three Pigs. She then engaged students in a brief discussion of this version during which students indicated that they knew other versions with different endings. After lunch, she asked students to become observers and to examine the "only" piece of evidence left from this "historic" event that had occurred in "Pigtown, USA." The evidence was a picture of three pigs walking down a road.

To illustrate how the different versions came into existence, students were asked to observe the picture from a particular point of view and to record their observations on the notetaking side of their observation sheet. Each table group was asked to take a different perspective: the perspective of mother pig, the third pig (the pig with the brick house), the stick salesman, the wolf, and Ana the ethnographer. The class then discussed what might be recorded. Students recorded their observations and shared these observations, first in their table groups and then with the whole class. Following the discussion of what the different groups recorded, Beth introduced the idea of interpreting or notemaking. The 2-minute excerpt shown here is from a 65-minute lesson. In this excerpt, Beth is framing the notemaking activity that students will do later in the lesson.

Beth: Introducing Notemaking, Interpreting A Common Text Differently

One of the things, now that historians do or ethnographers do is they take a look at what their notes mean to them (2-second pause) And (2-second pause) historians and witnesses, depending on their point of view do something called interpret the evidence, they interpret the evidence (4 second pause). They try to make, have it make sense to them

quiere que tenga sentido por eso ellos escriben lo que significa

So you just did that

Shyam said and Marcelo said, "we think they were moving and that's what the sticks meant" and "that's good for us cause maybe we can sell them sticks to make the house."

Of course it's possible they weren't moving. It's possible they were taking their lunch and going on a picnic. To the stick salesman, that's what they were doing.

Enrique said, "they're fat." To him, that might mean there's a good meal. They're gonna taste really good, I better get them.

   Enrique: "They're juicy"

   Junior: "There's going to be a lot of them"

There's going to be a lot of them, right.

The third pig said, "I'm wearing overalls, I can really work hard"

"puedo trabajar bastante en mis pantalones

"The mother said, "my children are all clean." To her, maybe that means, thank goodness at least they are safe if they are clean. Who knows?

Would you on the right side of your paper, of your "notemaking side" el derecho

would you please be the card at your table. Be the wolf, and write down what you think, write down what you think your observations mean to you wolves. If you observed these things, why are they important to you and what do they mean?

Escribe al derecho que significan sus notas porqué son importantes.

Por ejemplo, a los vendedores de palos, a los lobos, a las mamas, a los etnógrafos, a los, um, puercos.

What have you learned from your observation as a stick salesman ?

(turns to table with role of stick salesman)

José, what have you learned from your observations as an ethnographer?

What do your notes mean ?

In this excerpt, Beth invited students to think about what they had learned from their notes and from taking a particular point of view. She helped foreground the different points of view and, the fact that the students were in a role that was influencing what they recorded and how they interpreted the picture and their own notes. The following example illustrates the notemaking process:

From the Point of View of the Wolf: Raquel, Fifth Grade (1994)

Notetaking	Notemaking
Three pigs 1 pig is bricks 2 pig is stics 3 pig is dried hay with their bags going away from home the 1st pig is wearing a hat blue blue and / \ yellow / \ he is very fat with wight gloves 2nd is wering a sort of brick coler with wight gloves and blue bow tie with a brick colord hat. 3rd pig is wearing yellow with a yellow and brick collard hat with wight gloves. their all fat and their all allown going away from home with their bags on a stic over their sholder and their all happy and dancing sort of or skiping	I think their running in mud Their very fat so I'm going get a lot of food. I guess their moving to the forest so its going to be harder but their alloen with Know one to protext them so that macks one thing easy. The two in bacl look pretty dumb so it will be easy to get them but the one in front looks pretty hard to get.

Once students had recorded and interpreted their notes, they were then asked to use these data to complete a homework assignment—to write or draw the history of this event using the data recorded. Once again, students were asked to assume a role, in this instance, as an eyewitnesses, they used their notes and any other information that, as eyewitness, they knew about the story. The way in which this process was taken up is visible in the beginning of Ariana's history written in Spanish from the point of view of *ethnographer as participant observer.*

The Ethnographer's Perspective: Ariana, Fifth Grade (1994)

Original Version	Translation
Yo un dia iba a obserbar y mire que iban caminando muy contentos 3 puercos. Yo no sabia que si fueran hermanos porque hiban caminando uno atras del otro ni se podia saber que si se conosian. El primer puerco compro paja yo no podia saber que dijo el primer puerco porque yo estaba muy lejos y no podia escuchar.	*One day I was out observing and I saw three very happy pigs walking. I didn't know if they were brothers because they were walking one behind the other nor could I know if they knew each other. The first pig bought hay. I don't know what the first pig said because I was far away and could not hear.*

As indicated in the beginning of this history, Ariana was able to distinguish between what was observable and what was interpretation. Additionally, she was able to take up a position as ethnographer and to write from that point of view using a genre that was consistent with that role. Ariana also shows that students were able to view history as something based on data and informed by a point of view or stance. The Three Pigs cycle of activity framed the relationship of data to interpretation. The histories written from these data were viewed as one way to represent the information obtained. To extend students' understandings of ways of representing data, Beth adapted an activity used by Judith in her qualitative research course—using maps to examine ways the phenomena can be represented differently. In this activity, Beth used world maps and globes to show how different forms of representing information influence what can be known about the world. The types of maps included: political, endangered species, and topographical maps; globes showing land masses only; maps foregrounding oceans; and maps or globes produced by different countries. As in the earlier activities, students were asked to observe (notetake) and to compare and contrast the information represented. They were then asked to think about what their observations meant and to record their thoughts in the notemaking column. Thus, students had opportunities to extend their understandings of how point of view and purpose influence what is represented.

Two additional activities provided further opportunities for students to examine the relationship among the actions of observing, interpreting, and representing patterns of life. The first involved a detective story. Beth told the students a story and asked them to identify the types of evidence the detective used and to examine the mistakes and assumptions the detective made in interpreting that evidence. Students were then given a homework assignment in which they were to choose two events from their personal history timelines constructed in the second week of the school year. They were to provide written evidence that the event actually happened. Through this activity, she tied social science to writing in ways that supported student exploration of social science concepts and writing genres.

The second activity involved students in watching a PBS videotape entitled "The Ice Man." This video documents the work of scientists including social scientists, biologists, archaeologists and geologists in solving the mystery of an ancient skeleton found frozen in the Alps. Through the video, Beth helped students examine the processes and practices of members of particular disciplines working collaboratively. Students were provided an opportunity to observe how members of this team wrote or constructed a history of the Ice Man through observing and interpreting evidence, forming hypotheses, and constructing, testing, and revising theories. The students took notes on what occurred and wrote about the processes and practices of the scientists as homework. The information was then used to compare the processes and practices they used during the Island History Project with those of actual social and natural scientists. Thus, students were again provided with opportunities to compare the work within disciplines with their own actions as they took up the roles of historians, writers, and artists.

These four events formed a cycle of activity that established an orientation and approach to social science in Beth's classes. This cycle of activity introduced particular terms and concepts—point of view, perspective, representing data, interpreting data, notetaking, notemaking, theories, and evidence, among others. These terms formed a referential system that students used in all other aspects of social and natural science.

The Island History Project: Writing History

The Island History Project marked the onset of an extended cycle of activity in which students generated data and then used this data to identify patterns of culture and to write a history of a group of people. This project has been described extensively elsewhere (Floriani, 1993; Heras, 1993; Santa Barbara Classroom Discourse Group, 1995). For the purpose of this chapter, we highlight processes and practices that represent an ethnographic and historical perspective through the writings of students. Each example of writing was selected to highlight different aspects of this process. Together, the three examples provide a holistic picture of the Island History Project.

As indicated previously, students in this class were asked to compare their processes and practices with those of members of disciplines. In Chris' log entry, we see the process involved in the Island History Project up to the point of writing the final history, and how these processes compare with those of members of the scientific team researching the Ice Man.

Scientific Processes and Procedures: Chris, Fifth Grade (1994)

Ice Man	Island History
They discover Ice Man. They examened the remains and artifacts of Ice Man. They looked at the area near the place Ice Man died and made a guess at how he lived where he was from, how he died, how old he was, why he was on a journey, and other things. Then they drew a picture of how Ice Man might have lived. Next they ran tests on Ice Man and the artifacts to learn how old he was and what the artifacts are made of. Last they make an educated guess of the history of Ice Man.	*They discover the island. In groups we looked at what's left of the island civilization and make a guess at what they did and how they lived for the first week, 2 years later and 10 years later. Next we drew a picture of what the island might have looked like. We might run tests on the island artifacts to know more about how they lived, what they did and how they are, then we will write a history of the island.*

In his comparison between processes of the Island History Project and those of the Ice Man investigation, Chris provided a general overview of the Island History Project and identified the major activities within this 2-1/2-half month cycle of activity. In this project, students discussed what the island looked like, what members did, and how they lived after being abandoned on the island (for 1 week, for 2 years, and for 10 years into the history of the island). At each point in time, students, working in table groups, generated data about the life and about the changes that occurred on the island. These data were then shared with the whole class. Each table group also drew a picture that served to represent their theories of how people might have lived and what they might have done. These pictures became part of the evidence students used to write their histories of the island.

The charted data were then used to construct categories of activity and processes that represented the patterns of life and changes in patterns across time. These categories formed the basis for examining history and culture throughout the school year. Categories identified included: survival (food, clothing, shelter), family groups (education, socialization), communication (language, number systems, writing), science and technology, arts and recreation, economics (work, money, and trade), attitude toward the unknown and values (religion), and political organization (government, laws, ways of resolving conflicts).These categories represented cultural patterns identified by anthropologists in their studies of culture.

The overall process of data construction led to a final activity in which students used the data generated across this project to write a history of the island. In this phase of the project, students self-selected a partner to write the history. Each pair was to construct a chronological narrative as an historian or an anthropologist using the collectively constructed data. They were to support their interpretation and theories with evidence that was consistent with the data represented on the charts and other artifacts. The processes involved in writing the Island History are reflected in the following account of this event written by Joseph in response to a homework assignment asking him to recount a classroom event. This activity was assigned to provide practice in writing a history. It was assigned during the initial phases in which students were writing their Island Histories.

Classroom History: Joseph, Fifth Grade (1994)

Then we did are Island History Project. My partner and I put down as historians that we found evidence like pieces of wood that were damaged with some words on them that were faded. We looked at evidence that the classroom did but with different ideas. We gathered all of that evidence up and wrote what we think happened.

In this excerpt, Joseph demonstrated knowledge of how the same evidence can be interpreted and used differently. He also showed an understanding of history not only as a process of writing grounded in evidence but as involving interpretation—"what we think happened." He also made visible the collaborative aspect of history writing and that being a historian is a role one takes up. Thus, Joseph summarized the general orientation toward writing this history associated with membership in this class

The final example represents the presentation of a bilingual pair. This pair alternated turns at reading their history. Their presentation is followed by a question-and-answer period in which their interpretations were challenged by a fellow historian.

Presenting Theories: Omar & Salina, Sixth Grade (1992)

Omar: *In the early history of the island, we discovered that the people got there by boat. We found part of the engine to prove it. We haven't yet found out the reason of the crash.*

The first week their only interest was their lives. They were also concerned about food and shelter. The shelter was made out of palm leaves and bamboo sticks. Also on the first week their major food source was fruit and berries. After they had found food sources and shelter their main concern was leaving the island.

There were four lookouts on the island. Lookouts were on the highest parts of the island. We know this because it said so in the documents and because they needed to get off the island. Days passed. People died and others were born. To indicate that people were dead they were covered with leaves and a cross and grass on top. Laws were made and a council was elected.

This small island now became civilized. The reason for the laws was because people started to get out of hand. The people had voted to have a

council and we discovered documents that gave us other reasons why they wanted a law and a council.

The small island started with 10 people ended up with an estimated 350 people Some people were smart and made tools with their hands, just like pots with red sand and water.

Salina: People on the island made contact with other people on another island. We know this because we found bones on both islands and we know that they were different people because we found airplane particles. We found canoe parts. We think that the canoe was used to go to the other island. We also found monkey bones. We are not sure if the monkeys were pets or if they were eaten. We think they were pets because we found string around some of their necks.

We think that they were farmers. Some of the people knew a little about farming. We know because we found left over seeds to indicate that years passed. We discovered traps all over the island. We would have never known, but one of our men fell in. The traps were unnoticeable. There was just a big hole with leaves, sticks, sand, palm leaves and grass. Dead animals were found in two of the traps.

In the later history they had built a school. We found math books and other sorts of books. They made books by getting coconut shells and palm leaves and writing on the palm leaves

The next important thing that happened was a lot of people died.

Here are our theories. One of our theories is that they had a hurricane and it blew away [um] their major food sources and most people. Another theory is that they committed suicide. Some of the people couldn't handle living the way they had to live. Our last theory is that one of the people carried over a disease and other people caught it. The people never did get off the island but they 're hopes were high.

Class discussion following the Presentation of Omar and Salina's History.(Teacher facilitating discussion calls on KEITH whose hand was raised.) Keith: . . . *Now for Salina and Omar, um, about the the monkeys as pets. Omar: Uh huh. Keith: Or um, you said that they had um string or rope around their necks. OMAR: string. KEITH: String. It could be like hanging them. OMAR: no but um because um, um they put a leash, but it wasn't hanging them because it wasn't like high. Beth (Teacher): But Keith brings up a different, ah, an interesting point, and that is, that the same evidence can exist, but two different historians can look at it in two different ways. So that string might be there, and one historian might say, "Gee this is animal torture. They were hanging them." And one historian says, "Gee they were keeping them as pets. " And that's what happens in history* . . .

In their presentation, these sixth-grade historians showed the same pattern of understanding demonstrated in the other examples. Their language shows an understanding of history as a written text grounded in evidence and the role of historians as constructors and interpreters of data. They show an understanding of chronology of events and of how to "talk like" a historian. They also demonstrate that they understand that historians formulate theories, describe the evidence on which their theories are based, and show that alternative interpretations are possible while providing a rationale for their own interpretation.

The discussion among Keith, Omar, and Salina also demonstrates the students' understanding that being an historian, involves writing for, presenting to, and interacting with other professionals. Through his pattern of questioning, Keith demonstrates that he has internalized this orientation. His questions are appropriate. They challenge the basis of evidence and the interpretation of the other historians. Beth's response shows that she supports the process of challenge and intellectual debate. By restating the work of historians and how historians may interpret the same data differently, she helps students see that history is a construction of actors and not a statement of truth and that debate is a principled process. Thus, in the collective action of the student presenters, the questioners, and the teacher facilitator, a particular approach to history is framed and social norms and expectations are established for being social scientists in this class.

LEARNING TO SEE LEARNING IS AN INDIVIDUAL AND COMMUNITY PROCESS

In this final section, we examine how the ethnographic perspectives constructed by Beth and her bilingual students framed the ways in which they examined their own thinking, what they learned about academic content, and what they learned about being a student. To illustrate these relationships, we describe how Beth helped students construct showcase portfolios.

A showcase portfolio is the final stage of a year-long portfolio process. The overall portfolio process began in the second month of school when Beth asked students to construct a definition of portfolio and to explore what might go into one. In this way, Beth helped students shape a definition of portfolio that guided their selection process throughout the year. Therefore, portfolios, like ethnography, were an integral part of classroom life. Throughout the year, students (a) reflected on and evaluated their own work and learning, (b) kept records of the learning and thinking processes in learning logs, (c) shared their evaluations and reflections with others (e.g., teacher, peers and parents), and (d) periodically made selections of work that were placed in the portfolio.

The development of the showcase portfolio involved three steps. First, Beth helped students develop a set of questions that guided the construction of these portfolios. Second, students revisited the artifacts of classroom life they generated across the year (e.g., the learning logs, other projects, writer's notebooks). These artifacts become the texts that students used to provide evidence of learning in the final showcase portfolio. Third, this evidence was then summarized in a "Dear Reader" letter that served as a guide to the showcase portfolio. Thus, as in the Island History Project, students used all aspects of classroom life and all artifacts to provide evidence of their lives as learners in this classroom.

In the following "Dear Reader" letter, Maggie illustrates this process.

Maggie Defines A Showcase Portfolio, Sixth Grade (June8, 1993).

Dear Reader,

Hi my name is Maggie, I am writing to you because I want to tell you about my showcase portfolio. A showcase portfolio is a folder where you put all kinds of important papers that are evidence of how you are as a learner; what you have learned and how, The work that is in the portfolio is the main thing, the most improved work out of each section or question that I asked myself.

We made up several questions. We had to answer the questions by picking our best work. It has to be like evidence for the question.

This Portfolio shows how I can conduct an investigation, work effectively in a group, analyze a process and understand my own thinking, write clearly and thoughtfully to communicate my ideas, understand and respond to what I'm reading, solve problems, use creativity and imagination to communicate thoughts, ideas, and/or feelings. It also shows how I can revise my work and/or thinking and how I have changed and progressed as a learner in some area in the sixth grade.

I will tell or show you the answers and explain how and why each is evidence for the question . . .

Maggie's "Dear Reader" letter shows how the inquiry process, grounded in the ethnographic perspective provides a language and framework for students as they reflect on explore what they have learned and how they have grown as learners. What makes this approach to portfolios different from most others is that the students ask themselves what counts as learning in this classroom within and across discipline areas and how this way of learning defines what it means to be a student in this classroom. The ways in which students view themselves and represent learning across disciplines can be seen in the following excerpts from Salina's "Dear Reader" letter from her showcase portfolio (sixth grade, 1992).

Salina's Dear Reader Letter: Showcase Portfolio, Sixth Grade (1992).
Question 1: Can conduct an investigation?

As I looked through my portfolio, I saw different types of all the tesselation essay, any many other investigations, but rather than picking those I selected, I selected the Enchilada Dinner Investigation because I though that that was the best example of my ability to conduct an investigation. What's different with this investigation was that we worked in a sense of "out in the field" We got to go to the store to check the prices and also we sold the things. We stood there and passed out the food, collected the money and ran the dinner. We were in the middle of the operation the whole time and that is why I selected the Enchilada Dinner Investigation as evidence.

Question 2: Can I work effectively in a group?

I read this question and thought about the different activities I had done with my group. I decided to pick the Island History Project because my group had a lot of great ideas about how people could or should live on an Island and what they needed to survive, what was necessary and what wasn't. To draw the picture of the island wasn't easy. My group had to remember all the things that we said the island should have and we couldn't subtract anything because that wouldn't be all that we thought of and also we couldn't add anything because we hadn't said that before, so it was kind of a difficult process.

Question 3: Can I analyze a process and understand my own thinking?

I read this question over and over again, trying to understand what it meant. I finally understood it. It means, in simpler terms, can I explain a way to do something and understand my thoughts. Once I did that, answering the question was easy. I chose my Enchilada Dinner because I explained the process. I explained it step by step. At the beginning of the essay I wrote what the first thing we did was and at the end I wrote what we did last and my conclusion. So I think I analyzed it in a way where people who read it could understand it. Also I think that I can understand my own thinking, because before I wrote this piece, I had to reflect on myself, how I wrote the budget and how we came up with the numbers of people that were coming and so on.

Question 4: Can I write clearly, thoughtfully and effectively to communicate an idea or ideas?

When I read this question, within five seconds I knew what piece to use to show evidence. . . . My "Our Class Community" essay. The reason I chose it is because in this particular essay Ms. Yeager told me to use examples of things I was saying. I listened to her and thought it was a good idea and I did it. When I did it, I realized I had made the invisible visible. I had written it in a way where people who didn't know what I was talking about could understand.

In these questions, Salina, like Maggie, provides detailed evidence of how the ethnographic stance she has developed throughout the year has become a resource for thinking about her thinking as well as a language to describe the processes and practices of classroom life. The question most often asked when Beth presents this approach at in service meetings is, "How do you know that this approach makes a difference in how students approach learning in other classes?" To explore this question, we asked a student who was in the sixth grade class during the 1991-1992 school year with whom Beth has a continuing relationship to think about the impact of his sixth-grade learning experience on his seventh- and eighth-grade experiences.

In 1993, Sean Revisits Learning in the Sixth Grade (1991-1992)

Before the sixth grade I was unable to explain the way I thought and the way I learned. During that year, I was able to look at my way of learning in a more thoughtful way. Through investigations and reflections, I could understand my writing, my processing and thinking. Since that year, being now in eighth grade, I have experienced the opposite side of that learning. Even when experiencing the more structured side, the thinking and the processing stayed with me more than the grammar and the spelling.

The way I think about learning stayed with me but I really didn't know it. It's always been invisible but somehow I knew it was there. I don't think about it. I just use it.

POSTCRIPT

We have brought together many voices from our classroom community to make visible the stories of classroom life. We have also presented evidence to show how an ethnographic perspective is more than a set of techniques and tools. It is a way of thinking about the world and about the ways of participating and learning in the classroom. Through the individual and collective voices, we have sought to make visible how the language of ethnography can become an integral part of the language of the classroom.

In this chapter, ethnography was more than a means of studying other people. It was a resource for studying our own lives, for understanding the patterns of life, and for interacting with others. In other words, the ethnographic perspective Beth and her students constructed provided a basis for establishing common knowledge and a community of practice that shaped what counted as a learning, teaching, studenting, knowing, inquiring, and being a community member.

REFERENCES

Brilliant-Mills, H. (1993). Becoming a mathematician: Building a situated definition of mathematics. *Linguistics and Education, 5*(3-4), 301-334.

Calkins, L. (1990). *Living between the lines.* Portsmouth, NH: Heinemann.

Collins, E., & Green, J. (1992). Learning in classroom settings: Making or breaking a culture. In H. Marshall (Ed.), *Redefining student learning: Roots of educational change* (pp. 59-86). Norwood. NJ: Ablex.

Fernie, D., Davies, B., Kantor, R., & McMurray, P. (1993). Becoming a person: Creating integrated gender, peer, and student positionings in a preschool classroom. *International Journal of Qualitative Research in Education*, 6(2), 95-110.

Floriani, A. (1993). Negotiating what counts: Roles and relationships, content and meaning, texts and contexts. *Linguistics and Education*, 5(3-4), 241-274.

Green, J. (1983). Teaching and learning as linguistic processes: A state of the art. In E. Gordon (Ed.), *Review of research in education* (Vol. 10, pp. 151-254). Washington, DC: American Educational Research Association.

Heras, A. I. (1993). The construction of knowledge in a sixth grade bilingual classroom. *Linguistics and Education*, 5(3-4), 275-300.

Hymes, D. (1982). What is ethnography? In P. Gilmore & A. Glatthorn (Eds.), *Children in and out of school* (pp. 21-32). Washington, DC: Center for Applied Linguistics/Norwood, NJ: Ablex.

Lin, L. (1993). Language of and in the classroom: Constructing patterns of social life. *Linguistics and Education*, 5(3-4), 367-410.

Ringgold, F. (1990). *Tar beach*. New York: Random House.

Santa Barbara Classroom Discourse Group. (1992). Constructing literacy in classrooms. In H. Marshall (Ed.), *Redefining student learning: Roots of educational restructuring* (pp. 119-150). Norwood, NJ: Ablex.

Santa Barbara Classroom Discourse Group. (1995). Two languages, one community: Examining ways of constructing community in a bilingual classroom. In R. Macías & R. García Ramos (Eds.), *Changing schools for changing students* (pp. 63-106). Santa Barbara, CA: Linguistic Minority Research Project.

Spradley, J. W. (1980). *Participant observation*. New York: Holt, Rinehart & Winston.

Section II
Community as Curriculum:
Focus on Language

Although the chapters in the previous section did attend to language, their primary focus was on cultural aspects of students' lives in and out of school and on the use of ethnographic research and inquiry. The chapters in this section focus on language and employ modes of inquiry derived from sociolinguistics. The students in the three projects described in the chapters in this section become sociolinguists investigating the language of their communities.

In the traditional language arts curriculum, the study of language is dominated by the study of prescriptive grammar (hereafter Grammar) that is taught didacticly. Students rarely get any opportunity to study or research language the way it is actually used in everyday life or to investigate its variations (both dialect and register variations). Students traditionally do not encounter any of the means of inquiry associated either with formal linguistics or with sociolinguistics. Yet, students are not unaware that there are variations in language use and that these variations have social and perhaps even economic consequences. They are also aware that English is not the only language spoken in their communities, and that other languages play important roles in some families and some communities. Yet, in the traditional language arts curriculum little study is given to the multilingual nature of modern society.

The projects described in this section provide students with the opportunity to be researchers of language and to learn ways of studying language for talking about language. In the chapter by Thomas and Maybin, students examine the issue of "Talking Proper" and how that mandate has affected their lives and the lives of people in their families and communities. They create language autobiographies as a way to study how they learned language and languages. Through their inquiry, they were able to redefine language as human and community process, and not a prescriptive one that marginalizes them.

The chapter by Wolfram is an explicit attempt to use the knowledge base and tools of inquiry of descriptive sociolinguistics to create a unit on the study of language. Students were taught explicitly about language variation and how it is rule-governed, and then asked to use the knowledge they learned to study and reflect on their own language. As student sociolinguists they were asked to generate sociolinguistic rules.

The chapter by Cheshire and Edwards goes beyond redefining the traditional classroom study of language. After training, the students became co-researchers, helping Cheshire and Edwards, among sociolinguists in general, to generate and analyze a corpus of data that otherwise would be unavailable. Here, students are not only learning about language and modes of inquiry, they are also learning about how inquiry adds to an extant knowledge base and they are learning that being involved in extending a knowledge base is not beyond them.

7

Investigating Language Practices in a Multilingual London Community

Kit Thomas
Walthamstow School for Girls, London
Janet Maybin
Open University, United Kingdom

It is now generally accepted that students learn more effectively if they can build on and develop the language experience and skills that they already possess. Unfortunately, we are still remarkably ignorant about the full range of language practices that students (particularly those who speak more than one language) engage in across their lifetimes and about the ways these might be used as resources for learning in school. Often, the urgency to train students in the language practices required by national examinations leaves little space for the more open-ended, higher risk activities that starting from students' own language experience would involve. In this chapter we give an account of one way into making students' own experience of language and languages a central part of curriculum content, through involving them as researchers of their own lives and communities. The work generated through this research provided the 15-year-old students with a wide range of oral language experience and some of the most highly rated pieces of writing in their English examination coursework folder.

The activities we discuss here grew out of a multilingual East London school's interest in developing its students' linguistic knowledge to meet the new English National Curriculum requirements, and an Open University course team's interest in making a television program for an Open University Education faculty course on "Curriculum and Learning." In 1990 the then new English subject requirements within the National Curriculum included a strand of study referred to as Knowledge About Language. This involved students learning about:

143

1. Language variation in the community (e.g., variation among different geographical regions and different social groups),
2. variation within individual speakers' repertoires (e.g., how a speaker's use of language changes according to his or her purpose, audience, and context), and
3. some of the factors that influence people's attitudes to the ways other people speak (National Curriculum, 1990).

Associated policy documents and curriculum advisory materials suggested more broadly that Knowledge About Language should include:

1. knowledge about variety in and between languages,
2. history of languages,
3. language and power in society,
4. acquisition and development of language, and
5. language as a system shared by its users (e.g., Richmond, 1990).

Like many others in the country, the Walthamstow English teachers welcomed this strand of study, but most felt ill prepared to deal with it as they mainly had backgrounds in literature rather than linguistics. They therefore welcomed the opportunity to exchange ideas with the Open University course team in planning for this area of the curriculum. An additional factor that influenced the way the project developed was the teachers' concern to develop students' competence in informative styles of writing, which they seemed to find more difficult than narrative and expressive or persuasive writing.

We planned and developed a "Researching Language" unit of work with a class of 15-year-old students in Walthamstow School for Girls, using the National Curriculum guidelines and some specific ideas from ethnographic and psychological research that were being discussed in Open University course materials (some of which are listed in the bibliography). For more than 6 weeks, the students researched their own language practices and language histories, and we used these experiences and the data they collected as the basis for exploring issues about language acquisition and development, language variation, and language and power. In working with the students, the relationship between language and identity also emerged as a key area for investigation and reflection. Throughout the project, students learned primarily not from textbooks or other ready-prepared curriculum materials, but through sharing their own diverse language experiences and expertise. This experience provided the backbone for the "Knowledge About Language" curriculum content. The students' activities were filmed in 1990 for an Open University Education course television program.

After this initial project finished and the excitement of being filmed gradually faded, the ideas that we tried out were taken up and developed in various ways by other teachers within the school's English department. The work continues today, and this chapter describes some of these later developments as well as the original language project. However, we first explain the theory and research that informed the work.

THEORETICAL IDEAS UNDERPINNING THE WORK

Two areas of research discussed in the Open University course materials particularly influenced the project: first, Vygotsky's writings about language, culture and learning, and second, ethnographic literature about language and literacy practices in different communities.

Vygotsky's idea that talk is centrally involved in cognitive development and in socialization into a particular cultural environment, underpinned our determination to bring students' out-of-school experience and expertise in languages into the classroom, and to create a variety of contexts for different kinds of dialogues within classroom activities. Vygotsky viewed learning as occurring first through social interaction and dialogue before being internalized to feed into individual cognitive development. In addition, he suggested that learners can be supported through dialogue, typically with teachers or more able peers, to move toward understandings that they could not at that point have achieved on their own. Bruner (1985) called this *scaffolding*, implying that once these understandings have been achieved, the support can be withdrawn. An important part of the teacher's job, then, is to create the kinds of dialogues within the classroom that give students the most opportunity and support to move forward, using their own language and experience, to deeper and securer understandings about the curriculum and about their own lives. These dialogues will be as rich as the ideas that are fed into them—from other students, the teacher, printed and media texts. For Vygotsky and Bruner, the move into literacy involves another level of reflection, which again draws crucially on particular scaffolding dialogues. We were keen to observe and document the ways in which students were learning through talk during the project, and to look at the ways in which this talk supported and fed into individuals' writing.

The area of research that gave us the idea of involving students in researching their own language practices was the burgeoning literature about language and literacy practices in different communities, and the differences some children experience between language practices at home and at school. In theoretical terms, this literature has contributed to an important shift within the field of language and literacy studies, away from thinking about language and literacy mainly in terms of individual skills and competence and toward recognizing their role as part of social practice. For instance, it is now recognized that a particular act of writing or reading is always tied up with social activities, relationships between people, and values and beliefs. These factors are as much involved in why and how people read and write, as are the technical skills they may or may not possess. Similarly, talk is not just for conveying information but also for pursuing and playing out particular kinds of social relationships, exercising particular kinds of power, and negotiating cultural norms and knowledge. In practical terms, this theoretical shift raises important questions about how language practices within the classroom may be facilitating or inhibiting individual student language development, and affecting their conceptions of personal and cultural identity.

Within the Walthamstow School, 64% of the students speak English as a second language, and within the class with whom we were working languages spoken regularly in addition to English included Tamil, French, Kurdish, Urdu, Panjabi, Gujerati, Bengali, and French and English Creoles. Research suggests that bilinguals have greater and earlier awareness of language as a symbolic system (e.g., Saunders, 1983), for example, that objects and ideas can be represented by different words and in different ways, depending on which language is being used; it also suggests that bilinguals have greater sensitivity to the relationship between language and context. This should put bilingual children at an advantage in recognizing and coping with particular ways of using language in the classroom. On the other hand, these children are usually taught and assessed via their weaker language. And they may not find a basis of shared experience and understanding with teachers or receive positive affirmation of their own competence and experience in language use. As Miller (1983) pointed out: "A child with two or three non-European languages, in some of which he may be literate, may be regarded as quite literally languageless when he arrives in an English school where 'not a word of English' can often imply 'not a word'" (p. 5).

Home languages are an important part of pupils' own identity, and research is beginning to emerge that shows how drawing on these in the classroom can provide a powerful resource for learning (e.g., Burgess, 1984; Moll, 1991; Sola & Bennett, 1985). Through the language research project in Walthamstow School for Girls, we wanted to find out more, alongside students, about their own language resources and practices, and we wanted to explore how ideas from sociolinguistics and anthropology could contribute to students' research. As Cheshire and Edwards (Chapter 9, this volume) point out, language awareness work has most value when it takes place within a critical perspective. We found that approaching the study of language diversity and variation through students' own experience and involvement in language practices made it impossible to ignore the social and political implications of language use.

THE COMMUNITY AND SCHOOL SETTING

Walthamstow is in northeast London, in what was 150 years ago a leafy village in the county of Essex. Today it is a bustling area around a large lively market on the capital's fringes with a varied and fluctuating population. There is a large Asian community made up of mainly Pakistani Muslims, a smaller number of African Caribbean residents, and a significant number of White East London people. Many families are long established in the area, working in local light industry and in their own businesses. Property is relatively cheap and public transportation excellent, so Walthamstow has provided a home for people moving out from inner-city London and in from the Essex commuter belt, as well as from further away, including many refugee families.

Walthamstow School for Girls is popular with local parents and also attracts girls from further afield in London. Students stay at the school for 5 years, from the age of 11 to 16, before moving on to a mixed sixth form college for further study. "Neglect not the gift that is in thee" urges the school motto and the school values individual achievement, promotes equality of opportunity and is committed to raising the aspirations of the young women from the multicultural community it serves. Teachers are faced with mainly lively and willing students in groups of between 25 and 30 whose socioeconomic and linguistic backgrounds pose new challenges daily. There is a strong English department with a tradition of innovative curriculum development. Because of the wide range of texts used and the nature of classroom approaches adopted, the English department sees itself as pivotal in delivering the aims and policies of the school. Within the work of the English department there is a considerable amount of collaborative planning, both formal and informal, as teachers try to reflect on and improve their practice while they struggle to cope with the frequent changes and innovations in the national education system and the huge range of language ability and experience represented by students. The plans for the Researching Language project were seen by the staff in the English department as an interesting and uncharted area of research and development. Their contributions to the informal discussions Kit had with the Open University team and the BBC producer who filmed the work were an important additional aspect of the school's involvement.

Kit had been the English teacher of form 5N from when they first entered the school, so at the time of the project it was the fifth year he had been working with these students. Even though he was aware of the linguistic make-up of the class, he had only drawn on this resource as part of his teaching in an ad hoc way.

THE "RESEARCHING LANGUAGE" PROJECT

The "Researching Language Project" involved students taking part in initial class and small group discussion about "Talking Proper"; researching, recording and analyzing their own use of language across different contexts; researching and writing a language autobiography; and writing and delivering a speech concerning a language issue about which they felt strongly.

"Talking Proper"

We began by looking at accent and dialect. Although in purely linguistic terms one can talk about all varieties being equal, it was immediately clear that students' own experience of accent variation was closely related to issues of power.

As an introduction to the project, students watched "Talking Proper", a program from the BBC schools series Language File. It included a sequence showing a group of young upper class men talking together as they relaxed at their London club. Their accents and conversational style provided a sharp contrast to those of the students in the class, and Kit asked the girls what they thought the young men might think of them if they walked into the classroom at that moment. Some students responded immediately in terms of the assumption that the men might make because of the girls' Cockney accents—that the girls were "common," came from a lower class family and certainly didn't attend a private school. As Petra put it, "I think the minute they heard our accents, they would have an immediate image of us like oh our dad works on a market stall . . . and they'd think just cause they heard our voice they can completely tell our lives." Many students had experienced personal insults because of their accents: Nazia had been laughed at by her relatives from Pakistan for speaking Urdu with a Cockney accent and Kim had been told during work experience that her accent was not refined enough for telephone calls with customers. Kim felt her work experience employer knew he could criticize her accent freely (which she found personally insulting) because of his position of power over her. The discussion broadened out from accent and dialect to other personal experiences where the students felt someone had used language in a particular way to exert power over them. Many mentioned the way men talked to or about them. Petra said, "It's just like the way people make you feel like especially men like straight away people call you 'darling' or 'love' or anything, it's just to make you feel small, so like they feel they can control you."

Terms like "sexy" or "hotpants" weren't seen by the girls as necessarily complimentary; they could be a way of treating girls as objects rather than people. Neeshat suggested, "They wouldn't refer to you as like a person they might say 'her over there' but use some other word, not your name."

Following the whole class discussion, students divided into small friendship groups to discuss what they understood by a request to "talk properly," and to pick up any of the issues raised in the larger group that they wanted to go into in more detail. In this more informal setting, students could relate the discussion to their own experience, at greater length. For instance, in one group the girls questioned some of the points made in the larger group. "I mean if it was an attractive man saying 'darling' you would most probably like it, wouldn't you?" They started to explore the way "speaking properly" could be taken to mean both speaking standard English with a particular accent, and speaking appropriately for a particular situation. Rahilla said, "Like in Sheffield or Leeds when I went there I've got this accent and everybody said, 'You've got a London accent, are you rich or something, why can't you talk properly, like us?'" Students moved on to discuss how they changed the way they spoke, depending on whom they were with. Shellie said, "Trying to speak all like all proper you know it's like you're trying to be one of them when you're with them."

Some girls regularly switched between different languages, for instance, Anjana spoke Tamil to her mother, a mixture of Tamil and English to her father, and English to her brothers at home. Nazira spoke French Creole with relatives but was embarrassed and found it difficult to communicate with her cousins, who were being brought up in France and had a much more extensive French vocabulary.

This first session introduced students to what were to be major concerns within the project; the emphasis on personal experiences and histories, ways in which language use varies depending on context and relationships, and how language is tied up with issues of power and identity. Over the next 6 weeks, students worked on researching and writing up three major pieces of work that are discussed in the next sections.

Recording And Analyzing Their Own Use Of Language Across Different Contexts

The first piece of research involved students using small cassette recorders to collect recordings of themselves, their families, and friends in order to examine in more detail how people's language use varies depending on context and audience. Situations taped included:

- walking home from school with friends
- family members preparing the evening meal at home
- working in the family shop (and talking in English and Panjabi with different customers)
- playing or talking with young relatives
- friends styling each other's hair at home
- teacher/pupil talk in class

Students chose a short extract from their tape to transcribe. We discussed different ways of setting out transcription and some girls chose to use a column format (instead of setting it out like a play script) that can show up the interactive development of a conversation more clearly. A "context notes" column can be used to document important aspects of the nonverbal communication that are intrinsic to conversational meaning. For instance, Anjana wanted to indicate where her young brother Manajit was referring to the images on the television they were both watching while talking about what he had been doing in school that day (see Figure 7.1).

Students played their tapes back to the whole class or in small groups, and discussed how the situation, and the relationships between the people involved, were affecting the way language was being used. For instance, they quickly identified different degrees of formality in their own language use. In informal contexts like walking home together or doing each other's hair the girls used particular vocabulary or slang (e.g., "shut up," "Oh yea," "dude"), and nonstandard accent and grammatical forms (e.g., "ere," "It don't sound nothing like the song," "so what we gonna have, then . . .") that they wouldn't use in more formal situations, for example, serving customers in the shop, or talking to teachers. Charlotte (an English monolingual speaker) had taped her father talking on the phone to a work colleague about an estimate for building work, and then on a different occasion joking with his daughters. In the telephone conversation, he used standard grammatical forms and specialist terms and phrases, as in this extract from her tape: "I gave them lots of different permutations of how to send the fittings.... I upped the quantities very slightly . . ." Joking with his daughters, he spoke with a stronger Cockney accent and used phrases such as: "Wash yar mouth out, that's Bob Marley!"

In some of the recordings of talk with younger brothers or sisters, the girls noticed that they took on a teacherly role. Here is an extract from, Rahilla's recording of herself looking at a picture story

	Manajit	Anjana	Context Notes
A		Fantastic Max	
M	How do you know?		
A		Ah, I was just looking in the text and I saw it	
M	Mm		
		So what did you do at school?	
M	Worked		
A		On what? Did you paint, draw	
M	Drawed, colouring		
A		So what did you draw then	
M	I . . . I was in that I've seen in that		pointing to T.V.
A		Oh those, those that hmm, a fun fair	
M	that, the ones what went round		
A		The cups?	
M	the ones		
A		The cup one	
M	No it's fast. It goes it first goes slow and then it goes goes faster and goes like that and that and then it goes even faster		

Figure 7.1. Anjana's column transcript

book her 4-year-old sister Ansa in their bedroom at home. Rahilla said that she and Ansa usually talk to each other in Urdu, but here, where Rahilla is introducing her sister to a school type reading activity, most of the interaction is in English. Ansa does not speak English fluently and had only just started to attend the local first school.

Rahilla	*What colour is the flower?*
Ansa:	*White and green*
Rahilla:	*White and green. Ok. What's beside the em girl? What's beside her?*
Ansa:	*The thing*
Rahilla:	*The red thing. What's that?*
Ansa:	*Ladybird!*
Rahilla:	*What colour's the ladybird?*
Ansa:	*Red and black*
Rahilla:	*Oh look, there's a feather there!*
Ansa:	*Yai . . . white!*
Rahilla:	*What's on the page? What's this?*
Ansa:	*Boy teacher*
Rahilla:	*A boy teacher. What has he got in his hand?*
Ansa:	*(pause) . . . a . . . a sohti [stick]*
Rahilla:	*A sohti (yai!) That's a stick (. . .) Oh look, here's a teacher. What's he doing on the board?*
Ansa:	*. . . ehm . . . doing reading*
Rahilla:	*He's doing reading? (yai!) Isn't he doing writing? (laughs)*
Ansa:	*Aap nain teah on nar diya [you have turned the (tape recorder) on]*
Rahilla:	*Alright then . . . em . . . oh look, there's a wasp! Oh it's got the abc here. A . . . [Ansa repeats the letters up to J after Rahilla]*
Ansa	*Aur phir narain! [do it again]*

Rahilla explained her use of language in this extract first by the general observation that she was trying to teach Ansa. After listening to the tape a number of times and looking at her transcript with other students, she was able to comment on the interaction in more detail. She realized she was asking Ansa to name particular items in the pictures and their colors, and that Ansa was quickly picking up the question and answer patterns being used, for example, by giving the color of the feather ("white") before she is asked. Rahilla said she was trying to build up Ansa's confidence, and saw that she did this partly by repeating and confirming what Ansa says, including her description of the "boy teacher" that was not strictly accurate because the picture shows an elderly man. Ansa is learning that language is a symbolic system, where words can represent pictures and can be translated from one language into another (e.g., "sohti" means "stick"). It was interesting to see how Rahilla was introducing her to a particular way of having conversations about picture storybooks, including picking out specific features like color, which would be likely to prepare Ansa well for early reading activities in school.

In looking at Ansa's use of English and Urdu in the recording, we realized that in addition to using Urdu where she didn't know the English word (e.g., "sohti"), Ansa switched to Urdu for comments that were outside the frame of the immediate book conversation (e.g., "Aap nain teah on nar diya [you have turned it on], and "Aur phir narain" [do it again]). The question and answer routine about the book is thus framed as a particular language practice in English.

As well as noticing different degrees of formality of language in different situations, and the ways people moved between different languages, students realized that the relations of power between speakers affected the length of their speaking turns and their choice of topic.

Researching and Writing the Language Autobiographies

This was probably the most successful and rewarding part of the project for both students and teacher; for many students it produced one of the best pieces of writing (involving a blend of narrative and informative styles) in their examination coursework folder. We again used the stimulus of a program from the BBC *Language File* series, this time on language acquisition called, "The Hardest Thing You'll Ever Do." The program focused on very young children just starting to use words and phrases. This released a flood of memories for the students, and class discussion was full of stories about key moments in their own language histories. Kit asked the girls to divide up their draft workbooks into a few pages, each headed "0-5 years," "5-11 years," and "11-16 years." In pairs, they went through each stage of their lives trying to identify significant moments in their development as speakers, listeners, readers, and writers. Kit suggested various questions to use as starting points: When did you start to talk? Which language first? What was your first word? Who taught you to read? What embarrassing things did you say when young? What were the "in" words in primary school? Has your accent changed? How has your language use changed since you started secondary school? After the initial brainstorming and exchange of ideas in pairs, students compiled various questions they wanted to follow up with relatives at home about their early years.

By the next session they had collected an impressive amount of information in scribbled note form in their workbooks. To help with the style of actual writing of the autobiography Kit brought in copies of autobiographical writings both by professional writers, for example, London Morning (Avery, 1964) and Cider with Rose (Lee, 1959) and by young people, for example, Our Lives (The English Centre, 1979), Girls Are Powerful (Hemmings, 1982), and True to Life (Hemmings, 1986). These texts, which students read and discussed in small group and whole class settings, provided a range of styles and voices to act as models. Students tried out different styles, reading out their first few draft paragraphs to a partner and gradually beginning to develop their own writing voice. Different styles included adopting the voice of a time traveller, the voice of an adult talking from a baby's viewpoint, a third person narrative, a monologue, and a fairy tale.

In their writing, students drew on personal memories and research at home, the video programs the class had watched, their taping and observation of language in different contexts, and the various discussions. Several pieces quoted examples of conversations, songs, and rhymes in Urdu or Bengali. Equally valuable to the work and reflection that went into producing individual language autobiographies was the experience of listening to and discussing the autobiographies of others. The autobiographies of multilingual students were particularly interesting for the insights they provided about the experience of growing up with a number of different languages. For many students, memories of early language experiences were tied up with close, intimate family relationships. For example, Charlotte opens her autobiography:

> Picture a young child and her father on a cold November night, sitting on the edge of a large bed, or what seemed large to such a small girl. The only source of light being the warm, orange glow of a single candle, stuck firmly to a saucer by the hot trickles of wax. Both drinking tea for warmth. Then for some reason, though it was too long ago to recall it, the father picked up the saucer, lifted it across towards him and balanced it neatly upon his now empty cup. Then as a surprise to all, this chirpy little three year old came out with "Light on a cup of Teeeee ...." !! My dad laughed or so he tells me, and yes if you haven't guessed the little girl was me. This is the first sentence my parents remember me putting together. It is a funny tale I'm never going to live down.

For bilingual students, the first words they spoke could have a particular significance. Rahilla explains:

> [my parents] slipping in and out of languages reflected Very much on how I spoke later on in life. However, it was a great relief to my parents that the first couple of words I spoke were actually in Panjabi and Urdu. I had finally at the end of all that determination and enthusiasm spoken my first words in their language. These words were "Abu" and "Ammi" meaning "Dad" and "Mum."

In her autobiography, Rahilla also explains how as a young child she first became fluent in Panjabi but was soon also picking up words in Urdu and English from people around, books, newspapers, video, and television: "My brothers and I would sit in front of the television watching *Playschool, Rainbow* or *Tom and Jerry* then immediately after I'd switch on the video and start watching Urdu films." Rahilla says she now slips easily in and out of English, Urdu, and Panjabi, depending on where she is and whom she is talking to. She was never explicitly taught which language to use: "When we were younger we were not told how to speak to someone, we were only told how to behave. I was recognising that there were some situations where I had to completely change the way I spoke."

Other bilingual students echoed the naturalness of language switching for young children or of "slipping in and out of languages" mat students felt was a more accurate way of describing what they did. For instance, Nazira wrote, "I live in a Creole/English speaking household. To you this may sound difficult and confusing but when you've got 'stop being naughty!' coming in one ear and 'Arrêt faire mauvais!' in the other (which means the same thing) then you would have to get used to it."

Many students saw early bilingual experiences as a positive aspect of their emerging identity, but some also had unpleasant memories of times when language differences could make a strange situation more frightening for a young child. From Farhana's autobiography:

> "Na, naa, jabona." (No, no, I don't want to go). It's my first day at my childminder's and I don't want to go. I kick and scream at anybody and anything. Why do I have to come here? Why can't I stay at home? What's this woman saying?
>
> "Aah, don't cry, daddy's going to come back, but first we're going to play."
>
> "Abbuu," I scream that last word as my childminder closes the,door, reaching out for my dad.

For most of the students, the years between the ages of 5 and 11 involved increasing confidence in the use of language. It became an important part of the developing peer group culture, and could be used to resist and challenge authority. Charmain wrote in her autobiography under "Seven":

> Seven eh, do you remember those good old days? The days of "wicked," "shame," 'lergies" and "lickin's," "Jex" and "by ec" and "flippin" and "bloomin". Well, I do too. Yep, we sure did have fun. When "Suzy had a baby" and the "Bumper car" was still around the corner. Seven, that was when us kids claimed our new modern

language. Abbreviated swear words "flippin" and "bloomin," I suppose made some of us feel big and on top of the world.

And Kim wrote about confronting her teacher:

"Y-Y-Y Y You ROBBER." I certainly felt better for saying it, but would she get the point? I stood shaking, waiting for a reaction. There wasn't one. I felt a fool. I hat no knowledge of the very words that I wanted to say. So I attempted to explain myself with a definition of what I had said.

"You Robber . . . you robbed our playtime." She seemed to ignore me.

Students had found the opportunity to try learning a number of foreign languages a significant experience (the school operated a "taster" curriculum where students spent one term each learning French, Spanish, and Urdu). They had also become much more aware of having to consciously change the way they used language, for instance in their business studies course, and in out-of-school work experience placements. And they were reflecting on how other people reacted to the way they spoke, and made assumptions about their personality and background. For some monolingual and multilingual students, questions of personal identity were becoming explicitly related to conscious decisions about language use. It was clear from the autobiographies that questions about language use were very personal questions. They were also increasingly political, as students became more aware of issues of power relating to gender, race, and class. These issues were to surface more explicitly in their third major piece of language work for the project.

Writing and Delivering a Speech: "This is My Language, This is Me!"

Students all chose one or two aspects of language that had particularly interested them during their work so far on the project. These included prejudice about accents, "talking proper," the place of bilingualism in British society, sexist and racist language, and the way language and culture are bound together. The aim was for students to present a particular argument, and to persuade the audience to agree. As preparation, students looked at a collection of argumentative essays by other young people and discussed with Kit oratorical devices such as repetition, rhetorical questions, examples of points being made, and pointing words and phrases such as "therefore," "as a result," "I must stress here." The class came together to hear each other's speeches for a very powerful session. By this stage in the project, students not only felt able to bring their community languages and language practices into the classroom but also to share painful experiences of oppression and racism. A number of students focused on offensive jokes and racial abuse in their speeches; for example, Adama's speech:

> *I remember when I was walking down the market with my mum. She was talking to me in an accent, an African accent, speaking a mixture of French and English. Some boys were telling a joke. They heard my mum's accent and one of the boys said, "What's an ABC? An African Bum Cleaner!" All the boys started to laugh. We ignored them but I could tell my mum was hurt. Everyone has their own languages. Is it too much to ask that people an talk their own language in different countries? I wish people could be judged as people, and not by the languages or accents they speak, or the colour of their skin.*

Talk and Learning at Different Stages of the Research Process

As we said at the beginning of the chapter, we wanted to closely monitor the different talk contexts within the classroom to see how these contributed to students' learning and supported their research, particularly in relation to Vygotsky's ideas about learning occurring first in the context of social dialogue before being internalized as part of individual competence, and Bruner's concept of scaffolding.

We looked first at Kit's role within the first whole class discussion about "speaking proper," which we had taped. This discussion was particularly important in establishing a body of shared knowledge between teacher and students that would provide a common reference point for later small group work, and for individual research— a kind of common discursive resource that could be implicitly referred to in conversations and discussions. Looking at the discussion, we found that through the dialogue Kit often related students' individual personal examples to more general issues. For example, after a few contributions about girls' individual experiences of being made to feel small by men he said, "OK so now we're coming onto the whole issue of how language can be used in a sexist way, language can be used to keep somebody down...." Through these kind of statements, Kit offered more general principles for organizing experience that enabled students to move beyond the level of individual anecdotes.

Individual anecdotes became important again within the follow up small group discussions, but in spite of the rapid overlapping talk students showed they were listening carefully to each other through comments such as "Why do you do that?" "I bet it's embarrassing!" "Explain what you think it means." Through this close listening to individual experiences, students themselves began to draw out more general points, which were woven between the anecdotes and which would be taken up and developed in their autobiographies and speeches. Examples of these more general points emerging in the small group discussion were:

- You talk differently, don't you, in different situations?
- It depends what you mean by speaking properly.
- We're forever taking the micky [sic] out of people's accents when you think about it.

In a Vygotskian sense we would suggest that students' learning is being scaffolded through this kind of informal discussion with peers as well as in the dialogues with Kit. The way in which such discussion fed into later written work shows how anecdotes can provide the real-life evidence that is needed to support the construction of written argument (as illustrated in the extracts from Rahilla's and Nazira's language autobiographies quoted earlier).

These informal discussions were the first of a series of small group and pair discussions that occurred at intervals in the research, to support the analysis of tapes, and the turning of personal and family memories into a written language autobiography. As students were carrying out research independently outside the classroom, it was in particularly important for them to have opportunities within the classroom to share findings, and to be supported in expressing these through the various pieces of written work. They needed questions and comments from other students and from Kit to develop an analysis of how their language use changed across contexts, for example, to go beyond general comments about being polite to looking at specific uses of vocabulary, grammar, and different languages. Kit found that some students needed considerable help from him in constructing their written language autobiographies, and they then got additional help from each other. Some monolingual students who could not compare their experience and uses of different languages felt at a disadvantage in trying to tease out early language influences, and it was helpful for such students to explore early memories of literacy practices (such as having stories told and read to them).

The class had a tradition of using "talk partners" as sounding boards for the early stages of writing. For instance, Charlotte was having difficulty getting started on her language autobiography and Petra suggested:

What I did at first was like just thinking of something when I was really little that had something to do with language. What idea have you actually got down? Charlotte replied, Well me and my Dad who was sitting there in the darkness and he had a cup of tea, we were drinking tea and we had a candle and my dad put out the candle on top of the cup of tea and I said like "light on the cup of tea" and they started laughing so I just said that cause that was like the first sentence that I put two things together.

Petra's positive response to this encouraged Charlotte to produce the opening to her autobiography (as shown earlier).

This variety of talk contexts in the classroom—whole-class discussion, small group work, teacher/individual pupil, and pair work—provided a range of opportunities for students to talk about their own language practices and histories, to hear about others, and to move beyond individual experience to consider and reflect on more general issues. The teacher's role was crucial—to feed in video and printed texts to stimulate and extend ideas, to work intensively with individuals on their written work, and to knit together students' individual experiences and findings to create a shared discourse for learning. This shared discourse was constructed partly by students, as a result of their research experience (e.g., the expression "slipping in and out of languages"). This active and initiating role in creating a language of description for their research findings marked an important acceptance and valuing of students' own language as a valid resource for the school curriculum, and for their national examination.

Achievement of the National Curriculum "Knowledge About Language" Objectives

Students' research directly addressed language variation in the community, variation within individual speaker's repertoires across different contexts and factors influencing people's attitudes to the way others speak. In class and small group discussions about "talking proper" students were fascinated by different regional examples and the use of different words and phrases. They recognized that their own attitudes to accents often involved a double standard—they enjoyed mimicking and laughing at other people's but hated being teased themselves. Exchanging experiences throughout the project continually brought up new examples of variation within and between the languages they used in their own lives, and their reading and viewing introduced additional material about other aspects of social and geographical variation across Britain.

Issues of appropriateness in different kinds of language use came up early in the first small group discussions and the students' taping of a wide range of language interactions provided the linguistic data to investigate more precisely the way people's language use varies depending on context, purpose, and audience. Students looked at accent, vocabulary, grammar, and language choice and switching, and discussed the influence of formality of situation, and power relationships on language use. They could see how language varies across different types of spoken communication (e.g., joke, anecdote, teacher-pupil interaction). In looking at some of the recordings of themselves with young relatives, students were interested to see how talk became a vehicle for teaching and learning, and began to consider how this compared with their own learning experience through oral activities in English classes at school and in one-to-one student-teacher dialogues.

Students found looking at early language development patterns particularly interesting, through work on the child language development video, personal life history research, and recordings of talk with young relatives. As in all other areas of the Knowledge About Language work, the multilingual experiences and resources in the class opened up new areas of investigation: the significance of which language the young child's first words came from, the different situations in which they learned to use the different languages, the various kinds of literacy practices (including media viewing) that were associated with each language. Students reflected on how their language use had changed over the course of growing up: their experiences of the fashionable jargon of the playground, the vocabulary of new school subjects, and the use of words from other languages. The history of change in the English language over time was probably the area least touched on, although students' data included examples of older relatives in Britain and other parts of the world who spoke English or Urdu in what the students considered an old fashioned manner.

Factors influencing people's attitudes to the way others speak were extensively and critically explored in class discussion and through the girls' written speeches. Relationships between language and power, and between language and identity were themes that cropped up continually throughout the project, highlighted in particular ways because of the students' age, and their experience as multilingual speakers. Through their discussion, research, and writing they were constantly tussling with questions about how their own language choices, their positioning through language by more powerful others, and the broader social attitudes about language and languages within the community, affected their own emerging identity, their relationship with others and their potential for control over their own lives.

SUBSEQUENT DEVELOPMENTS

Filming for the TV program during the Fall 1990 term caused tremendous interest around the school, and the sight of camera crews and sound recordists in classrooms and corridors put Knowledge About Language and student research firmly on the agenda for teachers and students.

The Open University film is now a useful resource for incoming teachers and student/beginner teachers within the English department. It is a quick training tool with a built-in sequence of work, examples of students' oral and written work, classroom approaches, resources and materials needed. The 6 week project is, of course, not the only way for students to research and analyze their own language, but it does provide one realistic and workable model that teachers can adapt and improve to suit their particular students and to teach to their own strengths.

One solid foundation for the development of work from the original project was the use of part of a departmental in-service training weekend to view the film and to discuss how other teachers might use it, and what additional resources might be useful. The department decided to purchase new audiocassette recorders and tapes to facilitate recordings of language by students. It also brought new printed resource material to be used with future Knowledge About Language and Language Research work. This included: *My Personal Language History* (Harris & Savitsky, 1988), a collection of short personal accounts of people's language development, and the London English Centre's (1981/1993) publication *The Languages Book*, which provides useful background information and stimulus material on many Knowledge About Language areas. Many extracts from the original batch of language autobiographies were photocopied to use as stimulus material with new students—a practice that still regularly continues. In terms of classroom strategies, the project established a particular pattern of teaching and classroom organization as one possible model of good practice for this type of language work (launch to whole class—individual research—pair work—small group work—whole-class presentation).

Two sequences of work developed in the English department stand out as good examples of how two teachers at very different points in their careers used and developed ideas from the project. The first involved Sue, the head of the department, with some 10 years of teaching experience behind her, and the second involved Debbie, a student/beginner teacher embarking on her teaching career after a career change (Kit was her mentor). Sue was working with 14-year-olds and Debbie with 15-year-olds.

What's the Use of a Book Without Conversation?

Sue had expressed concern for some time that many students, particularly those from a Pakistani Muslim background, failed to draw on close experiences when writing fiction and narrative. The characters, the plots, and the settings seemed to bear little resemblance to the lives of the young writers and as a result much of the writing was unconvincing and bland. Within a sequence of work called "Lifeline Stories" developed for examination coursework, Sue had asked her students to interview a member of their family or an adult friend, and to try to get a rough overview of that person's life. They then chose one critical moment from the biography to write about in detail. The aim was to communicate a sense of place, for example England, Ghana, or Pakistan, depending on the student's choice, and to create characters appropriate to that place.

These lifeline stories were useful in presenting students with the process which many writers, including biographers, use—taking a set of skeletal facts and embellishing them to make a readable story fit for an audience. They were also successful in encouraging the girls to explore a variety of different cultural settings. However, the writing of the stories soon highlighted a particular problem: how to find a language appropriate for the story being told, both in terms of the narrative and in any use of dialogue. For example, the street language of Walthamstow did not seem appropriate for a daughter's conversation with her father in the Panjab 20 years ago! Relatives in the stories were frequently speaking Panjabi, Turkish, or Gujerati, or a mixture of their mother tongue and English. How could a writer capture the idiom and the tone of what was being said if the story was to be written in English? How was the dialogue going to be rendered to avoid on the one hand comic stereotypes of broken English or on the other a loss of personality through translation into standard English?

Sue started to explore these issues with students through exploring and writing about their own language histories, in order to gather the raw material for their writing of dialogue in the lifeline stories. Students were asked to choose an incident from their own language history and to role-play a scene from their chosen incident. This was done in English and in other languages with both expert speakers and beginner speakers taking the various roles according to their experience in particular languages. It was when the class was embarking on writing up the role-play in script form that students had to overcome the linguistic and writing problem of how, when writing in English, they could present their experiences from other languages.

One strategy that moved students toward solving the problem was to look at models from work by other writers. They plundered many stories set in other cultures or involving characters who spoke a variety of languages or dialects to see how the authors tackled the issue. The following were particularly useful:

- *We Are Mesquakie, We Are One* (Irwin, 1980), a novel in which a young native American Indian girl gradually becomes an adult and full member of her people;
- *The Laundry Girls* (Owen, 1973), a play about women working in appalling conditions in laundries in Victorian London;
- *"Drunkard of the River"* (in Anthony, 1973), a Trinidadian story that traces the development of a boy's relationship with his father;
- *London Morning* (Avery, 1964), an autobiographical novel set during World War II, which makes effective use of South London vernacular dialogue;
- *Pygmalion* (Shaw, 1983), the classic play about "talking proper," accent, and transcription of sounds;
- *The Red Box* (Sheikh, 1991), a Pakistani young woman's story in novel form, which uses a glossary to explain the words and phrases in Urdu and Punjabi;
- *Ridley Walker* (Hoban, 1980), a novel set in a post holocaust world where culture and language have become fragmented, and a new culture is being built up from the fragments.

Sue asked the group to write a story in which language played a major part. Following are three brief extracts from the students' script writing:

(From "That System of Theirs" by Serena):
"Voh uppir heh. Joow un koo bollow"
"Jee. Sana! Sana!" I shouted.
"What?" shouted Sana.
"Come down. Amie jaan is calling you to help her set the table for dinner," I shouted back.

(From "A Passage to India" by Saadia):
The Asian assistant walked towards Aniza and said, "Aap loag ya-haanh jayeah." He pointed towards the north west, where there was an entrance down the side."Hey, you guys! There's a passage!" said Michael excitedly.

(From "Fiery Eyes by Mubina):
The terrified boy remembered his mother's words and began chanting prayers "LA-I-LA-HA-n-LAL-LA-HOO!"
"No use. Dat won't elep you now," said the strange man in a deep and powerful voice.

Many of the Pakistani students wrote stories using Asian names for characters, and made use of a glossary of Panjabi words included in the story, written as transcriptions into the Roman alphabet. They loved it; this was writing not only by them but for them.

TAKING THE REGISTER

Debbie had a short half term of her teaching practice placement remaining and her class of 15-year-olds needed to complete a language study unit of coursework before she left the school to continue her teacher training. She and Kit decided to ask the girls to do a package of four short written pieces on the topic of language and school.

The first activity was to make a large display in the classroom as a backdrop and reference point for the project. This involved the students in captioning or writing speech bubbles for photographs of teachers and students based on what they might be saying or thinking. The class then watched the BBC/Open University video (1990) about the Knowledge About Language project and made notes on what language issues were raised by the program and what the program taught them. Much discussion about the different types of register used in class and around the school by the teachers and students ensued. The poem, "Taking the Register" was read as a stimulus for specific discussion about names called aloud, being addressed in public, having one's name mispronounced. The girls also watched a selection of school scenes from various television programs and discussed how classroom dialogues were being represented: *Beverly Hills 90210*, *The Cosby Show*, *Roll on 4 O'Clock*, *Grange Hill*, and *Home and Away*. Students read a number of extracts from several pieces of teenage fiction set in school: Francine Pascall's *Sweet Valley High* (U.S.), Berlie Doherty's *Tough Luck* (U.K. contemporary), and Anthony Buckeridge's Jennings (U.K., set in the mid-1950s). They also listened to a recording of Joyce Grenfell's *Nursery School*.

One of the most popular activities was recording an interview with Mudassir Kurshid, a beginner teacher of mathematics in the school, about his language history. The class planned the interview with great precision beforehand, to create a fluid, informal atmosphere. This method got everyone involved and allowed every student to notetake for some of the time during the taped interview.

Student written assignments included a play script involving role reversal between pupils and teachers, "Taking the Register" (a personal account and analysis of the school ritual of taking the register), a written report of the interview with Mudassir Kurshid that included direct quotations from the tape, and a parody of a school story.

Other Developments

Many teachers in the English department have used the personal language history sequence of work successfully and with some remarkable results, mainly with older students. Every teacher makes some new discovery about the language development of their students:

- *She didn't speak until she was 8;*
- *She was reading Lady Chatterley's Lover when she was 5;*
- *Yoruba was her first language but she has nearly forgotten it all.*

In one particularly striking assignment from one of the many projects, Narmida, who had a Sinhalese father and a Tamil mother, wrote vividly and movingly about her life moving between war-torn Sri Lanka and inhospitable England, and between the Tamil and English languages. She explained her feelings of confusion about her life, her language and her identity, and the reasons for her current determination to return to Sri Lanka and to a Tamil identity when she leaves school.

FINAL COMMENT

In the school in Walthamstow the original project continues to be spoken about: Students' own language histories are shared and passed around, written language autobiographies are copied and photocopied and used and shared in classrooms. Teachers now have a wider and more accurate set of vocabulary to describe language development and are more open and better prepared to explore students' discoveries about the languages they own and use. Moreover, they are excited by what each class's research and investigation will uncover, and believe most seriously that good learning and teaching takes place in an environment where the teacher-facilitator has vital knowledge about the linguistic heritage and current language resources and practices of their students.

REFERENCES

Anthony, M. (1973). *Green days by the river.* London: Heinemann.

Avery, V. (1964). *London morning.* London: Arnold Wheaton.

British Broadcasting Corporation. (1990). *The hardest thing you'll ever do.* Program 2 in the Language Files Series.

British Broadcasting Corporation. (1990). *Talking proper.* Program 4 in the Language Files Series.

Bruner, J. (1985). Vygotsky: A historical and conceptual perspective. In J.V. Wertsch (Ed.), *Culture, communication and cognition: Vygotskian perspectives* (pp. 21-34). Cambridge: Cambridge University Press.

Burgess, T. (1984). Diverse melodies. A first year class in a secondary school. In J. Miller (Ed.), *Eccentric propositions*. London: Routledge & Kegan Paul.

The English Centre. (1979). *Our lives*. London: Author.

The English Centre. (1993). *The languages book*. London: Author. (Original work published 1981)

Harris, R., & Savitsky, F. (Eds.). (1988). *My personal language history*. London: New Beacon Books.

Hemmings, S. (Ed.). (1982). *Girls are powerful*. London: Sheba.

Hemmings, S. (Ed.). (1986). *True to life*. London: Sheba.

Hoban, R. (1980). *Ridley Walker*. London: Jonathan Cape.

Irwin, H. (1980). *We are Mesquakie, we are one*. London: Sheba.

Lee, L. (1959). *Cider with Rosie*. Middlesex: Penguin.

Miller, J. (1983). *Many voices*. London: Routledge & Kegan Paul.

Moll, L. (Ed.). (1991). *Vygotsky and education: Instructional implications and applications of sociocultural psychology*. Cambridge: Cambridge University Press.

National Curriculum Council. (1990). *English in the National Curriculum* (Vol. 2). York: Author.

Open University. (1990). *Ways with words* (TV program 4 for Course E271, Curriculum and Learning). Milton Keynes: Open University Educational Enterprises.

Owen, B. (1973). *The laundry girls*. London: MacMillan Education DramaScript.

Richmond, J. (1990). What do we mean by knowledge about language? In R. Carter (Ed.), *Knowledge about language and the curriculum*. London: Hodder & Stoughton.

Saunders, G. (1983). *Bilingual children: Guidance for the family*. Clevedon: Multilingual Matters.

Shaw, G. (1983). *Pygmalion*. Harlow: Longman.

Sheikh, F. (1991). *The red box*. London: The Women's Press.

Sola, M., & Bennett, A. (1985). The struggle for voice: Narrative, literacy and consciousness in an East Harlem school. *Journal of Education, 167*(1), 88-110.

8
Dialect Awareness and the Study of Language*

Walt Wolfram
North Carolina State University

Within the language arts and English studies curriculum, the examination of language structure has evolved in several distinct traditions. A couple of these traditions concentrate exclusively on language structure per se, whereas other approaches within language arts include the examination of language form in connection with another primary interest, such as composition or literature.

The two most widely recognized traditions for examining language structure are the *grammar study tradition and the language usage tradition*. The *grammar study tradition* concentrates on segmentation and classification exercises with language structure, such as "parts of speech" identification tasks or diagramming the hierarchical constituency of sentence structure. Although a number of academic and practical justifications have been offered in defense of this practice, this approach to language study has come under severe critical attack in recent years, as many of the standard justifications have turned out to be unsupportable empirically (Cleary & Lund, 1993). And the National Council of Teachers of English (NCTE) has gone so far as to resolve that "isolated grammar and usage exercises not supported by theory and research is a deterrent to the improvement of students' speaking and writing . . ." (*Language Arts*, 1986, p. 103). In some circles of language arts education, grammar study is now viewed as little more than a set of deductively based taxonomic classification exercises of questionable value apart from familiarizing students with a common metalinguistic terminology for

---

*Thanks to Carolyn Adger and Natalie Schilling-Estes for helpful comments on an earlier draft of this chapter. It probably would have been judicious to follow their suggestions more closely than I did at times. My fault!

identifying some grammatical structures of English (Cleary & Lund, 1993). Notwithstanding objections, the study of grammar remains a continuing tradition in many language arts programs.

In the *language usage tradition*, the focus on language is reduced to an examination of the patterns of formal standard English as they contrast with their nonstandard English counterparts. The goal is utilitarian: Students learn about the patterns of formal standard English so that they can equip themselves to write and speak the prescribed standard variety. Its focus is selective and contrastive, in that it focuses exclusively on the specific structures of standard English that distinguish it from the nonstandard structures of vernacular or informal standard varieties. Traditionally, these patterns are called grammatical "rules" of English, which reduces the notion of a grammatical rule to a prescriptive norm of socially favored language use. This is in sharp contrast to the linguistic definition of a *grammatical rule*, which refers to the inherent systematic patterning of language apart from its social marking. In many educational circles, the notion of "studying grammar" is clearly associated with this prescriptively based language usage tradition. The strength of this interpretation is convincingly reinforced to me whenever I ask a class of undergraduates in a course entitled Modern English Grammar what they think they will be studying in the course. Overwhelmingly, students respond that they think they will be upgrading their skills in the recognition and use of standard English grammatical patterns, or the "grammatical rules" of English.

Although the underlying assumptions of the language use tradition have certainly been questioned because of its wanton disregard for the linguistic integrity of vernacular varieties (see, e.g., the position statement on students' dialect rights adopted by the College Composition Committee on Language Statement in 1974), this legacy of language scrutiny continues to flourish in one form or another. In fact, it is probably one of the sacred customs of language arts education despite the controversy that has surrounded it over the past couple of decades.

The study of language has also been combined with other traditional foci within language arts in a somewhat more ancillary way, which I refer to as the *associative tradition of language study*. In this practice, selective conventions of language structure and use may be examined as part of a more broadly based study of literary genre and expressive language registers.

The rationale for the *associative tradition of language study* may be both academic-interpretive and applied-utilitarian, as students are encouraged to understand and to appreciate representative literary works and acquire skills of literary expression themselves. Although the examination of language connected to literary study may serve a supplementary rather than a primary role, it must be recognized as an important type of language inquiry nonetheless that is based on a particular set of data, specific methods for examining language, and a distinctive metalanguage for discussing language structure and use in literature.

The role that language variation has assumed in the various traditions of language study is instructive, revealing important insight into how dialect differences fit into the study of English. In the traditional segmentation and classification exercises within the grammar study tradition, only standard English sentences are considered the proper object of scrutiny. Certainly, this selective practice has contributed to the myth that the structures manifested in nonstandard English varieties are simply "ungrammatical" approximations of "grammatical" standard English structures. It is quite understandable in light of this tradition that students might equate the notion of grammatical patterning with standard English grammar. This notion is certainly reinforced by the language usage tradition in which socially disfavored dialect structures are admitted only as objects to be eliminated in the process of learning their socially favored counterparts. Thus, we see an institutional heritage within language arts education that reinforces and derives from the myth that the only true grammatical patterns of a language are the standard ones.

Somewhat ironically, the one tradition of study that admits language variation to a degree is connected with the literary representation of language. In this tradition, diverse sociocultural characters in writing may be represented through so-called *eye dialect*, that is, the use of conventionalized spelling differences to indicate social and regional dialects. It must be pointed out, however, that eye dialect does not strive to depict the authentic structures of dialect but to portray for the reader the effect of dialect. In fact, many of the spelling conventions used to create the effect of dialect have nothing to do with the reality of dialect differences. Thus, the spelling of items like *wuz* for *was* or *cum* for *come* represents no actual difference in dialect pronunciation; instead it simply creates an effect that the speaker is not using the standard variety. The literary portrayal of dialect in many instances may simply be a caricature of dialect reality, the so-called *Li'l Abner syndrome*, rather than a genuine account of dialect differences in language.

Our discussion thus far has shown that there is no real tradition for including authentic language variation as a part of the study of language. Instead, there is a legacy for systematically excluding it as an object of study, including it only as a target for eradication, or including it only to represent a literary caricature of a dialect speaker. These traditions persist in language arts education despite the fact that social dialectology over the past several decades has challenged the basic linguistic and sociolinguistic tenets underlying the current treatment of dialects in the curriculum.

In the following sections, I propose a program of study in language arts that remedies this situation by introducing a curriculum of study on dialect variation. I first present a rationale for a curriculum of study on language variation, then discuss some of the components of such a curriculum. This is followed by the presentation of an experimental curriculum piloted recently in Baltimore. Finally, I discuss the educational outcomes and the consequences that may derive from the implementation of such a dialect awareness program.

A RATIONALE FOR DIALECT STUDY

There are several reasons for suggesting that there is a critical need for a curriculum on language differences. The current traditions for examining language as presented earlier make it all the more imperative to consider language variation as an object of study.

First of all, educational systems should be committed to a search for fundamental truth—the truth about laws of nature and matter. When it comes to language differences, however, there is an educational tolerance of misinformation and folklore that is matched in few subject areas. There exists an entrenched mythology about dialects that pervades the popular and educational understanding of this topic, particularly with respect to the nature of standard and vernacular varieties (cf. Wolfram, 1991). Myths about the basis of language variation, the linguistic status of dialect structures, and the socioeducational implications of dialect divergence are deeply rooted in language arts education, and they need to be confronted as honestly as any other unjustified set of beliefs in other disciplines. And the factual misinformation is not all innocent folklore. As we have seen, this mythology has influenced to a considerable extent what is studied under the aegis of language study and how it is approached. At the very least, then, a language arts curriculum should assume responsibility for replacing the established mythology about language differences with factual information.

The issue of educational equity is also tied in with the need for accurate information about language differences. Operating on erroneous assumptions about language differences, it is easy for educators and students to fall prey to the perpetuation of unjustified stereotypes about language as it relates to class, race, and region. The potential for dialect discrimination (cf. Milroy & Milroy, 1985) cannot be taken more lightly than any other type of discrimination. This discrimination may take place in education, in the workplace, and in society at large. For example, a recent examination of the basis for assigning students to special education classes in a large metropolitan area showed that language traits were often cited as primary objective evidence, without any regard for the necessity to distinguish between language difference and language deficit (Adger, Wolfram, Detwyler, & Harry, 1993). An educational system that takes on the responsibility to educate students concerning the truth about racial and social differences and the effects of this discrimination in other areas should feel obliged to extend this discussion to language as well.

Equity in education is hardly limited to how educators and professional specialists categorize students based on language differences. It also includes how students feel about other students and themselves. Students who speak socially favored varieties may view their dialectally different peers as linguistically deficient. Worse yet, speakers of socially disfavored varieties may come to accept this viewpoint about their own variety of language. Students need to understand the natural sociolinguistic principles that lead to the development and maintenance of language varieties apart from their relative social status. Furthermore, students need to understand that a dialect difference is not an inherent linguistic or cognitive deficit. Only then will we start seeing some change in the current practice of discrimination on the basis of dialect.

The equity issue also extends to the impartial representation of sociolinguistic history. As history and social studies texts strive to represent more fairly the contributions of various sociocultural and ethnic groups to the development of the United States, it seems only reasonable to extend this effort to language representation as well. Various vernacular dialects have had an important influence on the development of American English, but there is little or no acknowledgment of this role. For example, it is a curious but significant omission that the celebration of Black History Month rarely if ever includes any discussion of the historical development of African American Vernacular English (AAVE), as this is one of the most significant of all dialects of American English historically and presently.

The study of language differences offers another enticement, namely, the investigation of language patterning as a kind of scientific inquiry. In its present form, the study of language in the schools has been reduced to laborious, taxonomic exercises such as "parts of speech" identification, sentence parsing, and other comparable metalinguistic exercises of questionable value. Few students understand this type of inquiry as scientific in the sense that hypotheses are formed based on a particular type of language data and then confirmed or rejected using a specialized argumentation structure. The study of language differences, as any other study of language data, offers a fascinating window through which the dynamic nature of language patterning can be viewed. Looking at the nature of language differences can provide a natural laboratory for making generalizations from carefully described sets of data. Students can hypothesize about certain forms of language and then check them out on the basis of actual usage patterns. This process is a type of scientific inquiry into language that is generally untapped in students' present instruction about language. It also happens to be a "higher order thinking skill" that is becoming a central goal in contemporary education that extends beyond the mere accumulation of facts.

Finally, there appears to be a practical reason for studying about language differences that relates to mainstream education goals. As students learn in a nonthreatening context to pay attention to details of language variation and even to manipulate selected dialect patterns in learning about the systematic nature of language differences, they should become more equipped to transfer these skills to other language related tasks, including the acquisition of a standard variety. Studying about various dialects from a sociolinguistic vantage point hardly endangers the mainstream sovereignty of standard English. Instead, it simply provides an informed sociolinguistic background and a heightened sensitivity to language variation that can be applied appropriately by students and educators.

COMPONENTS OF A DIALECT AWARENESS PROGRAM

A curriculum of study based on the rationales discussed previously falls under the general category of what is now referred to as a *language awareness* program. Language awareness is defined as "*a person's sensitivity to and conscious awareness of the nature of language and its role in human life*" (Donmall, 1985, p. 7). A language awareness program may concentrate on a cognitive parameter, in which the focus is on the patterns of language, an affective parameter, in which the focus is on attitudes about language, or a social parameter, in which the focus is on the role of language in effective communication and interaction. Programs that have been developed over the last decade have encompassed a range of topics related to native language and foreign language considerations (James & Garrett, 1991). In the United Kingdom and other European countries, a number of language awareness curricular programs now exist (e.g., Hawkins, 1984, 1985), although there remains considerable controversy surrounding the nature and goals of such a curriculum (e.g., Clark, Fairclough, Ivanic, & Martin-Jones, 1990). In the United States, there has been no widescale curriculum related to language awareness although some of the central notions about language found in these programs have certainly been applied in sociolinguistic education for several decades now.

Based on our previous discussion, one of the most obvious areas for a language awareness curriculum relates to dialect diversity in English. In keeping with the range of concerns that might fall under a comprehensive *dialect awareness program*, an appropriate curriculum might include materials related to the affective, the cognitive, and the social parameters. Given the status of dialect awareness on all of these levels, it appears important to include curricular units of several different types as part of such a program. Thus, one component should consider the naturalness of dialect variation in American English. Students need to confront popular stereotypes and misconceptions about dialects. This is probably best done inductively. An easy method of doing this involves having students listen to representative speech samples of regional, class, and ethnic varieties. Students need to hear how native standard English speakers in diverse regions such as New England, the rural South, and urban North compare to appreciate the reality of spoken regional standards, just as they need to recognize the difference between standard and vernacular varieties in these regions. And students in the Midwest need to consider some of the dialect traits of their own variety as it compares with others in order to understand that everyone really does speak a dialect. Although most tape-recorded collections of dialect samples are personal ones that are not commercially available, the video production *American Tongues* (Alvarez & Kolker, 1987) is an especially effective tool for having students confront the affective parameters related to dialect diversity. It offers an entertaining introduction to dialects while, at the same time, exposing basic prejudices and myths about language differences.

It is important for students to contribute examples of dialect variation from their own community in a unit on the naturalness and inevitability of dialect diversity. For starters, students should at least be able to offer regional names for short order, over-the-counter foods (e.g., *sub, hoagie, hero,* etc.) and drinks (e.g., *soda, pop,* etc.). In phonology, they can start with a simple exercise focused on how they produce sets of vowels in a limited context (e.g., the vowel before -r in words like *Mary, merry, marry, and Murray*). In grammar, they can focus on one of the syntactic features of their region or neighboring regions they might be familiar with (e.g., positive *anymore* in sentences such as *Anymore we watch a lot of videos*). The goal of the unit is quite straightforward, to get students to acknowledge that they, too, speak a dialect. Of course, we need to be recognize that dealing with the underlying attitudes about dialects that students bring with them is a formidable challenge, equal in magnitude to confronting any other prejudice students bring with them to the classroom.

One of the most fundamental notions for students to master about dialects, or about language for that matter, is that language patterns or "rules" have their reality in the minds of speakers. The cognitive parameter of a language awareness program flies in the face of the popular stereotype that various dialects, particularly vernacular varieties, are simply imperfect attempts to speak the standard variety. And, as pointed out earlier, students tend to think of "grammar rules" as prescriptive dictums that take on life through their written specification in grammar books. Inductive exercises on the systematic nature of dialects can go a long way toward dispelling this notion. They also can set the stage for generating a nonpatronizing respect for the complexity of systematic differences among dialects.

Exercise 1 is a sample exercise of this type that I have used successfully in various dialect awareness workshops to demonstrate inductively the cognitive basis for language patterning. The exercise is based on the placement of the *a*- prefix in structures like *He was a-huntin'*. The idea behind this exercise is simply to demonstrate that students can make intuitive, systematic judgments about the linguistic contexts for *a*- attachment—judgments that correspond to its patterned distribution as an authentic "linguistic rule" in a vernacular dialect. The advantage of this particular example is that it involves a form for which

---

[Exercise 1]

A- Prefix: An Exercise In Dialect Patterning

Some dialects of Appalachia and other rural parts of the United States put an a type sound before words that end in **-ing** as in **They went a hunting**. This form may occur with some **-ing** forms but not with others. In the following pairs of sentences, choose one of the sentences that "sounds right" for the placement of the **a-**. Choose only one sentence for each pair. If you're not sure of the answer, simply make your best guess. Do not look at the answers and questions given below until you have made all of your selections.

1. a. John likes sailing.
   b.John went sailing.
2. a. The woman was coming down the stairs.
   b. The movie was shocking.
3. a. He was charming.
   b. He was running to the store.
4. a. They kept hunting for a snake.
   b. They thought hunting was great fun.
5. a. Sarah was following the trail.

    b. Sarah was discovering the cave.
  6. a. The dog was eating the food.
      b. The dog was drinking the water.
  7. a. The man was repeating the chant.
      b. The man was hollering at the dog.
  8. a. Raymond kept asking the question.
      b. Raymond kept telling the answer.

Questions:

1. One observer of the English language wrote that "in popular speech almost every word ending in **-ing** has a sort of prefix, **a-**." Based on your reaction to the sentence pairs, do you agree with him? Are there some sentences where the use of **a-** "feels" right and others where it doesn't? Check the choices you made above with the following correct answers for this dialect pattern: (1) **b** (2) **a** (3) **b** (4) **a** (5) **a** (6) **b** (7) **b** (8) **b**.

2. The language pattern, or "rule," that explains the use of the **a-** turns out to 6e very complicated and detailed. Few people can say exactly how the rule works, yet practically everyone makes The correct choices for the placement of the a- prefix.* Based on this observation, what can we say about the nature of language rules? Are language patterns based on written "grammar" books or are they based on an inner system of patterning that governs how we use language?

3. You are involved in a conversation with a person about dialects, and the person says, "Dialects don't have rules; they're just deviations from real English." Based on this exercise, how would you respond to this statement?

*Note: The rule for **a-** prefixing operates as follows: If the **-ing** form functions as a verb or adverb (e.g., 1a, 2a, 3a, 4a), then it may attach **a-**; however, if it functions as a noun or adjective (e.g., 1a, 26, 3a, 4b) it may not attach **a-**. However, the **a-** form may not attach to a form when the initial syllable is not stressed (e.g., 5a and 7b are acceptable, but not 5b and 7a) and typically attaches only when the form begins with a consonant (e.g., 6a and 8b). For more detail, see Wolfram (1980).

---

the intuitions of native and nonnative *a*-prefix speakers are alike (Wolfram, 1982). This fact makes the exercise appropriate for native speakers of English regardless of their original dialect.

An exercise like this one is an effective way of confronting the myth that dialects have no patterns of their own; at the same time, it effectively demonstrates the underlying cognitive basis for all language patterning and introduces students to the linguistic notion of a grammatical rule. The kind of reasoning involved in searching for the pattern also moves the study of grammar away from the mere classificatory exercise that it has so often been reduced to in traditional grammar study, to a search for systematic language patterning.

Another fundamental notion for students to understand about language is its organization on several different levels. Language patterning and language variation take place on several different levels simultaneously, including phonology, syntax, and semantics, and the study of dialects can be a basis for probing the various levels of this language organization. It is, of course, possible to present students simply with some of the dialect rules found on different levels, but it is more effective for students to work with dialect data to arrive at some of these dialect rules on their own. Working with data of this type also introduces students to the methods of dialectologists as they formulate hypotheses about language patterns and then check them out with actual language data. An example of such an exercise for phonological patterning is given in Appendix A. In this exercise, students consider how r-lessness operates in the regional variety spoken in eastern New England. Students first examine the phonological environment that triggers r-lessness, namely, a preceding vowel (e.g., [ka] *car* but not [kip] for *creep*). Then they examine how the rule in this variety is affected by following segments. In this variety (the rule does not operate the same way in all r-less varieties of English), r-lessness typically occurs when the following segment is a consonant or pause; r-lessness does not occur, however, when followed by a vowel (e.g., [ka bay] *car by* but [kar In] *car in*). Students arrive at this conclusion by examining data sets, formulating hypotheses, and confirming their hypotheses based on the data. Inductively, they learn that dialect patterns are regular and predictable, and therefore "systematic."

The advantage of these types of exercises should be obvious: Students learn how linguists collect and organize data to formulate rules. It also provides a protocol for students to apply to data that they might collect from their own community. For example, one of the exercises used to understand the systematic basis of grammatical rules in an AAVE-speaking community focuses on the so-called habitual *be* in sentences such as *She usually be going to the store.* Students use their native speaker intuitions about the use of *be* to mark systematically an intermittent activity over time or space in the following exercise on the grammatical patterning of this form. In Table 8.1, student responses ($N = 35$) from a forced-choice task for the patterned use of *be* are given for a classroom of 9- to 11-year-old African-American students. These students live in a community where AAVE is the predominant community dialect. The percentage of correct responses is given for each of the sentence pairs in the exercise. In each case, the response pattern significantly favors the habitual use of *be*.

Table 8.1. Responses of AAVE Speakers to "Habitual be" Sentence Pairs.

% Correct (N = 35)

1.	91.4	a. They usually be tired when they come home.
		b. They be tired right now.
2.	88.6	a. When we play basketball, she's on my team.
		b. The girl in the picture be my sister.
3.		a. James be coming to school right now.
	88.6	a. James always be coming to school.
4.	68.6	a. Wanda be going to school every day.
		b. Wanda be in school today.
5.		a. My ankle be broken from the fall.
	91.4	b. Sometimes my ears be itching.

In such an exercise, students learn firsthand about the systematic nature of all dialects regardless of their social acceptability. In the best case scenario, students may record language data, extract particular examples from the data, and formulate linguistic rules themselves.

In addition to seeing dialect investigation as a kind of scientific study of language, students should be encouraged to see how dialect study merges with the social sciences and humanities. This study can be viewed from the perspective of geography, history, or sociology; it also can be linked with ethnic or gender studies. In this far-reaching role, the examination of dialect differences offers great potential for students to probe the linguistic manifestations of other types of sociocultural differences. A student, or group of students, interested in history may thus carry out independent research to determine the contributions of various historical groups to a particular locale by researching the migratory routes of the original settlers of the area and showing how they are reflected in the dialect. Similarly, a group of students interested in sociology may examine status differences in a community as manifested in language. Or a group of students may probe the linguistic manifestations of in-group behavior by examining the way new vocabulary items are formed in some special interest groups. The way in which new words are formed can be examined through the investigation of the jargon of athletic specialization (e.g., playground basketball) or through the investigation of slang as used by peer cohorts who hang out at the mall just as readily as it can through the study of how mainstream words have developed. Students can even create a new slang term and follow its spread among their peers to observe the social dynamics of language.

Although it is possible to develop specific lessons on this research phase of dialect study, its true value is realized by allowing groups of students to examine complementary topics and by having the groups share their investigation with other class members. The underlying objective of this component of study, to introduce students to the way in which language differences reflect deeper sociocultural variation, can obviously be realized in a number of creative and interesting activities for students.

In keeping with the social concerns of many language awareness programs, it is also essential for students to consider the consequences of using various varieties of language, including standard and vernacular dialects. To some extent, students are already aware of the respective roles that such varieties may play, but this often exists on an implicit rather than explicit level. Students should, however, profit from an investigation of the development of standard and vernacular varieties and the relative roles they play in society. It is important that this phase of instruction on dialects be realistic so that students fully understand the relative advantages and disadvantages of both standard and vernacular varieties in different social situations. There is no reason why students cannot even be involved in active debate about teaching standard English in the schools. In fact, some of the best debates I have witnessed on this topic were conducted by students who were asked, simply for the sake of argument, to defend a particular position on the need for standard English. The discussion of standard English by students can be as active and lively as any topic in the study of dialects, as long as their opinions are self-generated and open. This discussion may also allow students to confront the standard English question for themselves, instead of simply being preached at by the teacher about the marketplace value of the standard variety.

THE BALTIMORE PILOT PROGRAM

As part of a research project aimed at enhancing the delivery of services to AAVE speakers, Wolfram, Adger, and Detwyler (1992) piloted a dialect awareness curriculum in the Baltimore City Public Schools. The curriculum, *"All About Dialects,"* is a five-unit curriculum in language arts and communication that introduces fourth-and fifth-grade students to fundamental concepts about language variation. It has also been used experimentally with middle-school students. Teaching the curriculum realistically takes ten 45- to 60-minute sessions with students. The goals of the curriculum combine humanistic, scientific, and sociohistorical objectives. On a humanistic level, the object is to introduce students to the natural and normal range of language differences within some American cultural traditions. Students are introduced to fundamental premises about language differences, particularly as they contrast with common types of language prejudices and stereotypes associated with dialects in popular culture. The initial unit from the instructor's manual is included in its entirety in Appendix B. The overall goal of this unit is humanistic, although the lesson includes other goals as well.

On a scientific level, the objective of the curriculum is to introduce students to the notion of systematic language patterning in dialects. The facts about dialect traits set forth in the lessons allow students to examine data sets to discover systematic patterns in different language varieties. The exercise on r-lessness presented earlier (given in Appendix A) is taken directly from the curriculum. Other exercises include features of Southern and Appalachian dialects, and deliberately mix socially favored and socially unfavored structures so that students understand that systematic patterning in language has nothing to do with social acceptability.

On a cultural-historical level, the objective is to have students gain a sense of appreciation for the historical development of a variety of English dialects, in this case, African-American English. As students consider, in one of the curriculum units, the ancestral cultural linguistic traditions and circumstances that gave rise to the development of this variety, they understand how different sociolinguistic roots result in distinct dialects. In the process, authentic sociohistorical information should replace myths about language change and development.

The curriculum may be taught by a regular classroom teacher or a specialist, such as a speech and language pathologist, reading specialist, and so forth. It is preferable to teach the units in the curriculum on consecutive days, but units also may be taught at regular intervals over an extended period. Each unit, best taught in two sessions, takes from 90 to 120 minutes, although the time range will vary according to how much time is taken up in various activities. Instructors are encouraged to give ample time to small group activities and discussion.

As mentioned repeatedly, the curriculum is largely inductive, as students are encouraged to arrive at conclusions about dialects on their own. At the same time, the instructor needs to present some introductory concepts and to work through some preliminary definitions with students. Instructors also need to guide student discussion at various points. The program is also highly interactive and participatory, incorporating some of the principles of cooperative learning into the small group format that is used for much of the student discussions. Students are asked to manipulate language, to formulate.

hypotheses about language patterning, and to reflect on some of the popular misconceptions about dialects.

Responses of students in various exercises indicate that students do indeed confront some of these misconceptions in critical, reflective ways that challenge existing stereotypes. For example, through selected vignettes from *American Tongues* (Alvarez & Kolker, 1986) used in the first unit in the curriculum, students are introduced to the naturalness of culturally based and regionally based linguistic diversity. These natural reflections of linguistic diversity are then contrasted in the video presentation with a set of excerpts (taken from real-life interviews about language attitudes) in which people resort to unjustified stereotypes in describing other people's speech. After student-led, small group discussions of the video presentation, students in one of the pilot classrooms were asked to write their impressions of the portrayal of dialect diversity. Out of 27 essays written by the students in one classroom, 21 included unsolicited comments about the unfairness of some of attitudes depicted in the interviews about dialect diversity. The following comments (reported in full) are representative of the students' comments after the presentation and discussion:

> Today I learned that not all people speak the same. I liked the way some people talk differently. I did not like the way some people teased others because of their language. I would like to see Dr. Wolfram improve the attitudes of the people in the video.

> I like how some people talked on the video. I did not like how some people talked about other people saying that their language was crazy. Dr. Wolfram has a weird name. What country was his ancestor from. He is very funny. I hope I learn more about dialects.

It is clear from such comments that the students were beginning to understand that it is natural and normal for people to speak different dialects and that many popular attitudes and stereotypes about dialect differences are unjustified. This is an initial step in learning the truth about dialects, but, unfortunately, one that needs considerable effort to promote and reinforce even at the earliest stages of education.

EDUCATIONAL OUTCOMES AND CONSEQUENCES

There are a number of positive results that might derive from a unit of study on dialects. If students simply replace the current stereotyped mythology about dialects with informed knowledge, the curriculum is probably justified, given the far-reaching effects of dialect prejudice in our society. Along with this perspective, students should develop a positive understanding of the complexity and naturalness of dialects.

One of the greatest attributes of a curriculum on dialects is its potential for tapping the language resources of students' indigenous communities. In addition to classroom lessons, students can learn by going into the community to collect live dialect data. In most cases, the language characteristics of a local language community should make dialects come alive in a way that is unmatched by textbook knowledge. Educational models that treat the local community as a resource to be valued rather than a liability to be overcome have been shown to be quite effective in other areas of language arts education, as demonstrated by the success of Wigginton's Foxfire experiment in Rabun Gap, Georgia (Wigginton, 1986). There is no reason why this model cannot be applied in an analogous fashion to the study of community dialects. A model that builds on community strengths in language, even when different from the norms of the mainstream educational system, seems to hold much greater potential for success than one that focuses exclusively on language conflicts between the community and school. In fact, the community dialect may just turn out to contain an educational lodestone for the study of language arts. The study of dialects can, indeed, become a vibrant, relevant topic of study for all students, not just for those who choose to take an optional course on this topic at a postsecondary level of education.

Given the nature of current educational concerns about language differences and the dynamics of the sociolinguistic confrontation in education that has taken place over the last several decades, it has become necessary in the implementation of the dialect awareness program to guard against possible misinterpretation. The road leading to such a program has hardly been a smooth one; in fact, we finally piloted the program in Baltimore only after a string of rejections from other school systems over the past decade. Part of the difficulty comes from the ways in which such a program is perceived by administrators, practitioners, and parents. It is thus necessary to state quite explicitly what the program is and is not in order to meet potential objections due to misinterpretation. There are also a number of ethical considerations that have to considered in the implementation of such programs as discussed in Wolfram (1993). These include: (a) the *ethics of persuasion* (i.e., the rationale used to convince educators of the need for the program), (b) the *ethics of representation* (i.e., the types of dialects that are included in the curriculum), (c) the ethics of presentation (i.e., how the dialects are depicted), (d) the *ethics of social educational change* (i.e., the sociopolitical agendas that undergird the educational changes), and (e) the *ethics of accommodation* (i.e., how the coexisting but complementary roles of a standard and vernacular varieties are reconciled).

It is important to understand that the curriculum is focused on the nature of dialect variation and is not a program that teaches students to speak AAVE. The possibility that the program might be interpreted as teaching school children to speak a vernacular variety may seem outlandish, but our experience over the past several decades has taught us to anticipate this possible misinterpretation. Past media reports often have depicted programs related to dialect awareness as efforts to teach students to speak AAVE. This is simply untrue, but it is an interpretation we have had to anticipate in the past and there is some reason to anticipate this misinterpretation once again.

Curiously, the disproportionate sociolinguistic attention publicly paid to AAVE vis-à-vis other vernacular varieties over the last three decades has resulted in an unfortunate representation of dialects in many educational and public settings. With regular media coverage, countless "studies," and continued socioeducational concern, the term *dialect* has in some educational circles become a new synonym for AAVE. This is unfortunate because it singles out this dialect group disproportionately while creating a distorted picture of dialects in the United States. Furthermore, such unbalanced attention understandably has sometimes been resented by African-American communities as once again African-American behavior is assigned marked, peculiar status. In the presentation of our dialect awareness program, we have been careful to represent other dialects, but we must always be vigilant about disproportionate representation. In our Baltimore program, we start out, with dialects other than African American to demonstrate that this is not a curriculum about AAVE; it is a curriculum about dialects that includes AAVE as one of the important varieties of English.

It is important also to make explicit where the program stands in relation to teaching standard English. We have tried to be honest in noting that our program is not intended to provide the teaching of standard English, nor is it even intended at this point as a step that leads to the eventual teaching of standard English. It is our position that students deserve the truth about dialect diversity and exposure to the rich dialect heritage of the United States whether or not they ever choose to buy into the mainstream values that lead to the acquisition of a standard variety. At the same time, our program is not philosophically opposed to learning standard English and some of the perspectives on dialects and the productive manipulation of language should position students to learn standard English more effectively. In actual classroom experimentation with the program, we find ourselves performing balancing acts between the traditional language usage viewpoint on diversity and the humanistic and scientific goals of our program. This dilemma is perhaps best summarized by a situation that took place in one of the pilot classrooms. As I conducted a dialect exercise in which African-American students selected the grammatical context for habitual *be*, I noticed that the classroom teacher became increasingly uncomfortable with my affirmation of students' responses to the grammaticality of sentences such as *Sometimes my ears be itching* (vs. the ungrammaticality of a sentence such as *My ears be itching right now*). I must confess that I "compromised" as I sensed that the teacher might feel my lesson was directly opposing her traditional efforts to teach standard English. I concluded the exercise by asking the students how they might be expected to say these sentences when performing in an academic, classroom context. Without hesitation, they translated the sentences into their standard English counterparts. The teacher was happy, and I didn't actually feel as sociolinguistically compromised as I thought I might. In fact, I realized that there is a very tender balance between promoting the legitimacy and beauty of linguistic diversity and accommodating traditional socioeducational goals that embrace dimensions of the standard variety.

Throughout this discussion, I noted that the dialect awareness curriculum is not a program focused on the collection of unrelated museum-like dialect artifacts, but one that introduces a systematic examination of language data that constitutes a critical approach to language inquiry, that is, a "higher order thinking skill" in current educational jargon. We therefore do not view the program as an educational luxury that is incidental to the traditional ways of approaching the study of language. In fact, the program is basic to how language, including language diversity, needs to be approached as a kind of linguistic science.

Finally, it should be noted that the dialect awareness program is not a program of detached knowledge accumulation. Students use their own language knowledge and become involved in issues of dialect structure and attendant attitudes about dialect in a way that should move the study of language forward in exciting, informative, and responsible ways, affectively, cognitively, and socially.

REFERENCES

Adger, C., Wolfram, W., & Detwyler, J. (1992). *Enhancing delivery of services to Black special education students from non-standard English backgrounds* (Cooperative agreement ho23400008-92). Washington, DC: Office of Special Education Programs.

Adger, C., Wolfram, W., Detwyler, J., & Harry, B. (1993). Confronting dialect minority issues in special education: Reactive and proactive perspectives. In *The third national symposium on limited English students' issues* (pp. 737-762). Washington, DC: Government Printing Office.

Alvarez, L., & Kolker, A. (Producers). (1987). *American tongues.* New York: Center for New American Media.

Cleary, L., & Lund, N. (1993). Debunking some myths about traditional grammar. In L. M. Cleary & M. D. Linn (Eds.), *Linguistics for teachers* (pp. 483-489). New York: McGraw Hill.

Clark, R., Fairclough, N., Ivanic, R., & Martin-Jones, M. (1990). Critical language awareness, part 1: A critical review of three current approaches to language awareness. *Language & Education, 4,* 249-260.

College Composition Committee on Language Statement. (1974). Students' rights to their own language. *College Composition & Communication,* 25 (special issue, separately paginated). Champaign-Urbana, IL: National Council of Teachers of English.

Donmall, B. G. (Ed.). (1985). *Language awareness: National Council for Language in Education reports and papers.* London: CILT.

Hawkins, E. (1984). *Awareness of language: An introduction.* Cambridge: Cambridge University Press.

Hawkins, E. (Ed.). (1985). *Awareness of language series.* Cambridge: Cambridge University Press.

James, C., & Garrett, P. (Eds.). (1991). *Language awareness in the classroom.* London: Longman.

Milroy, J., & Milroy, L. (1985). *Authority in language: Investigating language prescriptivism and standardization.* London: Routledge & Kegan.

Wigginton, E. (1986). *Sometimes a shining moment: The Foxfire experience.* Garden City, NY: Anchor Press.

Wolfram, W. (1980). A-prefixing in Appalachian English. In W. Labov (Ed.), *Locating language in time and space* (pp. 107-142). New York: Academic Press.

Wolfram, W. (1982). Language knowledge and other dialects. *American Speech, 57,* 3-17.

Wolfram, W. (1991). *Dialects and American English.* Englewood Cliffs, NJ: Prentice-Hall.

Wolfram, W. (1993). Ethical considerations in language awareness programs. *Issues in Applied Linguistics, 4*(2), 225-255.

Wolfram, W., Adger, C., & Detwyler, J. (1992). *All about dialects* (experimental curriculum). Washington, DC: Center for Applied Linguistics.

Wolfram, W., Detwyler, J., & Adger, C. (1992). *All about dialects* (instructor's manual). Washington, DC: Center for Applied Linguistics.

APPENDIX A: A SAMPLE EXERCISE DEMONSTRATING THE SYSTEMATIC STUDY OF LANGUAGE PATTERNING

A. EXAMPLE 1: NEW ENGLAND *R*-DROPPING
HOW PRONUNCIATION DIFFERENCES WORK:
DROPPING *R* IN ENGLISH DIALECTS

In New England and other dialects of English, the r sound of words like *car* or *poor* can be dropped. In these words, the *r* is not pronounced, so that these words sound like *cah* and *poo*. However, not all *r* sounds can be dropped. In some places in a word, the *r* sound may be dropped and in other places it may not be dropped. By comparing lists of words where the *r* may be dropped with lists of words where it may not be dropped, we can figure out a pattern for *r*-dropping.

List A gives words where the *r* may be DROPPED.
1. car
2. father
3. card
4. bigger
5. cardboard
6. beer
7. court

List B gives words where the *r* sound may not be dropped. In other words, speakers who drop their *r*s in List A, pronounce the *r* in the words in List B.
1. run
2. bring
3. principal
4. string
5. okra
6. approach
7. April

To find a pattern for dropping the *r*, look at the type of sound that comes before the *r* in List A and in List B. Does a vowel or a consonant come before the *r* in List A? What comes before the *r* in List B? How can you predict where an *r* may or may not be dropped?

In List C, pick those words that may drop their *r* and those that may not drop their *r*. Use your knowledge of the *r*-dropping pattern that you learned by comparing List A and B.

_____ 1. bear
_____ 2. program
_____ 3. fearful
_____ 4. right
_____ 5. computer
_____ 6. party
_____ 7. fourteen

Think of two new words that may drop an _r_ and two new words that may not drop an _r_.

MORE ABOUT R-DROPPING PATTERNS

In the last exercise we saw that _r_ dropping only takes place when the _r_ comes after a vowel. Use this information to pick those words in the list that may drop their _r_ and those words that may not drop their _r_. Tell why the words can or cannot drop the _r_.

Review List
_____ 1. pear
_____ 2. practice
_____ 3. teacher
_____ 4. rich
_____ 5. board

Now we are going to look at the kinds of sounds that may come **after** the _r_ in some dialects of English. This pattern goes along with the one you already learned. Let's see if we can figure out the pattern.

Here are some words where the _r_ may not be dropped even when it comes after a vowel.

List A: Words that do NOT drop R
_____ 1. bear in the field
_____ 2. car over at the house
_____ 3. garage
_____ 4. caring
_____ 5. take four apples
_____ 6. pear on the tree
_____ 7. far enough

What kinds of sounds come after the _r_ in List A? Are they vowels or consonants?

In **List B** the *r* may be dropped. What kind of sounds come after the *r* in this list?

List B: Words that Drop *R*
_____ 1. bear by the woods
_____ 2. car parked by the house
_____ 3. parking the bus
_____ 4. fearful
_____ 5. take four peaches
_____ 6. pear by the house
_____ 7. far behind

How does this pattern or rule for *r*-dropping work in terms of sounds that come after *r*?

Use your knowledge of the rule for *r*-dropping to pick the *r*s that may and may not be dropped in the sentence given below.
    1. **The teacher picked on three students for an answer.**
    2. **Four cars parked far away from the fair.**

APPENDIX B: EXAMPLE OF AN INTRODUCTORY CURRICULUM UNIT ON DIALECTS

UNIT 1: The Nature of Dialects and Language Attitudes

OBJECTIVES
1.1 To recognize dialect variation as a natural product of cultural and regional differences in society
1.2 To observe the range of language attitudes that are manifested about language, including the unwarranted stereotypes and linguistic prejudice often associated with language differences
1.3 To learn the distinction among dialect differences in pronunciation, grammar, and vocabulary
1.4 To begin making independent observations about language differences

ACTIVITIES

    1.1.1 Video vignettes from *American Tongues*
    1.1.2 Small group discussion
    1.2.1 Video vignettes from *American Tongues*
    1.2.2 Small group discussion
    1.2.3 Class discussion
    1.3.1 Workbook reading

    1.3.2 Small group discussion
    1.3.3 Class discussion
    1.4.1 Language journal
          (Ongoing)

Requirements: Class distribution into small groups of four to five students each, with a leader, a recorder, and spokesperson for each group

Materials: Student workbook (page 1)
                  VCR player, TV monitor
                  Video *American Tongues: Elementary School Version*
                  4" x 6" file cards for each group

Initial Organization: Students are broken into small groups of four to five students. Each group should have a leader responsible for coordinating student activities, a recorder who writes down responses for the group, and a spokesperson who reports for the group in general class activities. These roles may be rotated or designated for the duration of the curriculum, although group membership should be the same for all lessons. Working groups may be given names reflecting dialect variation for some type of item, for example, groups may be given names for dialect variants of sandwiches (e.g., *sub, hoagie, hero*, etc.) or drinks (e.g., *shake, frappe, cabinet, frost* ("milkshake"); *soda, pop, tonic*)

Warm-up Activity: (whole class) Introduce students to the notion of dialect diversity by having students think of experiences in which they traveled to a different region or someone from a different region visited their area. Have them recount the kinds of things they noticed about language differences. Guide them to give specific examples of accent or language rather than vague overall characterizations such as "nasal," "twang," and so on. After eliciting reactions to others' speech, have them relate experiences in which someone might have commented on something about their or their families' speech. ("Did someone from another area ever say anything about the way you speak?")

Introduce the notion that everyone speaks a dialect. This notion may be introduced by using the metaphor of a pie that is cut into pieces. It is impossible to eat the pie without eating a piece of the pie. Similarly, a person speaks a language only by speaking some dialect of the language (all major languages have dialects).

Video Vignettes and Small Group Discussion: Introduce the video *American Tongues* to the students by saying that they are going to see some examples of dialects about different places and different people in America. As students watch the video, they should think about the following set of questions. Place the questions on the chalkboard or on a display board at the front of the classroom.

What is a dialect?
What do people think about dialects?
Are people's feelings about dialects fair? Why or why not?
What do you think about dialects?
Can you give one example of a dialect difference from the video and one that is not on the video?

Time for Introduction of Video and Presentation of Questions: 25 minutes
Following the video, each group will discuss the questions and the group recorder will write down the group's response to each of the questions on a different 4" x 6" file card. In the case of disagreements among group members, different viewpoints should be represented by the recorder and spokesperson.

Group Summary: Each group summarizes its answers to the questions for the entire class.

Introduction of Levels of Dialect: Introduce students to different language levels of dialect by referring to the definitions of **dialect pronunciation, dialect vocabulary**, and **dialect grammar** in the workbook. The examples in the definitions attempt to illustrate by using examples from other dialects as well as dialect variants found in the local area. Introduce the students to the definitions and ask them to give examples not found in the definitions.

WORD DEFINITIONS

Dialect: A form of a language spoken by a group of people from the same regional or cultural background. *Everyone speaks a dialect, even though some dialects are more noticeable than others.*

Dialect Pronunciation: When people from certain regions or cultural backgrounds *pronounce the same words differently*, it is called a *dialect pronunciation*. For example, some people from New England pronounce the word *car* and *far* without the r. Also, some people from the South may say *greasy* with a z sound in the middle of the word, so that they pronounce it as *greazy*. In Baltimore, the way different people say the name of the city, *Baltimore*, or the different ways they say the word *dog* is a pronunciation difference.

Dialect Vocabulary: When people from certain regions or cultural backgrounds use *different words for the same thing, or the same word means something different* it is called a *dialect vocabulary* difference. For example, some people in Philadelphia and New Jersey use the word *hoagie* for the same kind of sandwich that other people call a *sub*. Also, some people in Pittsburgh, Pennsylvania, use the word *gumband* when people in other parts of the United States use the word *rubberband*. In Baltimore, some people may ask if they may *hold a dollar* when people in other parts of the United States may say *borrow a dollar*. This is a vocabulary difference.

Dialect Grammar: When people from different regions or cultural backgrounds *put together their sentences or their words in different ways*, it is called a *dialect grammar* difference. For example, some people from western Pennsylvania say *The house needs painted* when people from other parts of the United States say *The house needs painting*. Also, some people from the Appalachian mountains say *The man went a-hunting* when other people say *The man when hunting*. When African Americans in Baltimore say *They always be going to the park* where other groups say *They are always going to the park*, it is called a dialect grammar difference.

Introduction of Language Journal: At the back of each workbook are several pages entitled *language journal*. Instruct students to write down dialect forms that they observe outside of class (e.g., in the neighborhood, home), identifying what type of dialect difference it is. They may also write down reactions to activities and discussions in class. Instructors are encouraged to use a *dialogue journal* format for this curriculum. A brief overview of dialogue journals is given in the appendix.

9
Knowledge About Language In British Classrooms: Children as Researchers*

Jenny Cheshire
Queen Mary and Westfield College,
University of London
Viv Edwards
University of Reading, United Kingdom

In this chapter we report on an unusual collaboration among linguists, teachers, and school children. The main aim of our project was to collect data on English dialect grammar from a national network of schools. In the process, however, there were many opportunities for teachers to enhance their students' knowledge about language.

The overwhelming majority of our young collaborators were speakers of nonstandard dialects. But whereas educators, in the main, choose to approach the relationship between the standard and nonstandard dialects within a descriptive framework, there is growing pressure from right wing politicians in the United Kingdom for a return to a more prescriptive approach (as is true in other countries as well). Any discussion of the role of school children as sociolinguistic researchers must thus address the tensions between politicians, on the one hand, and linguists and educators, on the other.

---

*An earlier version of this chapter appeared as "Schoolchildren as Sociolinguistic Researchers" in *Linguistics and Education*. The present version has been revised to take into consideration both the ongoing debate on standard English within the context of the National Curriculum and the clearer articulation of the notion of critical language awareness in British education. The research reported in this chapter was supported by ESRC research award no. C-00-23-2264.

LANGUAGE STUDY IN BRITISH SCHOOLS

Interest in language in education and in the involvement of children as classroom researchers has a relatively long history in the United Kingdom. Linguistics was developing as an independent discipline in universities throughout the 1950s and 1960s. It argued for a move from prescriptive to descriptive language teaching, a position that proved attractive for many teachers disillusioned with traditional grammar teaching. As early as 1964, the Secondary Schools Examination Council recommended that the advanced level (A-level) in English (a course of study undertaken by some 16- to 18-year-olds) should offer opportunities to study, among other things, the structure of language, the relationship of standard English and nonstandard dialects, and the social implications of language use (Lancaster & Taylor, 1992). Although it was to take more than 20 years for the introduction of an A-level (designed for 18-year-olds) syllabus on English language (rather than literature), the potential of language as an area of study in its own right (cf. University of London, 1992) had finally gained recognition on the educational agenda.

The Nuffield program in linguistics and English teaching also began work in 1964 to examine the implications of linguistics for teaching language in school. The materials developed from this program (*Language in Use*; Doughty, Pearce, & Thornton, 1971) received a disappointing reception from teachers largely unfamiliar with developments in linguistics. Nonetheless, interest in this area was growing. In 1976, for instance, the National Congress on Languages in Education (NCLE) was set up as a forum for teachers, researchers, examiners, advisers, publishers, and others committed to promoting language study as part of the curriculum.

THE LANGUAGE AWARENESS MOVEMENT

Language awareness has been defined as "a person's sensitivity and conscious awareness of the nature of language and its role in human life" (cf. Donmall, 1985). Throughout the 1980s, there was a burgeoning of programs in British schools promoting such awareness. A central tenet of work in this area is that children themselves are the experts because they are all competent users of at least one language

Several developments within British education have been identified as giving rise to language awareness programs (Jones, 1989). These include the child-centered approach to education that became popular through the 1960s and that encouraged children to become active learners rather than passive recipients of knowledge; the educational impact of immigration from the Indian subcontinent and the West Indies that demanded a reassessment of both the content and delivery of the curriculum; the influence of the "language across the curriculum" movement that advocated that all teachers are responsible for the language learning of the children in their care (Department of Education and Science [DES], 1975); and growing dissatisfaction with the highly routinized audiolingual approach widespread within modern language teaching.

The number of teachers involved in language awareness activities increased dramatically; and, for the first time, there were opportunities for cross-departmental collaboration among colleagues in English, English as a Second Language, community languages, and modern languages (Anderson, 1991). From the late 1980s, however, there was a change in emphasis, with evidence of a more rigorous and questioning approach than had previously been the norm. Writers like Clark, Fairclough, Ivanic, and Martin-Jones (1990, 1991) and Fairclough (1992) began making a case for critical language awareness in which children are encouraged not simply to observe and catalogue information about language and language use but to draw on this knowledge to understand and explain a wide range of social and political issues.

KNOWLEDGE ABOUT LANGUAGE (KAL)

The late 1980s also marked a watershed in other important respects. The 1988 Education Reform Act heralded the introduction of a national curriculum that included a description of the issues that teachers need to address under the heading of KAL. Significantly for present purposes, there was considerable support for what is labeled a fieldwork approach (DES, 1989) and the notion of children as researchers. It is suggested, for instance, that: "Work on knowledge about language can be based on pupils' own fieldwork, collecting and classifying their own data, learning about the methodology of observation, classification, description, hypothesis-making and explanation" (p. 6.12). There is also an expectation that, at least in the case of older children, KAL should be assessed through children's own researches: "At 16, they should undertake a small-scale investigation of any aspect of language in the programmes of study that is appropriate to their level" (p. 6.51) Attention is also paid to the potential of bilingual children a a classroom resource. It is suggested, for instance, that they can help to "provide examples of the structure and syntax of different languages" that can form a focus for discussion about language forms and be used to contrast and compare with structures in English (DES, 1988a, p. 12.9).

Although KAL marks an important point of departure, the recommendations of the National Curriculum documents have not escaped criticism. Great concern has been expressed at the prescriptive approach to standard English that has been promoted by the National Curriculum (which we discuss in greater detail later). Warnings have also been sounded at the dangers of presenting KAL as a series of unrelated facts to-be tackled by teacher and student at different stages (Bhatt & Martin-Jones, 1992; Fairclough, 1992).

Although government guidelines do not advocate a critical approach to language study, many writers draw comfort that they do not actually rule out such an approach. Reactions to the Language in the National Curriculum (LINC) project, however, do not auger well for the future development of critical language awareness. LINC was a £21 million project funded by the British government between 1989 and 1992 (Carter, 1991). A primary aim was to enhance teachers' and pupils' knowledge about language, and attention was paid, among other things, to the intimate relationship between language and social power. In July 1991, in a political climate in which standard English was increasingly associated with maintaining both educational and moral standards (cf. Graddol, 1988) and where pressure was mounting for a return to traditional teaching methods, the DES banned the publication of the materials.

THE SURVEY OF BRITISH DIALECT GRAMMAR

The 1970s and 1980s, then, marked a growth of interest in language study in schools during a period marked by increasing political polarization. Against this background, we offer a description of a survey on British dialect grammar that we undertook with the help of teachers and school children between 1986 and 1989. Our aim was to obtain information on dialect syntax and, eventually, to present this in a way that would be helpful and accessible to teachers. We planned the dialect survey before the introduction of the National Curriculum, already seeing that this type of information was urgently needed. Research in Britain had shown the problems that could be caused by an incomplete understanding of the differences between the linguistic forms of standard English and those of nonstandard varieties: Edwards (1983), for example, discussed some of the inappropriate teaching strategies that teachers may use when teaching reading skills; and Edwards (1979) and Cheshire (1982a) gave examples of hypercorrect forms produced by school children in their written work.

We did not set out to address the differences between spoken and written standard English, which continue to elude linguists who have been working on spoken English for many years (see, for discussion, Crystal, 1980). Instead, we aimed simply to increase the amount of information on local dialect syntax that is available for teachers to consult, and to involve school children and their teachers in gathering that information. In Britain, dialectologists and sociolinguists know far less about dialect grammar (by which we mean morphology and syntax) than about dialect vocabulary or phonology (Edwards, Trudgill, & Weltens, 1984). Teachers can consult various general accounts of differences in dialect grammar (e.g., Edwards, 1983; Milroy & Milroy, 1985), but more detailed information is available on just four areas of the British Isles (Scotland, Northern Ireland, Southern England, and Newcastle upon Tyne; see Milroy & Milroy, 1989, 1993). For the most part, teachers have had to try to understand the differences between standard and nonstandard dialects of English without the help of linguists. There is widespread public confusion of dialect grammar with "sloppy English" or "incorrect" English, and in the absence of any proper linguistic or sociolinguistic training for teachers there seems little reason to expect this group to be any less confused than the rest of the general public.

The importance of standard English achieved fresh prominence in 1989 with the introduction of a national curriculum in British schools. The Kingman report on the teaching of English (DES, 1988b) stated the following:

> Schools should develop their own coherent policies, which are sensitive to their local circumstances on exactly how and when Standard English should be taught. In general terms, we advocate that there should be explicit teaching about the nature and functions of Standard English in the top years of the primary school; that there should be the beginnings of the expectation of Standard English in written work when appropriate by the age of 11; that there should be the provision of opportunities for oral work where spoken standard English would be a realistic expectation in the secondary school; and that all pupils should be in a position to choose to use standard English in speech when appropriate by the age of 16.

There has been a sustained and vigorous criticism of the failure of the English national curriculum to address the social and political realities of language use. There has been a similar disillusionment with the notion of "appropriateness" that is advanced to justify the teaching of standard English in schools (see, e.g., Cameron & Bourne, 1988; Fairclough, 1992; NATE, 1992). Given the growing preoccupation among British conservatives with the concept of nationhood and of national community and culture, it is perhaps inevitable that standard English should have emerged as a symbol of this national identity in the late

1980s. Marenbon (1987), for instance, in a pamphlet published by the right wing Centre for Policy Studies, prayed that politicians be granted "sharpness of mind and firmness of resolve" to resist "experts" influenced by fashion, since "in the future of our language lies the future of our nation" (p. 40). The influence of right-wing thinkers such as Lawlor (1988) and Letwin (1988) is now well documented. The decision of the Secretary of State for Education in 1992 to review the English Orders because they "place insufficient emphasis on the requirement that all pupils should become confident users of standard English," came as a great disappointment to many, but as a surprise to very few.[1]

Political considerations aside, there are also serious practical problems in the implementation of the English national curriculum. There is an assumption, for instance, that teachers "themselves have an accurate understanding of the differences between written standard English, spoken standard English and spoken local varieties of English" (DES, 1989, p. 4.40). Such an assumption would appear, at the very least, to be optimistic. A study of the level of linguistic knowledge and awareness among student teachers training to be primary teachers (Chandler, Robinson, & Noyes, 1988) indicates considerable gaps in their understanding of language.

The time was ripe for an initiative such as the Survey of British Dialect Grammar not only because of the fresh emphasis on standard English in the national curriculum but also because of the marked increase of the language awareness programs discussed at both primary and secondary levels of schooling. We established a nationwide network of teachers who were willing to take part in collaborative teacher-pupil projects on language use in the local community (see Edwards & Cheshire, 1989, for details). The collaboration between schools and linguists is an important development. On the one hand, teachers are interpreting for their pupils the accumulated knowledge of linguists and, in particular, of sociolinguists. On the other hand, the rapidly developing awareness of language in teachers and children opens up many new possibilities for linguists. There had, of course, been notable previous initiatives in this area, including the survey of languages and dialects of London schoolchildren (Rosen & Burgess, 1980) and the much larger Linguistic Minorities Project (LMP, 1985). However, to our knowledge, our own survey is the first attempt in the United Kingdom to involve schools in directly gathering detailed linguistic data rather than general information about language use.

For reasons of economy, the survey had to take the form of a questionnaire, which we sent to all the participating schools. The

---

[1]At the time of writing the new orders for English had not been published.

questionnaire consisted of 196 linguistic features, drawn from the main areas of dialect grammar described in Edwards et al. (1984). We felt it essential that a period of language awareness work (see Hawkins, 1984; Jones, 1989) should precede the administration of the questionnaire, in order to ensure that children provided reliable information, rather than simply the answers that they assumed their teachers wanted. In order to reinforce this point, we developed a series of lesson outlines and materials, tried these out during the pilot stage of the research, and sent the modified version to all teachers who participated in the survey. The lesson outlines covered topics such as multilingual Britain, language variation, language change, standard English, and "talking proper." The questionnaire on local dialect usage was presented as the end point of the work on language awareness, with the intention of consulting pupils as the experts on their local variety of English, and asking them to tell us whether the forms listed on the questionnaire were used locally.

The results of the survey provided the information that we had hoped for, giving us a general picture of the regional distribution of those features of dialect grammar that had been included on the questionnaire. We were also able to form some preliminary hypotheses concerning dialect leveling in the British Isles. We briefly discuss part of the analysis of the completed questionnaires later in this article; fuller details are given in Cheshire, Edwards, and Whittle (1989). In addition, we obtained some sociolinguistic information of a more general kind, as a by-product of the lesson suggestions that were sent to the teachers participating in the survey.

Teachers who returned the questionnaires were invited to comment on the usefulness of working on dialect issues in the ways that we suggested in the lesson outlines, and on practicalities surrounding the completion of the questionnaire. Their responses were, without exception, favorable; the general feeling was that the topics used as a basis for classwork were very successful, generating a great deal of constructive discussion and, in many cases, written work (Edwards & Cheshire, 1989). Some teachers offered us extensive examples of the written work that their pupils had produced as part of their exploration of dialect. These examples were of considerable interest to us as sociolinguists. In some cases, they provided a qualitative counterbalance to experimental research on attitudes to regional variation in English; in other cases, they gave us direct evidence of children's reactions to linguistic diversity and of their interest in exploring the everyday realities of language use in their local community. The work that we received convinced us of the value of incorporating language work in the classroom which will allow children the opportunity to explore their personal reactions to linguistic variation and to develop their skills as sociolinguistic researchers in the local community. In the following sections we give some examples of the work that we found the most interesting.

REACTIONS TO LINGUISTIC DIVERSITY

The work that we received covered a range of topics. We were particularly interested in the topic of correction, both because we wanted to see which linguistic variables are salient to the teachers, parents, and other adults who feel the need to monitor children's language and because we were curious about the children's reactions to being corrected. We were also interested in some written work that illustrated the way in which language functions as a symbol of individual and social identity, and in work that revealed children's attitudes to regional variation.

Correction

Part of the lesson outline on the topic of "talking proper" invited children to reflect on whether teachers or other people corrected the way they spoke or wrote. They were also to consider the kinds of things that these people said, and to explore their feelings about correction. Two teachers sent us the written work that their classes of 14-year-old pupils had prepared on this topic. This work was of interest for a number of reasons. First, we were interested in the identity of the forms that pupils said were corrected because there is little precise information available on stigmatized forms in the research literature, and few hypotheses offered to explain why some variables are more salient to speakers than others. Condemnation of *h*-dropping, for example, is very widespread in Britain, but people do not seem to be concerned about vowel alternations (such as regional variation in the pronunciation of a word such as bus, which may be [b s] or [b s].

Trudgill (1986) suggested that overt stigmatization occurs when there is a high status variant of the stigmatized form which tallies with the orthography, while the stigmatized form does not. Many of the corrections concerning pronunciation that schoolchildren wrote about gave support to this view. Sometimes (as in Examples 1-3) corrections were expressed in terms of dropped letters or additional letters:

1. Mum corrects my speech when I drop letters especially h and it annoys me but I suppose she's right.
2. Yes they moan at me when I start to speak like a Scouser [someone from Liverpool]. I say *married* as if there's about 7 rs in it—*marrrrrrried*.
3. Yes like when I say *ye* they always correct me and say *yes*.

Predictably, other corrections concerned features of nonstandard English grammar, which were denied existence (Example 4) or said to be "not English" (Example 5):

4. Yes because I use words like *worser* and other things like that when there's no such word.
5. Yes they correct me when I am saying something and say that's not English. If I say *what* they say *that*. If I say *can I borrow this* they say it's not *borrow* it's *lend*.

A second reason for our interest was the information that we received, indirectly, on whether correcting children's language is a worthwhile exercise. Teachers in England and Wales are sometimes advised on the kinds of corrections that they should make. For example, the Cox Report (DES, 1989, p. 4.46) rightly points out the dangers of indiscriminate correction, but suggests that teachers should correct nonstandard forms and highly stigmatized forms (such as the past tense forms of see) that occur frequently. The work that we received, however, did not lead us to share the view that correction is worthwhile. Several children reported "corrected" versions of their speech that we are confident were not made in that form:

6. Teachers normally correct me when I say can I lend a pen but you should say *can you please borrow me a pen*.
7. Yes. When I say *I saw something* they (teachers) say to say seen but my parents say it the opposite. This confuses me.
8. When you ask to lend something they always say *borrow* is the right word then your next lesson you ask to borrow something and they say *lend* is the right word.

Examples such as these indicate to us that correcting pupil's speech is a waste of time and is likely to lead to confusion about the linguistic relationship between features of standard and nonstandard English.

Sociolinguists stress that language is closely bound up with individual and social identity. It is certainly not difficult to envisage a scenario in which persistent corrections of a child's language can lead to a reticence in oral work and even, in extreme cases, to alienation from the school. We were interested, therefore, in the reactions that children expressed to being corrected. Examples 9-12 illustrate a broad range of professed reactions:

9. I feel very angry because I know what I am saying and so does the teacher.

10. I am not really bothered: I know what I mean and so do they.
11. My mum corrects me and it annoys me but I suppose she's right.
12. It doesn't bother me because they (teachers) know how to speak better than I do.

With the possible exception of the sanguine response in Example 10, this range of reactions confirms our view that it is not a good idea to correct children's speech. In this respect, the repeated complaints of older dialect speakers also consulted during the course of the survey present a point of comparison. One northern octogenarian commented:

> Any child using dialect speech would be severely reprimanded or ignored, depending on which teacher was in charge. Some teachers would endeavour kindly to explain that this was not on, others, less sympathetic, would perhaps resort to sarcasm or pretend to deliberately misunderstand.

Although tolerance of the spoken word has certainly increased in recent years, it is extremely doubtful whether the attempts of present-day teachers to change dialect speech or writing will be any more effective than those of the past. As one fourth-year pupil in Rotherham reflected:

> Teachers always correct the way I write. They correct the way I write more than anything. When I write a story and include talking I write it how I would speak. But sometimes teachers cross it out and put in how they would talk. I don't think they should do that. They should leave it as is.

Although we remain skeptical about the usefulness of correcting nonstandard forms, we are convinced of the value of including discussion of this aspect of "talking proper" in the school curriculum. We agree with the Cox Committee's view that every child is entitled to learn not only the functions but also the forms of standard English (DES, 1989). However, it is is by no means clear how this should be achieved, nor how teachers are to achieve the Cox Report's instructions to teach children the grammatical differences between the speech of their local area and spoken standard English (DES, 1989). Nonetheless, the opportunity to air personal reactions to corrections and to see the range of reactions amongst classmates seems a necessary prerequisite for constructive teaching of the linguistic differences between standard and nonstandard English.

Attitudes To Regional Variation

The research literature in sociolinguistics and social psychology is unanimous about the nature of attitudes toward regional varieties of English. A series of matched guise experiments has shown that accents associated with rural areas of Britain tend to be perceived by British speakers of English as more attractive than accents spoken in heavily urbanized areas (see Trudgill, 1983), and further experiments have repeatedly shown that speakers with Received Pronunciation (sometimes called "the Queen's English") are considered to be more intelligent and more competent than speakers who have a regional accent. This perception has been found to be shared by standard and nonstandard speakers alike, although nonstandard speakers may have strong feelings about the value of their own speech, associating it with friends, family, and neighborhood, with social attractiveness and with integrity (Giles & Powesland, 1975; Ryan & Giles, 1982).

The lesson suggestions invited children to consider which types of accents they liked best, and which they liked least, and to give reasons. One teacher in a school in the urban center of Widnes, Lancashire (in northwest England) sent us some written work that her class had prepared on this topic. This work did not give us any insights into attitudes toward Received Pronunciation, but it did show us that "talking posh" was often associated with the south of England, particularly London:

13. I dislike London accent. It sounds really posh.
14. I dislike London accent because they are stuck up snobs.

As for other accents, the most striking feature of the children's comments was the complete lack of unanimity in their likes and dislikes, and the very wide range of reasons that were given in support of these opinions. Many of the attitudes that were expressed within a single class of pupils directly conflicted with each other. Compare, for example, 15 with 16; 17 with 18; 19 with 20; and 21 and 22 with 23 and 24:

15. I like Cockney because it gives you a laugh. I also like American because it's dead cool. Geordie is OK as well.
16. I dislike Geordie accent because of the way they say it, it just gets right up my nose.
17. I detest American accents because there is too much of it going on TV.
18. I don't like Cockney accents because it sounds like they're talking out of their nose.
19. I like the Welsh, Manchester, and Australian accents because they're good.

20. I dislike Manchester accent because I don't like Manchester and everything's slower.
21. I like Scottish because of the way they say it and when they say it fast it sounds dead cool
22. Scottish is the best because it sounds so easy going.
23. I dislike Scottish because I can't understand what they are saying.
24. I dislike Scottish accent because they speak so quick I can't understand it.

The comments that pupils made about different regional accents revealed a very interesting selection of idiosyncratic likes and dislikes, which they justified in equally idiosyncratic ways:

25. Norfolk accent is the best. The people sound like farmers.
26. I like the Australians and the French because they're different
27. Scousers speak terrible. Apart from that I don't really mind the rest of them except the people from Devon, they're really stuckup.
28. I hate the Birmingham accent because it makes them sound thick.
29. I dislike Newcastle. They talk really slow and drawn out.
30. I like Welsh: it's got a nice sound to it.

This diversity of attitudes within a single class of schoolchildren is in stark contrast to the unanimity that has been found among participants in matched guise experiments. Perhaps this is because experiments direct participants to choose from a preselected closed set of characteristics (usually, of course, characteristics that have been elicited previously by open questioning); in a less structured situation, when people are invited simply to express their personal likes and dislikes, it is easier to see the very wide range of opinions that individuals hold and to appreciate the very personal and idiosyncratic nature of attitudes toward linguistic variation. Airing these personal views in the context of a class discussion is a valuable educational experience, showing those individuals who have very strong linguistic prejudices that others may have equally strong, but different, prejudices. Such a discussion can never be neutral. However, if children are to understand the reasons why some accents and dialects are more prestigious than others, they need to be introduced to the historical development of English and to the intimate relationship between language and power. Although the national curriculum does not advocate a critical approach of this kind, it does not exclude it.

Linguistic Variation as an Expression of Individual and Social Identity

Another aspect of the lesson outline on "talking proper" invited pupils to consider what they liked and what they disliked about speaking the way they did. The statements about what they liked confirmed the function of language as an expression of personal identity:

31. I enjoy speaking the way I do as I think it's me.
32. I feel comfortable speaking the way I do and I think it's good.

Similarly, there was confirmation of the role of language as a symbol of loyalty to the neighborhood (Examples 33 and 34) and to the peer group (Examples 35 and 36):

33. I like the way I speak because it sounds normal in this town.
34. I like Widnes accent best because it goes with the town and it's different from all the others.
35. I like it because you don't feel stupid, because all your mates speak it.
36. I like the way I speak because my friends all speak the same way and I can understand them.

The territoriality of language was mentioned by one cautious student:

37. If you go to Liverpool you might change the way you talk because you might get beat up.

There were few comments, however, about aspects of their speech that children disliked. We were surprised by this because research carried out in Britain has sometimes shown that individuals who speak with an accent typical of a heavily urbanized part of the country experience linguistic insecurity about their speech. Macaulay (1977), for example, noted the comments made by one Glaswegian about his own speech:

> I mean I'm not a speaker as you can see. I don't . . . I'm just a common sort of, you know I'm not . . . I've often wished I'd gone to some sort of elocution lessons because I meet so many people in my job and I feel as if I'm lower when it comes to speaking, you know.

Trudgill (1983) similarly noted that linguistic insecurity may cause individual speakers who have stigmatized accents to become inarticulate and reluctant to express themselves, in certain circumstances. Some of the comments that we received showed that pupils were aware of the social prestige associated with certain kinds of speech:

38. When I am talking to posh people I feel terribly common.

but other comments, such as 39 and 40, revealed an antipathy to "talking posh," and we were interested, and encouraged, to note that most children commented as in Example 41:

39. What I like is that I speak just like anyone else and not like a Yuppie (posh person).
40. I like it because it doesn't sound posh.
41. I don't really dislike anything about the way I speak.

Thus, we found little evidence of the linguistic insecurity that has been reported as typical of children who speak with a regional accent. Perhaps insecurity develops later, if individuals mix with people from outside their region after they have left school; or perhaps times are changing, and attitudes to regional accents are becoming more tolerant. We would like to believe in the latter explanation; after all, some newsreaders and program presenters on the BBC now have (slight) regional accents, especially on local BBC stations, and accents other than Received Pronunciation are increasingly heard in public life. One recent study, however, suggests that this explanation is overly optimistic: Collins (1988) found that the prestige of Received Pronunciation is still firmly entrenched, at least in London schools. Even those school teachers who had been teaching in an equal opportunities school for 15 years and who professed to have liberal attitudes toward regional accents nevertheless gave the highest ratings to the Received Pronunciation guise in a matched guise experiment. Trainee teachers who participated in Collins' study also gave the highest ratings to Received Pronunciation.

Resources for Diversity

Classroom discussions of dialect are useful not only for raising children's social and linguistic awareness, but also for their development as writers. The work that teachers shared with us demonstrated not only that children write with interest and enthusiasm about dialect but also that they write most competently in dialect. Teachers who participated in the project used a wide range of stimulus material—texts about dialect, short stories, and poems in dialect, records, tapes, and television programs. Children have recorded an equally wide range of responses. They have improvised plays that they have later transcribed. They have written plays in dialect that they have then performed. They have also composed poems and stories in dialect. Yasmin, a 12-year-old Pakistani girl from Blackburn, wrote 10 poems in Lancashire dialect, including this memorable one about her grandmother's wish to visit a disco:

T'disco

I wer the best looking un there
Wi mi jumper an mi mini skart.
Mi dad wer reet proud of mi.
O'boys ran far mi.
I loked like on' of them Miss World
Wi mi hair done and mi face.
I've been t'disco 'ut none like this.
Mi granny ses she wana go, er.
An ah ses, "Yer t'old granni, love!"
An she ses she's 'oing there today,
So ah as sum sharp words ready.
Wah! Mi old granny going t'disco!

Work on the project made it clear that dialect continues to be a source of fascination for a wide range of people—for academics who believe that the description of dialect is as important to linguistic theory as standard English; for teachers who feel that education should acknowledge and build on children's speech, rather than criticizing and rejecting it; for writers and performers who find dialect a versatile vehicle for their work; and for the large body of laypeople who identify with regional speech and want to find out more. It also became clear that there was a very great need for a central source of information on dialect resources. A secondary development, the compilation of a Directory of English Dialect Resources (Edwards, 1990), therefore attempted to bring together as comprehensive as possible a' range of books and commercially available sound recordings, together with information on dialect societies, resource centers and sound collections.

RESEARCH IN THE LOCAL COMMUNITY

The children taking part in the dialect survey carried out two kinds of research in the community. One was systematic research into the distribution of the specific features listed on the questionnaire, which was carried out as collaborative classroom projects and analyzed by ourselves. The other type of research consisted of mini-projects on various aspects of linguistic variation, which were carried out as individual research projects by the children, and written up as part of their schoolwork.

Small Scale Projects

The lesson outline on language variation invited schoolchildren to write down in a notebook the different phrases that they heard used during the course of a single day for greeting, thanking, or taking leave of people. This activity produced a great deal of written work, with some children carrying out detailed analyses of the phrases used by people of different ages and different genders. The value of this kind of work can perhaps be seen most clearly from the comments of one 16-year-old, who recorded seven ways of thanking people (*ta, thanks, thanks a lot, cheers, good on yer, proper job, many thanks*) and five ways of taking leave of them (*see you, tara, bye then, cheerio, cheers then*), and wrote that she was amazed to find that she had not recorded a single occurrence of *thank you* or *goodbye*. Carrying out mini-research projects of this kind, then, can challenge preconceived ideas about language and help pupils to develop linguistic sensitivity.

Another mini-project that resulted in written work was research into dialect vocabulary, with pupils noting down some words that were used locally and that they thought might not be understood by people from outside the locality. Thus, we learned that a 60-year-old man from Lydford, Devon used *gaiky* (ugly), *emmett* (tourist or visitor) and *dashels* (thistles); that in Leicester people said *cob* (bap), *me duck* (term of address from a man to a woman) and *mashing tea* (brewing tea). Another pupil in Devon recorded different ways of giving emphasis to what people were saying, mentioning intonation, swearing, and the use of *you* (as in *he was a big man you*). All these projects seem to us to be invaluable ways of extending the linguistic awareness of schoolchildren. They also provided us with some useful information that we did not have before (e.g., the use of *you* for emphasis has not, as far as we know, been reported before).

The Questionnaire on Local Dialect Grammar

From our own point of view, the most useful information on linguistic variation was contained in the questionnaires that were returned. We suggested to teachers that classes working collaboratively should divide into three groups, each dealing with one page of the questionnaire, and that each group should report on the forms of dialect grammar listed on their page, that were used in their local community. If more funds and research staff had been available it would, of course, have been preferable for our purposes to have based this part of the survey on audio recordings of a sample of speakers in different parts of Britain. However, teachers reported that the questionnaire provided a useful end point for the series of lessons on language awareness, with pupils seeing themselves as experts on local speech; it therefore served as a further way of developing pupils' linguistic sensitivity. And because the questionnaire responses had been systematically collected, they could be used in the way that we had intended—as a principled basis for providing classroom material on dialect grammar. We found that they could also be used to generate hypotheses about dialect leveling in

Britain, although these hypotheses could only be put to the test, of course, by making future audiorecordings of actual speech.

We were, of course, acutely aware of the limitations of using questionnaires to collect linguistic data and we took steps to guard against these limitations, as far as possible. A pilot study was carried out in the town of Reading, Berkshire, where a previous empirical study of morphological and syntactic variation had taken place (Cheshire, 1982b). Children's appraisals of dialect forms regularly heard in Reading coincided closely with those that we know, from the previous study, actually do occur. Each completed questionnaire that we received during the survey proper was examined to see if any examples of dialect usage were reported that, on the basis of existing knowledge, were unexpected for the area. Such examples were infrequent but did occasionally occur. Our procedure was to write to the teacher concerned to query the feature and to ask for further examples of utterances in which it occurred. This allowed us to judge for ourselves whether misreporting had taken place. Wherever possible, we also cross-checked examples of this kind with linguists working in that area of Britain.

Fewer questionnaires were returned than we had anticipated: The survey had to contend with several problems in data collection, many of which resulted from the effects of the industrial action taken by teachers during 1985-1986, and from the work involved in preparing for the introduction of the new GCSE public examinations in 1988. Two hundred questionnaires were distributed, and 87 completed questionnaires were returned. Although this was a smaller number than we originally expected, the returned questionnaires in fact covered all except two of the major urban areas of the British Isles (see Cheshire et al., 1989). The Survey of British Dialect Grammar therefore contrasts sharply with the only previous survey of English dialects (see, e.g., Orton, 1969), not only in its focus on syntax rather than on phonology, but also in its emphasis on urban rather than rural areas.

This predominantly urban distribution of responses allowed us to make a contribution to the controversial question of dialect leveling. Earlier analyses of English dialects based on SED material found it possible to define regional dialect areas in terms of the phonological features that occur in different parts of Britain (see, e.g., Lass, 1987; Wakelin, 1984), but could not identify any clearcut regions of England in terms of morphological features (again, see Wakelin, 1984). Lass (1987) suggested that one reason for there being no major morphosyntactic isoglosses is that regional English morphosyntax has remained relatively stable throughout its history; this would confirm Hudson's view that syntax is a marker of cohesion in communities and that there is, on the whole, less syntactic variation in language than phonological variation (Hudson, 1983). The massive social and demographic changes that have taken place since World War II, however, appear to have had an effect on this putative stability. Urban dialectologists agree that the growth of cities has been accompanied by very rapid mixing of a number of different dialects from surrounding areas (see Milroy, 1984), as former rural populations become increasingly urbanized. Dialects of English are now usually thought of as falling into two groups: traditional dialects, spoken by a probably shrinking minority of speakers living mainly in remote and long-settled rural communities, and mainstream dialects, spoken in various parts of the English-speaking world, including most of the urban areas of Britain (see Trudgill & Chambers, 1991). While traditional dialects may differ from each other and from standard English in unpredictable ways, mainstream urban dialects are thought to closely resemble one another and to have relatively few grammatical differences from standard English. In other words, it is thought that in some cases dialect diversity is reducing and being replaced not simply by standard grammatical forms but also by a development toward a leveled nonstandard dialect. This is a controversial question that can only be properly addressed by empirical investigations of actual usage, but the survey responses allowed us to make a preliminary, informed contribution to the question, by determining those features that were reported most frequently as used in the urban centers of Britain.

Certain nonstandard grammatical features are sometimes listed as common to most urban varieties of English (see, e.g., Hughes & Trudgill, 1987). Coupland (1988) suggested that seven of these grammatical features are so widespread that they are best seen as British social dialect characteristics rather than as marking regional provenance; these are negative concord, *never* as a past tense negative, *them* as a demonstrative adjective, absence of plural marking with some quantified nouns after numerals, adjectival forms with adverbial function, reduction of complex prepositions such as *up to*, and regularizing of the reflexive pronoun paradigm. These assumptions, however, have been unsupported by systematically collected empirical data.

The survey responses formed the basis for a more principled approach than has previously been possible. It emerged that a large number of features were reported infrequently (61 of the 196 features—31%—were reported by fewer than 5% of the schools). One dialect feature (demonstrative *them* as in *them big spiders*), on the other hand, was reported by more than 90% of the schools who took part in the survey, and a further 10 features were reported by more than 80% of the schools. We list these 11 features, together with the percentage frequency with which they were reported and the questionnaire item that was used to ask about them. Note that we attach no importance to the actual percentage frequencies; these were calculated simply as a way of distinguishing those features that were reported more widely than others.

them as demonstrative adjective (item 125: Look at them big spiders) 97.7 %

should of (item 196: you should of left half an hour ago!) 92.0%

never as past tense negator (item 7: No, I *never* broke that) 86.2%

absence of plural marking (item 95: To make a big cake you need two pound of flour) 86.2%

what as relative pronoun (item 115: The film what was on last night was good) 86.2%

there was with plural notional subject (item 58: there was some singers here a minute ago) 85.1%

there's with plural notional subject (item 29: There's cars outside the church) 83.9%

present participle *sat* (item 46: She was sat over there looking at her car) 83.9%

nonstandard *was* (item 51: We was singing) 83.9%

adverbial *quick* (item 86: I like pasta. It cooks really quick) 82.8%

ain't / *in't* (items 9 and 10: That ain't working / that in't working) 82.8%

present participle *stood* (item 47: And he was stood in the corner looking at it) 80.5%

The survey thus confirms that the following features are widespread throughout the urban centers of Britain, as suggested by Hughes and Trudgill (1987) and Coupland (1988): *them* as demonstrative adjective, absence of plural marking on nouns of measurement, *what* as relative pronoun, nonstandard *was*, adverbials without the *-ly* suffix (note, however, that the questionnaire included only one such form), and *ain't/in't*. In other words, regional dialect appears to be a misnomer for these features. We think it important to report, however, that their social distribution has yet to be determined, so that, despite Coupland's (1988) suggestion, we do not yet feel ready to label any of them as social dialect features.

Some features were not reported as frequently as we had expected. These include multiple negation; the use of simple prepositions such as *up*, *round*, and *over* where standard English has complex prepositions such as *up to*, *round to*, or *over at*; the regularized reflexive pronoun forms *hisself* and *theirselves*; and the past tense form *done* for full verb do. With the exception of the nonstandard reflexive pronoun forms, all these features were reported much more frequently by schools in the south of England than by schools elsewhere in Britain, suggesting that there may be a hitherto unsuspected regional distribution to these forms.

Some of the syntactic features that were most frequently reported are not usually thought to be widespread features of urban varieties of British English, although they appear from the survey responses to occur throughout the urban centers of the country: These are *should of;* and the present participles *sat* and *stood.* Some of the frequently reported features are thought to be used by "educated" speakers and should not, perhaps, be considered as nonstandard; these include *there's* and *there was* with plural subjects; *never* as past tense negator; and, possibly, adverbial *quick* (Hughes & Trudgill, 1987; Quirk, Greenbaum, Leech, & Svartvik, 1985). The relationship between standard English and nonstandard English is by no means straightforward. All the most frequently reported grammatical features discussed here are characteristic of spoken English, whether they are considered to be features of dialect, features of nonstandard English, or features of educated colloquial English. Some of these features reflect the interactive nature of speech, having discourse functions such as addressee-orientation (*never* is an example; see Cheshire, 1989) or the structuring of information (invariant *there's* and *there was* are examples). With the possible exception of *never* as past tense negator, the features have in common the fact that they are not used in formal written English, and children have to learn not to use them in their school writing. Now that we have established which features appear to occur throughout the urban centers of Britain, and which features have a more limited distribution, we are in a better position to decide on the best way to convey this information to schoolteachers.

CONCLUSION

The Survey of British Dialect Grammar was an attempt to incorporate sociolinguistics directly into the classroom, with the short-term aim of enlisting teachers and their pupils as researchers, asking them to help us in the systematic collection of data on local dialect grammar. We have used these data to formulate hypotheses on dialect levelling, which now await empirical testing (see Cheshire et al., 1989).

We also found that schoolchildren were interested in acting on their own account as sociolinguistic researchers, exploring their personal reactions to linguistic diversity as well as investigating the linguistic variation that exists in their local community. These personal explorations seem to us to be an essential first step toward achieving the aims of the national curriculum, paving the way for an understanding of the differences between written and spoken English that can be linked to discussion of standard and nonstandard English, and toward the addition of standard English to the repertoire of those children for whom standard English is not their native dialect (DES, 1989). These explorations, however, are also a valuable educational experience in the own right, allowing children the opportunity to share their experiences of linguistic diversity with their peers and their teacher, and empowering them to face the adult world (see Fairclough, 1992, for further discussion).

Activities of this kind also offer interesting challenges for teachers. Children are allowed to assume the role of expert and, in most cases, will be able to speak with greater authority on the local dialect than their teachers. Children's views on nonstandard speech may, on some occasions, cause teachers to reappraise their own classroom practice, particularly in relation to the "correction" of nonstandard forms.

The scope of work on standard and nonstandard language is *impressive. Children can be encouraged to explore the use of dialect in role-play and drama. They can express their views on dialect through the writing. They can be presented with examples of dialect literature and invited to discuss the particular effects that dialect can create as a prelude to the* own dialect compositions. Small-scale research projects on language provide experience of questionnaire design, data collection, and analysis. It seems to us that this approach to language study offers ample opportunities for a wide range of educationally valuable activities that can be actively promoted within the framework of the English national curriculum. We would agree with many of the contributors to Boume and Bloor (1989) and Fairclough (1992), however, that such work can only be of value when it takes place within a critical perspective that encourages children to explore the social, political, and historical reasons for the way things are today, empowering them to reflect on their own language use and to consider the choices they can make.

REFERENCES

Anderson, J. (1991). The potential of language awareness as a focus for cross-curricular work in the secondary school. In C. James & P. Garrett (Eds.), *Language awareness in the classroom* (pp. 133-140). London: Longman.

Bhatt, A., & Martin-Jones, M. (1992). Whose resource? Minority languages, bilingual learners and language awareness. In N. Fairclough (Ed.), *Critical language awareness* (pp. 285-301). Harlow: Longman.

Boume, J., & Bloor, T. (Eds). (1989). *Kingman and the linguists*. Birmingham: Committee for Linguistics in Education.

Cameron, D., & Bourne, J. (1988). No common ground: Kingman, grammar and the nation. *Language and Education, 2*, 147-160.

Carter, R. (Ed.). (1991). *Knowledge about language and the curriculum*. London: Hodder & Stoughton.

Chandler, P., Robinson, W.P., & Noyes, P. (1988). The level of linguistic knowledge and awareness among students training to be primary teachers. *Language and Education, 2,* 161-173.

Cheshire, J. (1982a). Dialect features and linguistic conflict in schools. *Educational Review, 34,* 53-67.

Cheshire, J. (1982b). *Variation in an English dialect: A sociolinguistic study.* Cambridge: Cambridge University Press.

Cheshire, J. (1989). Addressee-oriented features in spoken discourse. *York Papers in Linguistics: Festschrift R.B. Le Page,* 49-64.

Cheshire, J., Edwards, V., & Whittle, P. (1989). Urban British dialect grammar: The question of dialect levelling. *English Worldwide, 10,* 185-226.

Clark, R., Fairclough, N., Ivanic, R., & Martin-Jones, M. (1990). Critical language awareness, part 1: A critical review of three current approaches to Language Awareness. *Language and Education, 4(4),* 249-260.

Clark, R., Fairclough, N., Ivanic, R., & Martin-Jones, M. (1991). Critical language awareness, part 2: Towards critical alternatives. *Language and Education, 5(1),* 41-54.

Collins, P. (1988). *Teachers' evaluations of accent in a GCSE simulation.* Unpublished master's dissertation, Department of Applied Linguistics, Birkbeck College, University of London.

Coupland, N. (1988). *Dialect in use: Sociolinguistic variation in Cardiff English.* Cardiff: University of Wales Press.

Crystal, D. (1980). Some neglected grammatical factors in conversational English. In S. Greenbaum, G. Leech, & J. Svartvik (Eds.), *Studies in English linguistics* (pp. 134-152). Harlow: Longman.

Department of Education and Science. (1975). *A language for life* (The Bullock Report). London: HMSO.

Department of Education and Science. (1988a). *English for ages 5-11* (The first Cox Report). London: Author.

Department of Education and Science. (1988b). *Report of the committee of inquiry into the teaching of English language* (Kingman Report). London: HMSO.

Department of Education and Science. (1989). *English for ages 5-16* (The final Cox Report). London: Author.

Donmall, G. (Ed.). (1985). *Language awareness.* London: Centre for Language Information on Language Teaching and Research.

Doughty, P., Pearce, J., & Thornton, G. (1971). *Language in use.* London: Edward Arnold.

Edwards, V. (1979). *The West Indian language issue in British schools.* London: Routledge.

Edwards, V. (1983). *Language in multicultural classrooms*. London: Batsford.

Edwards, V. (1990). *A directory of English dialect resources*. London: Economic and Social Research Council.

Edwards, V., & Cheshire, J. (1989). The survey of British dialect grammar. In J. Cheshire, V. Edwards, H. Munstermann, & B. Weltens (Eds.), *Dialect and education: Some European perspectives* (pp. 200-215). Clevedon: Multilingual Matters.

Edwards, V., Trudgill, P., & Weltens, B. (1984). *The grammar of English dialect*. London: Economic and Social Research Council.

Fairclough, N. (Ed.). (1992). *Critical language awareness*. Harlow: Longman.

Giles, H., & Powesland, P. (1975). *Speech style and social evaluation*. London: Academic Press.

Graddol, D. (1988). Trapping linguists: An analysis of linguists' responses to John Honey's pamphlet "The language trap." *Language in Education, 2*(2), 95-111.

Hawkins, E. (1984). *Awareness of language: An introduction*. Cambridge: Cambridge University Press.

Hudson, R. (1983). *Sociolinguistics*. Cambridge: Cambridge University Press.

Hughes, H.A., & Trudgill, P. (1987). *English accents and dialects: An introduction to social and regional varieties of British English*. London: Edward Arnold.

Jones, A.P. (1989). Language awareness programmes in British schools. In J. Cheshire, V. Edwards, H. Munstermann, & B. Weltens (Eds.), *Dialect and education: Some European perspectives* (pp. 269-281). Clevedon: Multilingual Matters.

Lancaster, L., & Taylor, R. (1992). Critical approaches to language, learning and pedagogy: A case study. In N. Fairclough (Ed.), *Critical language awareness* (pp. 256-284). Harlow: Longman.

Lass, R. (1987). *The shape of English*. London: Dent.

Lawlor, S. (1988). *Correct core*. London: Centre for Policy Studies.

Letwin, S. (1988). *Aims of schooling*. London: Centre for Policy Studies.

Linguistic Minorities Project. (1985). *The other languages of England*. London: Routledge.

Macaulay, R.K.S. (1977). *Language, social class and education: A Glasgow study*. Edinburgh: Edinburgh University Press.

Marenbon, J. (1987). *English, our English*. London: Centre for Policy Studies.

Milroy, J., & Milroy, L. (1985). *Authority in language*. London: Routledge.

Milroy, J., & Milroy, L. (Eds.). (1989). *Regional variation in British English syntax*. London: Economic and Social Research Council.

Milroy, J., & Milroy, L. (Eds.). (1993). *Real English: The grammar of English dialects in the British Isles.* London: Longman.

National Association for the Teaching of English. (1992). *Made tongue tied by authority: New orders for English? A response by the National Association for the teaching of English to the review of the statutory order for English.* Sheffield: Author.

Orton, H. (1969). *Survey of English dialects (A): Introduction.* Leeds: E.J. Arnold for University of Leeds.

Quirk, R., Greenbaum, S., Leech, G., & Svartvik, J. (1985). *A comprehensive grammar of English.* Harlow: Longman.

Rosen, H., & Burgess, T. (1980). *The languages and dialects of London schoolchildren.* London: Ward Lock Educational.

Ryan, E.B., & Giles, H. (1982). *Attitudes towards language variation.* London: Edward Arnold.

Trudgill, P. (1983). *On dialect.* Oxford: Basil Blackwell.

Trudgill, P. (1986). *Dialects in contact.* Oxford: Blackwell.

Trudgill, P., & Chambers, J. (Eds.). (1991). *Dialects of English: Studies in grammatical variation.* Harlow: Longman.

University of London. (1992). *London examinations: English (8177, 9170-9175) Advanced Supplementary and Advanced Level Syllabuses May/June 1994 and January 1995.* London: University of London Examinations and Assessment Council.

Wakelin, M. (1984). Rural dialects in English. In P. Trudgill (Ed.), *Language in the British Isles* (pp. 70-93). Cambridge: Cambridge University Press.

Section III
Community as Curriculum:
Focus on Social Action

In the previous chapters, students became ethnographers and sociolinguists, simultaneously learning modes of inquiry and learning about the culture and language of their own communities. They used what they learned to improve their academic learning and to redefine themselves. Classrooms too, were redefined. Rather than being sites of text reproduction and displays of "textbook" knowledge, classrooms became workshops for conducting inquiry, reflecting on experiences, analyzing and discussing findings, sharing across cultural and linguistic communities, and synthesizing new knowledge with academic knowledge. Even if it is not named explicitly, there is a social action dimension to each chapter in the book: validating students' home cultures and communities as sources of knowledge, valuing the language and languages spoken at home and in the diverse communities in which students live, demystifying knowledge and modes of inquiry and making them accessible, redefining relationships among students, parents and teachers, redefining what it means to be a writer, among the other social and political actions.

The chapters that follow are explicit about their social action agendas, indeed their social action agendas guided the projects. Montero-Sieburth describes a Foxfire-inspired project by high school students and others to study, record and publicize the history and culture of the indigenous people in the Talamanca region of Costa Rica. The chapter provides a description of the broader political and educational contexts in which the project was conducted, and how that broader context influences how such projects evolve and what can happen. Projects that link education and social action—explicitly or implicity—do not happen in a political vacuum, and they affect and are affected by many different political and social contexts.

Schaafsma's chapter is similar in many ways to Montero-Seiburth's chapter, although Schaafsma describes a project with younger students in a major, North American urban center. To many the area in which the students live is only a wasteland, a decaying urban neighborhood. Without trying to hide the problems that exist, what the students found were communities alive with history, poetry, art, a rich cultural life, and with people working for a change and creating a community with an ethic of caring. They found inspiration and strengthened their personal and social identities. What they found they recorded, published and distributed—the first of several booklets on the neighborhoods in which they lived. The teacher involved in the project was Toby Curry, coauthor of chapter 2. Thus, Schaafsma's chapter can be read as one way in which projects evolve into other projects.

The final chapter in this section, and in the book, is by Egan-Robertson. With a small group of young women, Egan-Robertson formed a writing club that supplanted the students' usual language arts instruction. They began by generating questions they wanted to investigate, and it soon became clear that the questions focused on racism and personhood. These questions were more than guides for inquiry, they addressed core dynamics in the alienation that the students felt about school, their communities, and themselves. After generating questions, the students started talking with people in their community who were addressing some of the concerns the students had about the racism they had experienced: community artists and playwrights, and other young people using drama and writing as a way to reclaim history. They found more than inspiration and encouragement, they found ways to reconstruct their personhood through their ethnographic inquiry and writing.

The project conducted by Egan-Robertson and the students she worked with—as well as all of the projects described in this book—can be called a kind of *native anthropology* As Egan-Robertson writes,

> Rather than exporting knowledge of a community for use by others, ethnographic research becomes a way for people to reflect on their own communities by developing a better understanding of the cultural [and political] dynamics in which they live. But the methods and theoretical frameworks that might be used in a "native anthropology" cannot be imported from outside, they must be recreated.

10
Reclaiming Indigenous Cultures: Student-Developed Oral Histories of Talamanca, Costa Rica*

Martha Montero-Sieburth
University of Massachusetts, Boston

Even before Wigginton's *Sometimes a Shining Moment: The Foxfire Experience* was published in the United States in 1986, Paula Palmer,[1] the coordinator of the Talamanca Community Research Project, and 10th- and 11th-grade students from an agricultural school in Costa Rica, produced the first student-developed oral history publications in a Spanish-speaking country during 1980-1983.[2]

The development of a student-based collection of oral histories, *Nuestra Talamanca—Ayer y Hoy (Our Talamanca—Yesterday and Today)* was a major feat, especially in a highly homogeneous, democratic, White

---

*It is very difficult to appropriately describe secondhand the experiences that Palmer, her students, and community members within Talamanca shared. Thus, I am indebted to Palmer for her insights and comments that have broadened my own understanding of Costa Rica and its people. Throughout the contact we have maintained over the years, her writing about the histories of diverse groups, reflection during our interviews and correspondence, conservation of cultural knowledge, and her commitment to keeping the environment safe, have all been enormous sources of inspiration.

[1]Palmer, an American sociologist, lived and worked in Costa Rica from the mid-1970s to 1993. Throughout those years, she was concerned with the documentation of the oral histories of the Black and indigenous peoples of Costa Rica and their environmental needs and has published their stories (see references).

[2]It is important to note that the *Foxfire* series from Rabun County, Georgia were a source of inspiration for the development of the student oral histories of Talamanca.

society where Black and indigenous[3] populations have been historically marginalized and maintained at the lower socioeconomic rungs of the society.

Traditionally, Costa Ricans of the Central Plateau have tended to perceive indigenous peoples of Talamanca as relics and artifacts of the past.[4] In the present, they are stereotypically viewed as quaint peoples of the coast who through their unique music, culture, and foods add cultural resources to Costa Rica's largely White population. In fact, there has been a mythologized cultural veil regarding the multiethnic and multicultural differences that exist in Costa Rica, in favor of White Eurocentric middle-class standards. Media programs tend to present an urban and White middle-class orientation, dominated with images, news, and information that highlight either programs from developed countries or Costa Rican national issues. Indians and Blacks are rarely depicted as part of the national consciousness.[5]

This mythologization of Indians and Blacks of Talamanca in Costa Rica has contributed to people's belief that both of these groups have been totally assimilated, hence the popular version of Costa Rica's history has been that there were few or no Indians left in Costa Rica. Such inaccuracies have been in recent years reassessed by Costa Rican historians, anthropologists, and educators who recognize the existence of thriving communities of Indians and Blacks with distinct cultures and languages. In fact, anthropologists and linguists have identified the trilingual proficiencies of the Black people of the province of Limón, who speak not only Spanish and English but their own patois. In spite of their achievements, they are still subject to racial prejudice and stereotyping. Moreover, the falsely presumed lack of Indian culture in Costa Rica prior to the Conquest, also gave rise to the myth that the Conquest of Costa Rica was kinder and gentler than the rest of Costa Rica's neighbors. Juan Vazquez de Coronado was diplomatic in his treatment of the Indians, but those who followed were less benevolent (McPhaul, 1990). Stressing the impact of this mythology, McKinney (1993) pointed out the following:

---

[3]In Spanish, the term *indigena* or indigenous is used as well as *indio* for Indian. Thus, both terms are used interchangeably throughout the chapter.

[4]Native Indian populations overcame the Spanish conquistadors' attempts to colonize the Talamanca region. West Indian Blacks have been in the region since 1828 when they began to settle the coastal communities. In 1970, Talamanca was established as a cantón, a subdivision of the Province of Limón, one of the seven Provinces of Costa Rica.

[5]For an excellent exploration of the influence of Blacks in Costa Rica, see Purcell (1993) and McKinney (1993). Eulalia Berhnard's poetry in Costa Rica is extensive and deals specifically with Black, White, and Indian issues. See also Chomsky (1996).

Official discourse has often forgotten or overlooked the presence and contributions of the country's indigenous inhabitants, as well as those of African slaves brought by the Spaniards in the second half of the seventeenth century to work on the Matina cocoa plantations and the Guanacaste cattle ranches, black fishermen from Panama and Nicaragua, and finally, the thousands of Chinese, Jamaicans, and other Antilleans who emigrated to Costa Rica's Atlantic Coast in the 1870's to construct the San José-Atlantic coast railroad and later developed the cocoa and banana plantations in Limón province. (p. 1)

Until 1949, Costa Rica's Black and indigenous populations were denied geographical and political access to the central plateau beyond the town of Siquirres. Citizenship was not granted to the descendants of Black immigrants until the 1950s. Some Costa Rican indigenous groups were not recognized as citizens until the 1990s. Through the creation of *Nuestra Talamanca—Ayer y Hoy*, the descendants of West Indian Blacks and Bribri and Cabécar Indians of the Talamanca cantón began to recover the oral histories of their ancestors. In the process of learning how to photograph, interview, and use tape recorders while eliciting oral histories, the students and community members regained a sense of their indigenous roots, thereby reclaiming, or rescuing to its right course the legitimacy of their backgrounds.

This was particularly significant in light of the context in which the publication appeared—at a time when there was limited support for qualitative research of the type initiated by Palmer or others including myself. The educational terrain was not fully prepared to support student-developed oral histories. Nevertheless, the Talamanca Community Research Project through the publication of *Nuestra Talamanca—Ayer y Hoy* was able to gain the attention and interest of the national government that published and distributed the students' oral histories nationwide.

This chapter is a portrayal of the student-developed oral histories within the context of community-based education and curriculum and within the national educational scene of Costa Rica during the 1980s and 1990s.[6] The chapter is divided into three sections. The first section locates the Talamanca Research Project and the publication of the student developed resource magazine within the context of Talamanca. The Talamanca Community Research Project and resource magazine *Nuestra Talamanca—Ayer y Hoy* is analyzed within the broader context of national, cultural, political, and economic dynamics to explain the survival and likelihood of such innovations taking hold beyond the local level in highly democratized yet hierarchical contexts.

---

[6]Although the publication of *Nuestra Talamanca—Ayer y Hoy* was primarily as a resource magazine, its educational value is considered by educators and others to fall within the unfolding of Costa Rica's curriculum development.

The second section attempts to describe, to the extent that it is possible, the process that Palmer developed with her students, using secondhand information that I have gathered from documents and descriptions.[7] The descriptions do not include actual classroom experiences because the resource magazine had been published by the time I arrived in Costa Rica in 1983, yet the interpretations about the research process and what Palmer's students learned were gathered directly from Palmer through a series of interviews conducted during 1983, 1989, 1990, 1991 and through telephone and written communications.[8]

This is followed by a brief content analysis that shows different emphases and interests derived from the local cultures, as well as the effects of this community-based effort on the Talamanqueños' sense of community development. My purpose in exposing the reader to its content is to show how the selection of content, pictures, and stories carries political and empowering messages.

The last section concludes with a discussion of the implications of the Talamanca Community Research Project and the resource magazine in terms of political and educational policies. Although Palmer's work in this chapter is central to the discussion of student-based oral histories and text, the essence of this chapter is the short-lived existence of the Talamanca Community Research Project and *Nuestra Talamanca—Ayer y Hoy* under less than promising circumstances in Costa Rica. Questions about apparent contradictions between educational policies and practices as well as the types of strategies (political lobbying, research, and curricular platforms) that are needed at the national level to guarantee the longevity of such projects are raised for reflection:

- How can space for oral history and qualitative research of indigenous peoples be created without posing a threat/challenge to the educational agenda within democratic countries?
- How can a diverse community of learners retain their individual and unique cultures against the encroachment of urban pressures and modernity?
- What are the intrinsic and extrinsic values of oral history student-produced texts?

---

[7]The actual process employed by Palmer has been described in Palmer (1983b).

[8]Informal interviews with Palmer were conducted during the summers of 1983 and 1989, 1990, 1991. Subsequent telephone and written communication have kept me up to date with her work. In addition, this chapter relies on the corpus of data gathered from extended field trips to Costa Rican schools, videotapes of Costa Rican classrooms, structured interviews with Ministry of Education personnel and University of Costa Rica students and faculty, as well as gathered historical documentation from 1983 to 1993.

- Under what conditions can student writing become the community-based texts for classroom study?

THE TALAMANCAN CONTEXT

Talamanca is a 2,828 square kilometer area in the south Atlantic coastal region of Costa Rica, extending from the Caribbean Sea to almost 13,000 feet along the continental divide in the Talamanca mountains. The mountains extend from Costa Rica's Central Valley into Panama, and include the Sixaola River basin and its tributaries. The name of Talamanca comes from a place in Castille, seven leagues from Madrid, which was the birthplace of the Spanish "founder" of Talamanca in Costa Rica.[9]

The original indigenous residents of the area (Térrabas, Cabécares, and Bribris), dating back to before the 16th century, have lived in the highland Talamanca mountain range that in 1976 was named the Indian Reserve of Talamanca. Of these groups, the Bribri and Cabécar Indians have survived in the area.[10]

Until the 1950s, the lifestyle experiences of Talamancan Indians had changed little from the 1600s. Historian Francisco Montero Barrantes pointed out in *Elementos de la Historia de Costa Rica* (1892a) and in *Geografía de Costa Rica* (1892b) that the Talamanca region was constituted as a separate territory in 1610 in order for the Spaniards to conquer and control the Indian tribes who lived there. The Spanish Crown through military force and the Church sought to subjugate each Indian tribe. The Indians of Talamanca were never fully subdued even though the Conquest of the Talamancan Indians was one of the cruelest in Costa Rican history. The uprising of the Indians in 1709 attested to their resistance.

The region's natural landscape provided a refuge for the Indians during the Conquest, and at the same time contributed to ensuring the survival of the original cultures. In isolation, the Indians of Talamanca maintained their native language, cultivated plantains, beans, cacao, and maize. However, with the arrival of the United Fruit Company in 1910, the Indians were forced to move inland. When the company left in 1930, they returned to the area (Palmer, 1983a).

The Blacks in Talamanca arrived on the Atlantic coast during the first half of the 19th century from the West Indies. Some of them wanted to make new lives for their families in freedom; others hoped to earn enough money to return to Jamaica and the West Indies. They settled and developed fishing villages, in which they maintained

---

[9]According to Francisco Montero Barrantes (1892a).

[10]At the time of Costa Rica's settlement by the Spaniards, there were more than 60,000 Indians according to Costa Rican historian, Francisco Montero Barrantes (1892a).

themselves using English and their Protestant religion without being directly influenced by the surrounding Spanish culture even though by the 1920s Spanish-speaking teachers and schools were evident in the region. Community life for them revolved around the cultivation of cocoa and coconuts for more than 100 years. Talamancan Blacks sustained men's social lodges, English schools, games such as cricket and baseball, and calypso dances and concerts reflecting their West Indian heritage (Palmer, 1983a).

Isolation for the Indians and Blacks created a unique set of circumstances for the people of Talamanca. The exchange between Indians and Blacks led to linguistic mixing, according to Nuria Fonseca, Paula Palmer, and Danilo Acosta.[11] Indian elders learned to speak Caribbean English as well as their native language. Yet because of the national government's efforts to provide universal education, Spanish-speaking teachers and schools came into the region, thereby making Spanish the second language.

The 1970s brought the establishment of the first permanent Catholic mission in the Talamanca Valley, the creation of the Indian Reservation of Talamanca, the development of Cahuita National Park and a road from Puerto Limón to the Talamanca region. The 1977 beachfront coastal law had limited private property rights along a 200-meter strip along the shoreline. Petroleum explorations of the area in the 1980s as well as the introduction of roads and electricity, logging companies, land speculators, tourism,[12] and the migration of peasants, all contributed to shattering the privacy and isolation that Talamancans once had enjoyed. The lifestyles of Indians and Blacks in Talamanca, including the natural resource management of their region, yielded to outside pressures.

Palmer, an American journalist and educator, settled in the largely Black coastal village of Cahuita in 1974, and helped the local school board develop a program to revive its tradition of English education. By interviewing, tape recording, and transcribing the stories of the older residents of the area, she was able to create reading texts for her students based on local history. She learned about the concern that Talamancan adults had about the lack of knowledge young people in Indian and Black communities and schools had about their own histories and cultures. She was convinced that the process of doing oral history research could fill these gaps. The result was the publication of

---

[11]See Fonseca, Palmer, and Acosta (1986).

[12]In 1986, the Costa Rican government established a 9,449 hectare terrestrial and maritime Wildlife Refuge in the coastal region of Talamanca, to protect one of Costa Rica's few remaining lowland tropical moist forest areas, and estuaries and coral reefs (Palmer, 1989).

What Happened: A Folk History of Costa Rica's Talamanca Coast (1977), which depicts the experiences of three generations of immigrants, starting with the first settlers (1700-1914); the community builders (1915-1948); and Costa Rican citizens (1949-1977). *What Happened: A Folk History of Costa Rica's Talamanca Coast* tells:

> Where the African-Caribbean peoples came from, what they brought with them, and what they found on the Talamanca coast; how they dealt with the natural environment in keeping with sound ecological principles and with the human environment in keeping with high school ideals; how they were able to create a society in which their basic needs were more than satisfied, leaving time for recreation, inventiveness and creativity; with whom they shared the skills and values of their culture and from whom they learned new skills and values . . . and for whom did they expend all this visible and invisible effort? (pp. 8-9)

From her research for *What Happened: A Folk History of Costa Rica's Talamanca Coast*, Palmer became aware that the informants, in knowing their stories would be published, reevaluated the significance of their experiences and found inspiration in them. She also reflected on the changes she experienced during that process:

> I, too, was changed by these conversations. A bond formed between the speakers and myself, and with it came a mutual sense of power and responsibility. I came to believe that the young people of Talamanca needed to experience this bonding to know themselves and to carry on building their communities. Young people had so much to be proud of, and they did not know it. (Palmer, 1983b, p. 29)

In 1981, with Coopetalamanca's sponsorship, Palmer had a series of meetings with the members of Coopetalamanca, a regional agricultural cooperative, who were equally concerned about the region's young people. They formed an education committee whose primary goals were to: (a) educate Costa Ricans about Talamanca so that government programs might be made more relevant to the local needs of Talamanqueños; (b) organize Talamanqueños in order to know how to defend their rights; and (c) enhance the self-esteem of the younger generations of Talamanqueños with a positive image of their culture, history, and themselves (Palmer, 1983b).

Palmer initiated the Talamanca Community Research Project with funding from the Inter-American Foundation at the Talamanca Technical Agricultural School in Grades 10 and 11.[13] Thirty-seven

---

[13]This project was done in collaboration with Coopetalamanca, a Talamanca agricultural cooperative, the local high school and the Ministry of Education in the region's only secondary school.

students from both grades, two Costa Rican teachers, and a photography instructor began the process that evolved over 2-1/2 years under her coordination. Students were trained in photography, audiotaping, and interviewing and were able to elicit the histories, customs, and cultural roots of the Talamancan peoples. In their interviews, they met *curanderos* (healers), fishermen, housewives, musicians, artisans, and farmers of Bribri Indian and Black West Indian backgrounds who shared their observations, perspectives, values, traditional skills, and knowledge (see Palmer, 1986). With editorial help from journalism students from the University of Costa Rica, the Talamanca Community Research Project published the three editions of *Nuestra Talamanca— Ayer y Hoy* (1981-1982).

In 1983, the Ministry of Education republished the three issues together as a resource book for use in high schools throughout the country. It had two immediate impacts. First, the Black and indigenous populations of Talamanca gained exposure within Costa Rica's assumed homogeneous White society. Second, it provided a template for community-based, student-developed oral histories that could be used to further curriculum development from a regional perspective.

The Role of Community-Based Education within the National Educational Framework

Throughout Latin America, the purpose of education is not only to impart instruction, but also to inculcate nationalism and forge future local citizens. Local educational communities depend on what is happening in urban centers for their cues. Extensive interviews with teachers in rural areas of México and Costa Rica over the past 12 years indicate that they tend to view their role as bureaucrats implementing the directives of the central office. It is quite common to hear teachers make the distinction between *what they know* and *what they must teach* in order to fulfill the demands of the Central Administration. Much of this dependency has grown out of the conditioning effects of organizational bureaucracies set up during colonial times, but it also comes from the notion that intellectual excellence emanates from the urban center to the rural periphery. In other words, whatever is worth knowing comes from the city. Moreover, it is commonly said "that anything of significance happens or occurs in the urban centers and specifically in the capital cities of Latin American countries." Consequently, political shifts in national educational policy become exacerbated as one moves from the urban center to the periphery.

The "official" curriculum used by the Ministries of Education for all regions of a country in most Latin American countries consists of a national plan of education prescribing both the programs (subject matter areas) and the plan's time frames, subject matter distribution, and general orientation, objectives, and evaluation methods. Thus, curriculum is limited by its emphasis on urban life and values. Not only does the national curriculum imply the superiority of urban values, but what is taught often has little or no relevance to the lives of rural or indigenous people. The national curriculum is also limited by its focus on national goals as defined by the political agenda of the government in power. With each incoming government, the orientation of curriculum will tend to shift accordingly.

Curriculum policies that are set during a 4- to 6-year period may altogether change with the new administration. The same curriculum can remain in effect for longer time periods, when the ruling party is reelected, especially if the Ministry personnel remain the same. But if the party in charge is different, the likelihood that the "new" curriculum will be used depends on a variety of factors. With few exceptions does the same curriculum survive over time, and often in connection with the number of years already spent in planning, implementing, evaluating, and pilot-testing a curriculum for each grade level. In some cases, the time and money involved in the production of textbooks requiring several years of development, are what saves a curriculum program and extends it from one presidency to the next. México's mass production of free textbooks with its specified curriculum, teacher guides, and resource books for elementary grades and Guatemala's bilingual curriculum development as part of the enactment of a National Program of Bilingual Education (PRONEBI) under federal law are two examples of Latin American curricula that have survived political changes until recently.

In other cases, the "official" curriculum is sustained year after year through disseminated plans and programs that sit in desk drawers or the offices of directors of schools and teachers, whereas experiments on alternative curricular practices are carried on by the Ministry of Education. A case in point is the production of free textbooks as a vehicle for curriculum carried out through U.S. funding in several countries. Costa Rica and Honduras are two such countries, where the official curriculum may be operant even though newly developed textbooks that have been pilot-tested are gradually diffused throughout the school system at different grade levels. Such experimentation of curricula has made it possible to adapt the national or official curriculum to meet specific school needs, as in the case of multigraded classrooms where teachers may have the six grades together.

Finally, there are instances in which policies drawn from the national or official curriculum are developed at the local level through grassroots efforts. Since the early 1960s, there has been a gradual shift in much of Latin America toward *decentralization*—the deconcentration of power in large urban centers—and *regionalization* of the national curriculum—actually moving the center of education to the periphery by developing regional capabilities and by delivering quality education to outlying areas.

Costa Rica was one of the first Latin American countries to consider plans for regionalization and during the late 1970s and early 1980s, it developed plans and programs for achieving such ends. During this period, the national curriculum was adapted to the local areas by including local language, agricultural issues, local customs and values, and so on, under the initiatives provided by aid from donor agencies and curriculum specialists. Despite massive decentralization and regionalization programs that were designed to effect change by Costa Rican educators and policymakers, local experiments centered on the curricula used in urban areas; this was not surprising given the history of reliance on the national curriculum.

Costa Rica's Curriculum Trends

The national curriculum in Costa Rica is the core of the educational system. It is the vehicle for policymakers and educational researchers through which the social and cultural values of the society are reproduced. Thus, the Division of Curriculum within the Ministry of Education is a bureaucratic agency equal to the Division of Supervision and Operations, which manages a sizable workforce dedicated to curriculum concerns. Decisions about *what is to be learned* and *how it is to be learned* are made at this level. *Why* certain knowledge is to be acquired, or *why* it should be formulated in certain ways, are relatively recent questions (Montero-Sieburth, 1987).

In the past 13 years, the revisions of the curriculum carried on by the Ministry of Education in Costa Rica have yielded several eclectic curriculum models: a behaviorist model, a systems model, a humanistic model, a cultural analysis model, an information-processing, technological computer-based model, and lately an ecology-driven model. In this respect, Costa Rica is one of the first Latin American countries since 1989 to develop a full-fledged ecology-driven curriculum that enhances conservation, care of animals, and the environment. The Costa Rican Humane Education Project continues to impact Costa Rican students at the elementary school level and has been targeted for national implementation (Zuman, 1990).

The development of curriculum models in Costa Rica has, for the most part, been preceded by research using a quantitative questionnaire or instrument for identifying needs. Many of these research studies have been adapted from the United States and other industrialized countries, using primarily the instructional theories of Ralph Tyler, Benjamin Bloom, Robert Gagne, and B. F. Skinner among many others. However, during 1982-1986, as part of the Ministry of Education's initiative toward "Qualitative Betterment in Education," more grassroots curriculum policies were instituted using integrative models of curriculum with a humanistic and scientific perspective. This was part of the Ministry of Education's response to developing a Costa Rican national identity in light of modernization and demographic changes.

The war in Central America brought immigrants from Nicaragua, El Salvador, Honduras, and Guatemala to Costa Rica in unprecedented numbers. The government responded by setting up refugee camps in various parts of the country and providing schools for the immigrants' children. The rise of shantytowns and urban-marginal living became experiences of poverty that were relatively unknown to many Costa Ricans of middle-class standing.

Lacking qualitative models of curriculum development, the Ministry of Education invited curriculum specialists in systems analysis, values orientation, and cultural analysis to help develop a national consciousness about the changes that Costa Ricans were undergoing (Magendzo, 1986). By 1986, the Commission studying the national curriculum, described that curriculum to be:

> an *applied scientific discipline* able to *operationalize* the *theories and principles of science* which explain educational phenomena and create and adapt *organizational models* to enhance educational action to its intended learning outcome (*La Investigacion Sobre Planes de Estudio Vigentes en la Educación Costarricense*, Document No. 134, Informe Final, 1986; emphasis added)

It was in this context of evoking scientific rationality—the dominance of scientific beliefs and systems—that the then Vice-Minister of Education, Francisco Guillermo Araya, who was predisposed toward the qualitative betterment of education, responded to the work of Palmer and the Talamanca students. In effect, the vice-minister surmised that their work coincided with the Ministry of Education's call for rescuing the cultural values and heritage of Costa Rican citizens (Palmer, personal communication, 1985). The project was developed by Palmer and her students over a 2-year period during which they published three editions of their magazine, *Nuestra Talamanca—Ayer y Hoy*. They gave presentations about their oral history project in three areas of the province of Limón in 1982 by invitation from the Ministry of Education. The next year the Ministry reprinted the three magazines together as a resource book for use in all secondary schools.

The project fit within the rubric of qualitative studies that the vice-minister supported, particularly the need to create space for qualitatively driven ethnographic research that had begun to gain a foothold in Costa Rica. Initially, qualitative research emerged in Costa Rica through seminars offered by Rolando Pinto at the University of Costa Rica. But it was in 1983, 1984, and 1985 that I began to teach qualitative research and curriculum development courses at the University of Costa Rica and National University of Heredia during the summers with the hope of engaging teams of researchers in doing ethnographic research.

Before traveling to Costa Rica, I came across Palmer's description of this project in an article published by the Inter-American Foundation entitled "History and Identity of Talamanca, Costa Rica" in 1982/1983. Her description of the cultural survival and identity of the Black and Indian peoples of Talamanca and how the *Foxfire* magazines had provided a model for the development of *Nuestra Talamanca — Ayer Y Hoy* intrigued me (see also Olmsted, 1988), particularly because I was unaware of the Indian and Black influences in Costa Rica as a Costa Rican, and because I knew of few attempts to develop community-based instructional materials despite massive regionalization.

Francisco Guillermo Araya's vision about the betterment of qualitative education created the type of space that helped the evolution of the project during critical moments. He and other Ministry personnel paid partial salaries for Costa Rican teachers who were assigned to the project and printed *Nuestra Talamanca — Ayer y Hoy* at the Ministry's publication unit. Furthermore, the Ministry of Education provided support to Palmer and her colleagues at the Talamanca High School, Nuria Fonseca and Danilo Acosta, who engaged in a series of activities including:

- Conducting workshops on oral history techniques for teachers of Limón province;
- Offering a seminar/workshop on curriculum planning to administrators and teachers of Talamanca High School, Regional Educational Directors for the Limón area, and administrators from the Ministry of Education and Ministry of Culture, Youth and Sports[14] that focused attention on the cultural and environmental characteristics of Talamanca;
- Involving 30 Indian and Black residents from Talamanca and students in planning curriculum change;
- Establishing institutional and departmental objectives responding to the needs expressed by the community;
- Initiating a long-range process of curricular modification;

[14]Financial support for the curriculum planning seminar-workshop was provided by the Organization of American States and the Ministry of Culture in Costa Rica.

- Establishing a regional commission to supervise, follow through, and evaluate the modification process; and
- Gaining the support of the Ministry of Education's Divisions of Curriculum, Operations, Planning, Technical Education, and Indian Education, plus that of the Limón regional office staff and advisors.

The structure of the seminars and workshops was effective in generating enthusiasm among the teaching staff of the Talamanca High School and the Ministry of Education's regional staff for community-based education. As members of the workshop learned how to use oral history, and interview community people about their assessment of educational needs, a process for educational transformation and curricular modification was created. The suggestions and recommendations generated through the interviews required involving teachers more closely in the community activities, developing unit plans based on the agricultural production of the area in conjunction with the students' parents so that they could also learn, including students in communal committees and cooperatives, developing bilingual/bicultural education, and changing attitudes toward Indian and Black Costa Ricans.

Francisco Guillermo Araya attempted to formulate qualitatively driven curricula during his term, yet the Minister of Education and other officials considered basic knowledge skills to be imperative and shifted their emphasis towards more technocratically driven curricular structures that included information processing, the use of computers, and the development of math and science skills. Before completing his 4-year term, Araya left the Ministry. The director of the school and the teachers Palmer trained continued the project after she left and when salaries were no longer paid after 1986, and the teachers were no longer supported, the project itself and the curriculum reform initiatives in Talamanca came to a halt.

THE RESEARCH SEQUENCE AND THE PROCESSES INVOLVED

Impressed with the fact that as a foreigner, Palmer could be influential in contributing to what other educators and I consider to be curriculum change, in a country undergoing evaluations of its own identity and education, I met with her in the summer of 1983 and continue to meet with her when I am back in Costa Rica visiting family or teaching at the University of Costa Rica. Lately, I have corresponded with her in the United States, where she has moved.

What has stood out about Palmer throughout our conversations and letters, is her ability to penetrate the collective consciousness of Talamanca's indigenous people from their perspective. Her concern about the destruction caused by the April 1991 earthquake in Talamanca and her seeking of funds to help the people is just one example of her commitment.

Undoubtedly Palmer has personally been as affected by the process of collecting oral histories as by her informants. She has gained both an insider's as well as outsider's perspective. Her observing, collecting data, interviewing, reflecting, recording, and analyzing on her own, appear to parallel many of the processes used in applied ethnographic research. She speaks about the basic principles and methods that are used in conducting qualitative fieldwork in her own research.

In a working paper describing the community research project (Palmer, 1980) she defined community research: "as an experience-based learning method in which students produce and publish a magazine focusing on the history and culture of their own communities" (p. 1). She continued:

> [It is] first of all an educational experience. High School students in the 10th, 11th and 12 grades already possess a basic knowledge of national and international history. But few have had the opportunity to be historians. They have studied fine literature, but few have had the opportunity to be writers. They may have taken business courses, but few have had the opportunity to run their own business. Community research in the high school curriculum makes of students historians, writers, and business men and women. It is a serious undertaking because the result of the students' work is a public product, a magazine. (p. 1).

Through another 18-page manuscript entitled *"Project to Rescue the Oral Tradition of the Cantón of Talamanca,"* she described the research process for collecting oral histories in detail. Attention is given to the use and care of the tape recorder, the strengths and weaknesses of the interview, the role of the interviewer and interviewee, the role of the photographer, secretary, the types of transcription (literal and connotative), the sorting of themes, and the actual process for formulating articles. Throughout the guide, questions are suggested for conducting interviews and for reflection such as: Who have distinguished themselves and continue to do so through their special skills, such as fishing, healing, sports, music, art, dance? How do each of the ethnic groups relate to each other? How has communal life changed throughout history?

Of particular interest is the distinction that is made between oral and written history at the beginning of the guide. Students are encouraged to see the lived or common history of people as different from the written history that is used to generally emphasize political and military events and that is based on relating the experiences of people in power. Questions such as "Where did the founders of the community come from?" "What are the actual problems of the community?" "How do the people of the community think about these?" are used to help students think and reflect.

In addition, the history that has been popularized by Costa Rican authors, the oral histories of farmers, and songs of composers are called to mind as examples drawn from Costa Rican culture.

In enumerating the stages of research, Palmer shared some of her own insights and her expectations for her students (field notes for 1983, 1984, and 1991). In order to carry out the data collection, a process is elaborated through the formation of study groups around important issues (the customs of the Bribris, use of medicinal herbs, fishing, etc.). The purpose of the group is to identify the ways in which one finds out about a topic. Each group learns how to use the tape recorders and cameras with meticulous care.

In these study groups, students focus on questions that explore what is known about the history of Talamanca, how it has been learned and from whom. Such groups also raise questions about the identity of the group, what is not known and needs to be sought and finally *how to rethink what the group wants to know*. The idea is to discover what people know by learning to use different kinds of interviews: For example, topical, open-ended interviews for finding out how to make something.

Once students are confident about their skills, they can select informants from among their family members and neighbors who can tell their stories. For such interviews, four or five students are involved and each is responsible for accomplishing tasks within the process. One person is to be in charge of taping, another is to be concerned with the introductions of both the students and the topic at hand, the third is to direct his or her attention to taking photos, and yet another is to record notes, and draw pertinent pictures when necessary.

In the process of collecting and assessing data, students use conversations as a way to clarify ideas, and they talk through the ideas they have come up with. After transcribing their taped interviews, they begin to organize the transcripts and references in order to develop a point of view that allows them to communicate clearly in writing. The main goal is to communicate. Any doubts that students have need to be recorded so that they may be clarified as additional data or information are gathered. This is the occasion when other informants who read the initial stories offer additional information to be audiotaped and photographed.

At the end of this process, an evaluation is made. In evaluating each interview, it is important to recognize what went well and what went wrong. During this phase, topics are delineated. Questions used to guide the learner include: *What have I learned? When are the data enough? Did I learn everything of this situation that I need to know and understand? Is this worth publishing? If not, how do I continue to uncover more information?*

In summary, the study groups progress through a series of stages that are discussed briefly as (a) collecting the data, (b) processing the data, (c) creating a data archive, and (d) disseminating the data.

Collecting the Data. This stage consists of conducting interviews with key informants of the community who know about the theme under investigation and who can share such experiences. These interviews need to take place in the informant's context and should be audiotaped in order to be shared with others. Taking photographs as well as using drawings and notes about the environment complements the data gathering. Interviews are to be transcribed so that a record of the informants' thinking and verbatim statements of the informants exists. It should be noted that notes about the personality, nonverbal communication, and innuendoes of the interviewee contribute to the interview and therefore need to be included.

Processing the Data. In this stage, the interviews that have been taped need to be transcribed exactly as they are heard. In addition, photographs need to be processed and complete descriptions taken from the field notes, and observations of the interview as well as drawings need to be made.

Creating a Data Archive. All data sources—interviews, the transcriptions, audiocassettes, photographs, drawings, field notes and any other related documents—are to be organized and filed appropriately so that they can be made readily accessible to museums, libraries, and state entities.

Disseminating the Data. Possible means for disseminating the data include using publications, radio, museums, festivals, food fairs, photographic exhibits, communal projects such as baptizing the streets or parks with the names of important local heroes or figures, and declaring regional holidays to commemorate local happenings. The Talamanca students disseminated information through the publication of their magazine, *Nuestra Talamanca—Ayer y Hoy.* They also gave free copies of the magazine to all their informants, as well as copies of the photographs.

The educational objective of this research process is not only to develop oral and written skills in writing and publishing an article, but also to be able to reflect about what is learned. Students are asked to reflect about the ways they relate to persons, especially what is positive about the person. They are also asked to reflect on the content and the kinds of impact they have. The value of engaging in this process is knowing about one's own history and being able to communicate with other humans.

Content Analysis of Nuestra Talamanca

The following section highlights the content of three separate editions of *Nuestra Talamanca—Ayer Y Hoy*. The goals that students stipulated for publishing their resource magazine were articulated by Maritza Rugama, a 12th grader and the president of the student body in the foreword to *Nuestra Talamanca—Ayer y Hoy* (1982/1983, p. 6):[15]

Why do the students of Talamanca High School publish a magazine about local history?

1. To learn about our own county and share this information with other Costa Ricans.

Talamanca is a unique region of Costa Rica in that it includes three cultures, each of which has its own language: the Indians, who speak Bribri and Cabécar; the Afro-Caribbean Blacks, who speak Creole English; and the White people of Spanish descent, who speak Spanish. The people of each of these cultures conserve their own history and customs, all of which are interesting and valuable.

We are all Talamancans, but our cantón is very large and lacking in roads telephones and other means of communication. Because of this we do not know each other. Also, we don't have textbooks about Talamanca, because this region of the country has always been isolated and ignored. That is why we are doing our own research, to get to know the Talamanca of yesterday and today, our history, our people, our problems and our needs. We also want other Costa Ricans to know the real Talamanca and to put aside their false impression that only savages live here.

2. To learn to value older people and make friends with them.

Many young people don't pay any attention to older people, but we have learned that the old folks are the only ones who can teach us the history of our communities. They have lived the history of our country, they have worked very hard, and everything we have here today we owe to their struggle. That's why we want to make friends with them now and hear what they can teach us.

3. To unite the high school and the community.

Our magazine is a product of the collaboration between the high school and the community. We need the people to help us because they're the only ones who have the information that we need to learn and publish. And the people benefit from the magazine because in it they learn about other Talamancans, and they also feel proud to be interviewed and featured in the magazine.

---

[15]Translation by Palmer.

4. To learn new communication skills.

Thanks to this project we've been able to learn to do interviews, use tape recorders and cameras, organize and analyze information, and write good articles for publication. This has helped us become more confident in expressing ourselves verbally and also in writing.

5. To learn to be responsible citizens.

By getting to know and understand the problems and needs of our communities, we become more active citizens. We learn to appreciate our home, and in future years we will be prepared to fight to resolve our problems and protect our communities from anyone who would want to destroy our way of life.

The first edition depicts several themes: the students' trip into the Talamanca Indian Reservation where they interview Indian elders, learn about childbirth practices and how to use the mortar stone, and interview a shaman (healer); the evolution of the coastal transportation system by foot, railroad, burro-rail (rail car pulled by a burro or a horse) and roads; the Kasawak clan; the community's fight to create a secondary school in Talamanca; Bribri Indian legends; the petroleum interest in Talamanca; and the memoirs of an Indian elder.

The second edition presents the use of different herbs according to Indian and Afro-Caribbean traditions, interviews with key members of the community about the future of Talamanca, interviews with the missionary priests in the area, the histories of two villages, deforestation, Indian legends, and letters from the readers.

Because one of the major concerns expressed in the magazine is the future of Talamanca and how to retain the young people in the community who are engaged in education and able to respond to the needs of their people, a call for technical assistance and quality teaching is markedly expressed throughout this edition. The issue is how to maintain the Indian and Black cultures while introducing educational and technical innovations.

The third edition, which focuses on the Black people of Talamanca, stresses the yesterday of *Nuestra Talamanca—Ayer y Hoy*. Using folk narratives, this edition explains how Puerto Viejo became a town, how Black Costa Ricans struggled to perpetuate their Caribbean culture through English schools, and why traditional festivities such as the anniversary of England's emancipation of slaves continue to be celebrated.

The next section catapults the reader into the present as he or she reads about the reactions of the people of Cahuita to the new beach front law that affects their land and the construction of houses on the beaches. The law in effect is to promote tourism but the townspeople question not only how it will affect them directly, but who is to gain from the development of tourism.

On this same line of questioning, one of the Indian leaders expresses that "the development for the White man" is "the death of the Indian." Against the encroachment by industrialists and petroleum developers, the rights of Indians are articulated in relation to land ownership, and the Indian's relation to the universe and his or her cosmology. Townspeople give examples of villages that have overcome odds by creating their own initiatives and developing cooperatives in order to save the small farmers. This section of the third edition alludes to the encroachment by tourism as well, and even though it is not stated, it forecasts what might lie ahead if the area is developed.

Interspersed between these issues are examples of the music and artifacts of the area—including the calypso songs of Mister Gavitt. Recipes for the local dishes such as "rice and beans and pati, bami and cassava pudding" are also included. The edition ends with a short article emphasizing the teaching of Bribri, one of the Indian languages.

Throughout the three editions, the message is clear that the need to reclaim one's culture carries with it linguistic, social, economic, religious, and political linkages. *Nuestra Talamanca—Ayer Y Hoy* contributes to stressing the universality of folk traditions and beliefs, and to identifying how race relations and multicultural understanding can be improved through their description. The fact that once isolated and seemingly "silent" members of a community can openly express their opinions, formulate critiques about changes in their region, and identify with the youth of Talamanca to carry forth such messages is indeed an achievement. It is comparable to what Freire (1985) described for people who "break out of the silence" to appropriate (regain) their own voice.

THE POLITICAL AND SOCIAL RAMIFICATIONS OF THE TALAMANCA COMMUNITY RESEARCH PROJECT AND NUESTRA TALAMANCA—AYER Y HOY

Questions remain concerning how a project of this magnitude came to a halt, especially at a time when it needed further nurturing and institutionalization beyond Talamanca. How was the space that had been created for collecting the oral histories of indigenous peoples, especially by its youth, curtailed in a highly democratic country? What have been the impact and aftermath of the efforts initiated by students and the community at the local and national levels?

It is clear that a diverse community of learners is able to reclaim its cultures, ignored or forgotten by the dominant mainstream culture, by knowing *who they are, what they can share of their diverse backgrounds,* and *how they can work together.* Having an identity within the context of an apparently homogeneous country like Costa Rica means gaining a visible foothold. To secure such a foothold requires more than collecting people's oral histories and their concerns. It requires helping a diversified community become aware of its own history, and its need to legitimize and affirm its status within the power structure of an "assumed homogeneous" society. In acknowledging Costa Rica's heterogeneity, the deculturalization of Indian and Black cultures that has been traditionally sustained, can be stopped. It is ironic that among the features of Costa Rican democracy, diversity is precisely the feature that is inhibited, despite attempts like the Talamanca Community Research Project.

The Talamanca Community Research Project, although not directly influencing the development of strategies that promote community involvement and that are primarily connected to the region's economic, educational, social, and cultural planning and development, indirectly contributed to the consciousness raising that has taken place in the community and has pushed the community into action.

The achievements to date for Talamanqueños are reflected in the solidarity of the Indian Association and the cultural center at Amubre, the development of the Indian crafts center at Rancho Grande, communal development of nurseries for agricultural diversification, cultural rescue projects such as *Nuestra Talamanca—Ayer Y Hoy* and the appointment of an Indian advisor to the Ministry of Education (Documento Base, p. 3). Coopetalamanca, the agricultural cooperative closed in 1992, and the cultural committee went out of existence several years ago.

However, the recent development of ecotourism, "the struggle to defend the earth and to protect and sustain traditional communities" (Salazar & Palmer, 1990, p. 4) has taken strong hold in Talamanca. Ecotourism in Talamanca seeks to establish a "cooperative relationship between the non-wealthy local community and those sincere, open minded tourists who want to enjoy themselves and, at the same time, enrich their consciousness by means of a significant educational and cultural experience" (Salazar & Palmer, 1990, p. 4). The problem is that these efforts are greatly overshadowed by the social and economic impacts of mass tourism and the buying of land by foreign-owned investors (see also Palmer, Sanchez, & Mayorga, 1991).

Costa Rica's national government has also responded to the needs of indigenous people of Talamanca by expanding its educational offerings. Consolidation efforts between the Ministry and the indigenous community only came about in 1985 when an assessment team from the Ministry became directly involved through additional projects requested by the community in the education of Indians at the primary and adult levels. The Ministry of Education is providing support to Indian schools by coordinating the development of curriculum with local teachers and Ministry personnel through Indian supervisors, despite some resistance from non-Indian teachers. As a consequence, the Ministry of Education's Division for Adult Education has involved the Talamanca community in diverse projects that include the creation of cultural circles for the education of Indians (influenced by Freire's ideas), the development of textbooks, and the training of teachers for Indians.

What has been the impact produced by the Talamanca Community Research Project and *Nuestra Talamanca—Ayer Y Hoy*? Currently, although copies of *Nuestra Talamanca—Ayer Y Hoy* have not been reprinted since 1983, some copies are still found in bookstores in San José, at the Ministry of Education,[16] and throughout the Talamanca area. Yet the impact of *Nuestra Talamanca—Ayer Y Hoy* cannot be measured simply by its level of distribution or utilization in Costa Rica. Instead, it needs to be viewed in terms of its community development effects reaching local, national, and international levels and its creation of space for participatory community research and education.

In a multicultural region such as Talamanca, where ethnic groups, principally Blacks, Hispanic, and Indians, are geographically separated, the unifying factor is the high school. Using the diversity of the students to create research projects representative of the peoples of the communities helped break down the racial and ethnic barriers that existed. More importantly, working together on issues that concern all eroded the generation gap among age groups by allowing elders to voice their ideas to the youth and by having the young make a positive contribution to the community.

On a more concrete level, research projects such as the Talamanca Community Research Project offer alternatives to the rote memorization and recitation that traditionally take place in schools. Students learn to raise questions on their own and take responsibility for thinking through the kinds of questions they ask and expect to have answered. For those communities where access to books and reading materials is limited and quite costly even when available, producing local information through collaborative human-labor intensive efforts can be cost-effective while developing the community outreach needed.

Beyond Costa Rica, Wigginton (1986) addressed Palmer's work publicly. First, in the Introduction to *Sometimes a Shining Moment* he discussed how different groups have used *Foxfire*:

---

[16]The Ministry of Education did distribute *Nuestra Talamanca—Ayer y Hoy* to all of the *colegios* (secondary schools) in Costa Rica. However, it is likely that the remaining copies have either been boxed, currently sit at the Ministry of Education or have been discarded given the changes in educational and presidential administration since the 1980s.

Many of them, for example, have taken some of our ideas and
applied them in ways more exciting than I could ever have imagined
ten years ago like Paula Palmer, whose students work in Costa Rica
has culminated in a social studies text that is so culturally
appropriate that the Ministry of Education there has printed and
distributed it to every secondary school in the country. (p. xiii)

And second at Harvard University in 1990, he spoke about the impact
of *Foxfire* as a transfer model to other countries.

The Talamanca Community Research Project and *Nuestra
Talamanca Ayer Y Hoy* exemplify a set of conditions that need to be in
place in order for such projects to become institutionalized. Beyond the
genuine humanistic interest in inclusive and multicultural education
that it displays, such a project will demand taking risks, being single-
minded in generating change, and finding individuals or groups willing
to participate, despite limitations and obstacles, in responsive processes
for change.

In many respects, the process of conducting the research by
students created the type of space in which students' voices and
community concerns could be heard within the bureaucratic maze of Costa
Rican education and politics. Today the space for expansion that was
denied to the project has been restored with other initiatives by the people
of Talamanca through ecotourism, reforestation projects in indigenous
reserves, curriculum reform, and innovative educational programs.

CONCLUSION

The lessons that can be learned from this particular project and its
process have intrinsic and extrinsic value. In collecting oral histories of
indigenous peoples, their funds of knowledge, that is, their underlying
social networks and "the essential cultural practices and bodies of
knowledge and information that households use to survive, to get ahead
or to thrive" (Moll, 1992, p. 21) are made evident. Although such
projects help to legitimize the regional and local variants of knowledge
learning (as these contribute to national development), at the same time,
they contribute to people's questioning the imposed knowledge of a
centralized national curriculum. More significantly, oral histories such
as those collected in *Nuestra Talamanca—Ayer y Hoy*, make it clear that
even in a fairly homogeneous country like Costa Rica with 3 million
inhabitants, approximately 25,000 Indians and 65,000 Blacks, there exists
a unique heterogeneity. Like most communities undergoing change,
guarding this uniqueness while breaking out of the isolation is a
necessary skill that future Talamanqueños will need to learn.

Palmer's work with the students has been a process of identifying and reclaiming indigenous cultures by recalling the historical past and inserting oneself in the present. Those who participated in the production of *Nuestra Talamanca—Ayer Y Hoy* also reflect a change in attitudes. Alphaeus Buchanan, manager of the cooperative pointed out:

> Only recently have we of the older generation begun to see ourselves as united Talamanqueños. Perhaps it is because so many outsiders have been coming in recent years that we are beginning to see the threads that unite us, the ways in which we are different from them. It is also clear to us that to maintain control over our own destiny we must be united. Our cooperative movement is the strongest expression of our unity. Our task and our intention is to draw all Talamanqueños into our movement for economic, political and social strength. To do this, we need to break down whatever barriers remain among our three major ethnic groups. We are not racist, but we may be ignorant of each other in many ways. We need to learn about ourselves and each other so that we can work together in mutual respect. (cited in McLarney, 1984, p.14)

Throughout its 120 pages, *Nuestra Talamanca—Ayer Y Hoy* reflects a student-developed grassroots community initiative, which was carried out within the formal system of the school and extended to the community. Its effect at the local level in raising the consciousness of Talamanqueños has been most significant, yet its most important contribution has been in opening critical spaces within the national educational framework, in which similar projects can continue to validate, affirm, and reclaim indigenous cultures.

REFERENCES

Chomsky, A. (1996). *West Indian workers & the United Fruit Company in Costa Rica, 1870-1940.* Baton Rouge: Louisiana State University.

Fonseca, N., Palmer, P., & Acosta, N. (1986). *Documento base para el I seminario-taller de planeamiento curricular.* Colegio Tecnico Profesional Agropecuario de Talamanca, Bribri.

Freire, P. (1985). *The politics of education: Culture, power and liberation.* South Hadley, MA: Bergin & Garvey.

Magendzo, A. (1986). *Curriculum y cultura en America Latina.* Chile: Programa Interdisciplinario de Investigaciones en Educacion, Academia de Humanismo Cristiano.

McKinney, K. (1993). *Costa Rica's Black Body: The politics and poetics of difference in Eulalia Bernards's poetry.* Unpublished manuscript, Bentley College, Waltham, MA.

McLarney, B. (1984). What happened: Nuestra Talamanca—Ayer y Hoy. *Annals of Earth Stewardship, 2*(2), 14-15.

McPhaul, J. (1990, June 22). Historians taking new look at Costa Rica's Indians. *The Tico Times*, p. 11.

Moll, L. (1992). Bilingual classroom studies and community analysis: Some recent trends. *Educational Researcher, 21*(2), 20-24.

Montero Barrantes, F. (1892a). *Elementos de historia de Costa Rica.* San José, Costa Rica: Tipografia Nacional.

Montero Barrantes, F. (1892b). *Geografia de Costa Rica.* Barcelona, Spain: Lit. de José Cunil Sala.

Montero-Sieburth, M. (1987). *Analysis of the actual conditions surrounding the application of curriculum in Costa Rica: Identification of policies and classroom practices for change* (Final report). Prepared for Development Technologies, Inc. Project of the World Bank and MIDEPLAN on General Education in Costa Rica.

Palmer, P. (1977). *What happened: A folk-history of Costa Rica's Talamanca coast.* San José, Costa Rica: Ecodesarrollos.

Palmer, P. (1980). *A community research project at the Colegio de Talamanca* (working paper). Limón, Costa Rica.

Palmer, P. (Ed.). (1983a). *Nuestra Talamanca—Ayer y Hoy.* Proyecto de Investigaciones sobre la Historia Local del Cantón de Talamanca, 1981-1982, Bribri de Talamanca, Provincia de Limón. San José, Costa Rica. Ministerio de Educacion Publica.

Palmer, P. (1983b). Self-history and self-identity in Talamanca Costa Rica. *Grassroots Development, Interamerican Foundation, 6*(1), 27-34.

Palmer, P. (1986). Guide for students. In N. Fonseca, P. Palmer, & D. Acosta (Eds.), *Documento Base para el I Seminario-Taller de Planeamiento Curricular* (pp. 1-18). Talamanca, Costa Rica: Colegio Tecnico Profesional Agropecuario de Talamanca.

Palmer, P. (1989). *Environment, development, and indigenous knowledge systems: A participatory action research approach toward natural resource management in Costa Rica's Cochles/KéköLdi Indian Reserve* (Sociology Working Paper No. 16), East Lansing: Department of Sociology, Michigan State University.

Palmer, P., Sanchez, J., & Mayorga, G. (1991). *Taking care of Sibö's Gifts. An environmental treatise from Costa Rica's KéköLdi Indigenous Reserve.* San José, Costa Rica: Editada por Asociación de Desarrollo Integral de la Reserva Indigena Cocles/KéköLdi.

Purcell, T.W. (1993). *Banana fallout; Class, color and culture among West Indians in Costa Rica.* Los Angeles: Center for Afro American Studies.

Salazar, M., & Palmer, P. (1990). *Local participation in ecotourism development, Talamanca, Costa Rica: Opportunities and obstacles.* Paper presented at Miami Conference on Eco-Tourism, Sponsored by the Sierra Club, WWF Conservation International.

Wigginton, E. (1986). *Sometimes a shining moment: The Foxfire experience.* New York: Anchor Books.

Zuman, J P. (1990). *Costa Rican humane education project. Second progress report.* Unpublished manuscript, World Society for the Protection of Animals.

11
Telling Stories With Ms. Rose Bell: Students as Authors of Critical Narrative and Fiction

David Schaafsma
Teachers College-Columbia University

What words will take us from the position of schoolgirls to that of powerful women? . . . We can tell other stories.
—Walkerdine (1990, p. xiv)

Grown-ups don't give kids credit for things. We observe. We experience things in the world and some of them aren't nice, but we need to speak about them. Many of us have friends who have been or might be threatened with the problem. We need to deal with these things. We need to get our feelings out instead of keeping them inside.
—Julia Pointer (sixth-grade student,
Dewey Center for Urban Education, 1989)

There is a crisis in contemporary research; increasingly, researchers are questioning their view of and ability to represent social reality.[1] Lather (1991), among others, argued that it is important for researchers to acknowledge uncertainty about what constitutes an adequate depiction of social reality. Lather wrote, "We live in a world full of paradox and uncertainty, where close inspection turns unities into multiplicities,

---

[1]Much has been written recently about this crisis in research. For example, postmodern and feminist theorists such as Nicholson (1990), Harding (1991), Minh-ha (1989), Lather (1991), Belenky et al. (1986), and Walkerdine (1990), have focused attention on subjectivity, positionality, and the extent to which experience might be considered as data. Anthropologists such as Van Maanen (1986), Atkinson (1990), Abu-Lughod (1993), Turner & Bruner (1986), Clifford & Marcus (1986), Wolf (1993), and Geertz (1986) have focused attention on the rhetorical and political dimensions of ethnography.

clarities into ambiguities, univocal simplicities into polyvocal complexities" (p. xvi). One way to view the contemporary crisis in research is as a challenge to what Lather (1991) called the "dinosaur culture" of the research establishment (p. xvi), dominated by unitary, elitist, and monolithic conceptions of culture. Scholars and researchers must rethink their conceptions of research and develop ways of writing about that research that allow space for multiplicity and ambiguity.

In this chapter, I explore some ethical and political issues involved in research and representation by examining the writing of two Detroit middle school students—Mianne Adufutse and Julia Pointer— who, through a student ethnography project, interviewed Rose Bell (a woman who runs a volunteer-based program for single, teenaged mothers) and wrote stories based on those interviews. The stories these students wrote constitute an ethnographic and particularly narrative form of research that is also a basis and a means for social change in their own community. For these girls, the ethnographic, the personal, and the political merge in interesting ways. In an attempt to better understand their perspectives on their stories, I talked with each girl about her writing. In part, on the basis of those discussions, I see their stories as examples of praxis-oriented and passionate ethnographic research into their community.[2]

PLANTING FOR PEACE: STUDENTS WRITING FOR SOCIAL CHANGE IN THE DEWEY CENTER COMMUNITY WRITING PROJECT

Mrs. Bell
Mianne Adufutse

mrs bell is a nice lady
so nice and neat
she is a lady that has faith in me
she is someone
that's really so sweet
God should give
her rest and peace
(The Dewey Center Community Writing Project, 1989, p. 38)

The Dewey Center Community Writing Project is a community based, collaboratively designed summer writing program in Detroit's inner city. During 3 weeks in June and July 1989—its first summer—30 fifth-through seventh-grade students from Detroit's Cass Corridor worked

---

[2]I have elsewhere written about student stories in connection with the project, analyzing them in those essays for sometimes rather different purposes; see Schaafsma (1993, 1994) and Schaafsma and Smith (1992).

with 7 teachers from the University of Michigan and the Detroit Public Schools and desk-top published their writing in *Corridors: Stories From Inner City Detroit*. Toby Curry, one of the cooperating Detroit teachers, had been involved in a previous student-as-ethnographer project (which she and David Bloome describe in Chapter 2 in this book). Toby wrote in her preface to the book:

> Physically, the writings in this book took place at the west end of the Cass Corridor, a wounded, healing, infamous neighborhood in Detroit's inner-city. In the process of living this community writing project we were blessed with the life stories of many long time residents and volunteers in Detroit's inner-city. Their interviews and experiences gave us our inspiration as writers and taught us a history of the community that can't be found in any textbook. For instance, Rose Bell opened our eyes and hearts to truly understand the meaning of "born to serve." (The Dewey Center Community Writing Project, 1989, iii)

Julia Pointer, one of the students, wrote in her preface to the book on behalf of her fellow student ethnographers and storytellers:

> Everyone involved in the Dewey Center Community Writing Project and *Corridors* can hold their heads up in pride. For most of us, including the adult staff, these stories, poems and essays are either our first writing or our first writing being published in a book. It was relaxing to be able to work, write, have fun, and get along with so many people of different ages. We must also give special recognition to the wonderful and inspiring guests we had. You'll find fictional and non-fictional pieces about a lot of them. And, I think I speak for all of us, especially the kids, when I say that this book and this experience is one that cannot be replaced. And an experience that none of us will forget. (The Dewey Center Community Writing Project, 1989, p. iv)

My fellow teachers and I were excited that year about putting into action principles of language learning like those Jaggar and Smith-Burke (1985) named:

1. Language learning is a self-generated, creative process.
2. Language learning is holistic. The different components of language—form, function and meaning—are learned simultaneously.
3. Language learning is social and collaborative.
4. Language learning is functional and integrative.
5. Language learning is variable. Because language is inherently variable, the meanings, the forms, and the functions of children's language will depend on their personal, social and cultural experiences. (p. 7)

Most of us had been incorporating such principles into our teaching for several years but we were excited, too, about developing a curriculum with students, colleagues, and community members together that might speak to the very real social concerns that our students living in this community would name as important to them. (A detailed account of this program can be found in Schaafsma, 1993.) As both Julia's and Toby's prefaces indicate, much of the program that evolved focused on the retelling of life stories of various area residents gathered through oral history interviews.

The Dewey Center for Urban Education, where the summer writing program took place, is located in Detroit's Cass Corridor, on the corner of John C. Lodge and Martin Luther King Boulevard, in the neighborhood of the Jeffries Homes, also known as the Projects. The summer writing program involved many activities, but central to the program were interviewing people in the community and using the interviews as a basis for writing. We prepared students for the interviewing by asking them to interview each other in pairs, through a "mock interview" with fellow selected students and teachers, and we also encouraged students to take notes, although we didn't require them to write about this interview at all. During the summer program we involved students in numerous experiences such as field trips to area sites, many of which they helped plan, and asked them to write at least one finished piece for publication.

On the second day of the Dewey Center program, students interviewed George, who had once gone to jail for protesting the fact that area residents were being evicted from their apartment building, and Ms. Bell, who runs a volunteer service for unwed mothers called 961-BABY. George told stories of several community rebuilding projects in which he had been involved, including stories of occasions when he had "been in trouble with the authorities" for some of his community activism. Ms. Bell brought with her baby clothes that had been knitted by women from a nearby extended care facility and shared stories of her work in various volunteer projects in the area. Both answered questions from students about their work and life, which inspired writing by teachers and students alike, including portions of verbatim transcripts, poetry, character sketches, "nonfiction" accounts of what the long-time residents had talked about, and fictional stories inspired by particular aspects of what we had heard. One piece, written by a girl who was a sixth grader at the time and shaped largely from her notes as a "nonfiction" account, was published in *Corridors* as follows:[3]

---

[3]I chose both Mianne's and Julia's stories because I saw them as representative of the writing done by students in the Dewey center program, and representative of the kind of writing done about Rose Bell in particular.

A Giving Woman

Mianne Adufutse

Mrs. Rose Bell lived in a small town called Oil City until she was nineteen. She lived with her parents, grandparents, ten brothers and sisters, plus her sister's husband and three kids. Mrs. Bell explains that Oil City was a small, cozy town nestled between the mountains just like God set it down there. It was divided in the middle by a river. The city is so small it's not shown on maps because you wouldn't be able to see it there.

When Mrs. Bell was young she liked to skate and play basketball and was raised strongly in the Bible and giving. She said even though her house was filled with people, if a needy person came to their door for food they had enough to give to them.

When Mrs. Bell was nineteen, she moved to Detroit and later moved to the Jeffries projects. Even though people might say it's a bad neighborhood, she says it has its good and bad times. She gives tours of the projects to visitors, city officials and people like that. Once she gave a tour to a minister and she told him, "Go ye into the vineyards and reap the harvest. This is a vineyard."

She has been living there for seventeen years and beautifies the projects by planting flowers for peace. As a young girl, flowers amazed her. She stated, "To be able to put a few seeds in the ground and have a little sunlight and rain and see what God can do; it turns into a little flower."

Mrs. Bell also started a nursery school before it was in the other cities, because she loved people and babies. She loves volunteering work and likes to help young women and their children get food and have clothing. But they have to earn what they get by working. As she stated, "No work. No food."

Mrs. Bell never complained about her job and enjoys it and helps people when they need her. She plans to start her own school and teach volunteers how to get next to people and how to be loving through volunteer work. She ends this statement by saying, "What a thrilling life it is."

At the time of this writing, Mianne lived in an area north of the Projects, although not far from the Dewey Center. After the completion of the summer program I talked with her about her story. As one of the program's teachers, I had worked with her on her writing, although other teachers had worked with her more closely.

I interviewed Mianne about her writing on Ms. Bell. I asked her why she wrote it. She said:

Well, at first I wasn't sure what I wanted to write, but I thought this was an interesting woman. I didn't know her like some of the others did. At first I wasn't sure what I thought of her, but then I got more interested in telling her story. I think she is doing very nice things for her people, her community.

"And God," I said, and she agreed. I asked her if she herself was a Christian. Mianne said she was: *"Most of us who live around here, we believe in God and go to church. I think Ms. Bell is one of God's children."* I asked what it meant for her to go to church, and she replied, *"Well, it brings us all together and it gives us strength."* When I asked Mianne what she felt was the point of her story about Rose Bell, she said:

> "I don't know. How she was helping herself and others. Like all those girls who are pregnant. . . . Many girls are having babies, even girls my age, which I think is too bad, because some of these girls are so young. They are too young to be having babies! So Rose Bell is doing something good in helping out and I admire that."

I asked her why she had written her piece in the form of a nonfiction report and not a made up story. She replied, *"I guess I wanted to just tell the facts in this story. I thought she might get mad if she read it and she thought it wasn't like she had said."* I asked her if she had hoped to convey her respect for Ms. Bell in this way and Mianne replied, *"Yes. Maybe it will help her in her work, too. Kind of like an ad."*

I asked her why she had chosen to include some of the details in her story, and named some examples. She said, *"Because that's what happened. I wanted to give a better picture, so people reading it can see what she is really like."* When I asked her why she had chosen specific details, such as her love of children and flowers, and her quotation from Ms. Bell: *"What a thrilling life it is,"* Mianne said, *"That's just the way she is. I wanted to give a positive impression of Ms. Bell. I thought people would want to hear of all the good things she had done, and you know, her personality. She's really happy and positive."* We had heard other, less happy details about Ms. Bell's life, so I asked her why she had chosen to exclude those details. She said, *"Well, partly because I didn't want it to be too long. Also, I didn't want to tell her business. That wasn't why I was doing it. She might not like it if I tell that to other people. That's up to her."*

A seventh grader at the time of writing her story, Julia, like Mianne, wrote a story of Ms. Bell, and like Mianne, shaped it in terms of her notes, although she took a rather different approach than Mianne's, constructing her story purposely as a fiction. Although the story is much longer than Mianne's and includes much greater detail, it draws from the same interview material.

Miss Rose Bell

Julia Pointer

Chapter 1

Stepping out of that taxi cab, I finally realized. This was real. This baby inside of me is real. The fact that my mama threw me out is real.

"What's wrong with you chile," she screamed when I told her. "Don't you see these five other kids running around me?!"

I glanced about. Mark, Janie, and Tony were an inch away from the TV watching a violent show. Millie was in the kitchen eating cookies, again. She never got enough to eat. And little Jimmy, the baby, was tugging at my mother's earrings that hung from her ears. Then, I looked back at my mother just in time to hear her say, "You go find your boyfriend. He got you this far, tell him to take care of you, feed you, and love you. Cause it seems to me you don't appreciate nothing I done for you!" I stood up in alarm.

"Mama you can't do this to me," I pleaded. "I'm only 16." "Yeah, I know," she said. "I'm your mama remember. But you sho' ain't think about your young age when you was messing with that good-for-nothing, irresponsible boy."

My eyes flashed. "Fine," I screamed. "I'll go to Doug. He's the only one who gives a care about me anyway!" I stormed out of the house. I was convinced Douglas cared enough to help me. I was trying to find a way to tell him anyway.

Chapter 2

When I got to the projects where Doug lived, I was exhausted. When that lady at the Volunteer Health Services told me I would need exercise, I didn't know walking a couple of blocks would wear me out.

Doug's mom opened the door. I had always liked her. She always had a hot meal waiting for Doug when he got home from work. Doug was her only child and she never raised her voice at him or questioned anything he'd said or done. Despite that, Doug never seemed spoiled or selfish.

"Angie," Ms. Jones exclaimed, opening the door. "Come on in. Doug's in his room getting ready for work tomorrow."

"Thanks," I said, walking into the fresh smelling room. Ms. Jones was a person who cared enough to keep her house neat. It stood out among the other houses as fresh and too good to be in the projects. I walked into Doug's room. I wasn't surprised at how clean the room was. (Ms. Jones cleaned it every day).

"Hi," I said, half cheery, half gloomy. "We've got to talk." "Hey babe," he answered looking up with a smile. "What about?" "My momma kicked me out." There was a pause. "What for," Doug said dumbfounded. He walked away from the closet and took my hand. I didn't say anything. What if he reacted like my mom? Doug dropped out of school when he was in 10th grade. His mom didn't dare say anything and he rarely listened to anyone else.

"Hey," Doug said, seeing the hesitant look on my face. "You know you don't ever have to keep anything from me."

"I'm pregnant, Doug," I blurted out, looking away. No noise came from Doug. Finally he just got up and walked out the door mumbling something that sounded like stay here. "Doug wait," I screamed after him. "We've got to talk." I ran out of his room and ran into his mother. "What was that all about?" she asked puzzled. I sighed. This was going to be a lot harder than I thought.

Chapter 3

I sat Ms. Jones down and filled her in on the confusing events that had plagued my whole day. When I had finished, she had the same astonished look Doug had. "Come eat," she said. "You look famished." Ms. Jones had to be the best cook in the world. I hadn't tasted pork chops that good in years. After I helped Ms. Jones with the dishes she sent me to bed. I couldn't sleep though. Doug hadn't gotten home yet and he was known to go off for days without giving word to anyone.

I must have dozed off because my eyes opened up to the glaring light of the sun. I smelled bacon so I got up and walked in the kitchen expecting to see Doug. Instead I saw Ms. Jones sitting in a chair with her head in her hands. "Ms. Jones," I said uneasily. She jumped up. "What's wrong?"

"I'll tell you later," she answered. "But, right now I want you to eat. You need your strength." I sat down. I didn't want to push her. But, I wondered what those tears were for. She never got that emotional when Doug left before.

The breakfast went down my throat without my actually tasting it. Something was definitely wrong and I was itching to find out what. "Are you finished," Ms. Jones asked. I nodded my head. "Then come with me." She led me over to the couch and sat me down. Then she went over to the closet and got out a suitcase. "Doug came by last night," she started. "He says he took care of everything." She put the suitcase on the floor. Then she put a $50 bill, a newspaper clipping, and a map on the table. "He stopped by your mama's house and got you some clothes. He also said he heard of this lady, Rose Bell is her name. She helps girls in your position. Dougie's real sorry, honest he is. It's just that he's not ready for this responsibility. I wish I could keep you here with me, but I can't." I stood there in a daze, knowing that in my mind I expected this but my heart just couldn't accept it. Finally I just picked up my things and walked out of Doug's house. All I had to my name was $50, a suitcase full of clothes, a newspaper clipping on Rose Bell, and a map to the Jeffries Projects, way on the other side of the city where she lived. I felt like everyone had given up on me. I didn't even know if I'd ever even see my family and friends again. Just about all my hope was gone.

Chapter 4

It was dark when I got to the Jeffries and very late. I didn't want to disturb anybody but I wasn't about to wander around the Projects at night. I knew from experience that that could be dangerous. (Sometimes fatal). But, even in the dark, I could see how clean and beautiful these Projects were: There were colorful flowers and a sign on the lawn that said, NO WORK: NO EAT. I decided to knock on the door that the sign was in front of since that's where the eats probably were and I was more than willing to work.

"Who's there," a scraggly voice said as a hand moved back the curtain that covered the pane of glass in the door.

"My name's Angela Thomas ma'am and I wondered if you could help me." The door opened and there stood a short slim woman with a black knit sweater and a yellow pleated skirt. She had thin graying hair. "Come sit while I make some tea," she said. I noticed that it was midnight and she had her clothes on. I guessed that a woman who did what she did had to be on call night and day. I looked around and there were bags and bags of baby clothes all over the room.

Just then Ms. Bell walked into the room with some tea and sandwiches. "Now, you can tell me why you're here at this time of night." I told her everything that happened ever since my mother threw me out. "Hmm," she said. "That's different. Usually the boy splits without giving nothing. But anyway, I must tell you this. I don't reward young mothers, I just help them. If you don't work you don't get." I nodded remembering the sign. "If you need a place to stay," she continued. "There's an empty place right next door. Plus, I'm a strong believer in education. And if you're gonna stay here you're gonna have to get your GED and then a job. Also I need your help. I don't run this thing by myself. I need help sewing, cooking, cleaning, etc."

I decided I liked this lady. She was direct, said exactly what's on her mind and didn't sugar coat anything with bull. I wanted to know everything about her. "Can I ask you a question?" I said. "Anything but my age," Ms. Bell answered matter-of-factly.

"Why do you plant flowers when you have so much else to do?"

"I call it planting for peace," she replied without hesitation. "Just because you live in the Projects doesn't mean they have to be old, shabby, and broken down. Just think about it. Flowers are an important part of us. For someone to take a seed, some sun, and the rain and make something as beautiful as a flower." I stared in awe thinking how much this place would put even Mrs. Jones to shame.

"You're helping all these kids. Don't you have any of your own?" I asked. Ms. Bell paused as if she was wondering whether or not to tell me something.

"I had three sons," she finally said proudly. "All of them helped a lot around here, 'specially the one that recently . . . recently passed away. He was really depressed and ended up jumping off the Belle Isle Bridge. He used to live in the empty place I told you about."

I cringed, wondering why she decided to tell me. "Where did you come from? Where were you born?" My curiosity made me ask even though that story made me queasy.

"Came to Detroit when I was 19, from Oil City, Pennsylvania. It was wonderful there. A cozy town with mountains and a stream right in the middle as if God just sat it down. I lived with 10 siblings and my grandparents. That was just plain chaotic. My grandparents always had something to give to somebody. But Detroit isn't bad either. It can be fantastic with the right leadership." I interrupted her to ask if she would consider running for mayor of Detroit. "If I was younger maybe," was her reply.

"The projects aren't bad either. There are good and bad times. We call this place 'the Grosse Pointe of the projects.' But, even though it's the responsibility of the city nothing much gets done. That's why we run this foundation by donations from the church and such, because we aren't funded. That's also why I need so much help. "What's your religion?" I asked, instantly wondering why.

"I just hope I'm one of God's children cause without God no one would be here. I was brought up to believe strongly in God. I was also brought up to save yourself for marriage. That's why I'm so hard on unwed mothers. I think it's because you kids have too much freedom in the home."

I think Ms. Bell was right. Maybe if my mother had set an example instead of just telling me what to do, all of this would have turned out differently. But I couldn't blame it on anyone but myself.

"Now, no more questions," Ms. Bell said suddenly standing up. "It's 3:00 in the morning. You can sleep on the couch tonight and I'll show you the place tomorrow." I laid on the couch as she got me a sheet and cleared away the teacups. I knew that Ms. Bell just changed my life forever. Just like she had changed girls before me and was going to change girls after me. All the doubts I had when I left home vanished. Ms. Bell was going to help me get back on my feet. I know that I'll be forever grateful to Ms. Rose Bell.

Julia wrote her story after being one of Ms. Bell's interviewers, incorporating elements of fact and fiction in her writing. The story, one of several pieces Julia wrote during the program, was written quickly, with little help from her peers, although she did consult several teachers about it in its various stages in workshop groups and received some advice. Julia's best friend Camille was her most influential reader; they responded to each other's stories candidly and often.

One September day after the summer she had written her story, I discussed it with Julia. In the course of our conversation I asked her what she thought was successful about the story. She said,

I think the moral is that here's a lady that lives in the Projects who is just living in the same environment as the people she helps, and is just as bad off. But she's bringing so much joy, and it shows you that if you are in a hole, it doesn't mean that you can't help somebody else and get out of it. And at the same time, I think that she has a sense of self-fulfillment about this thing that she's doing. So, both parties are benefiting, and I think that that's the basic moral of the story. And when you think about it, here she is living in the projects, and here I am living in a middle-class neighborhood less than 2 miles away, and she's going through all of this, as poor as she is, and I'm not doing anything. I do little things, but it makes you think about how much you really care about what is going on. For example, when you get a Christmas card from the Salvation Army, asking for money, some people throw it out without even reading it. Some people get angry, and say they can't afford it. But here's a lady that is helping people and barely making it herself. She's just wonderful. Like I said in my story, I don't know how she's made it this long time. It has to be God that has let her make it. But that story has to be told, and I wanted to tell it, in my own way.

I asked her how she came to write "Miss Rose Bell." She said:

Sometimes when I hear things—a movie, or a song—I'm inspired. Well, Ms. Rose Bell inspired me when I heard about her work and all the good she is doing. It just came to me that if I could 'make up' a person that had met Ms. Bell and learned from her, then I could tell the story in a more complete way. It would be more real.

But why fiction, I asked her? Why not just tell the facts?

Well, fiction is my thing, That's what I do best. I thought it would be better to mix the fact with the fiction than just give you the facts about her life. The things about Ms. Bell, that's the fact part, but the fiction: I just can create stories in my mind, put myself in a person's life, imagine what it would be like to be there, and hopefully I can get readers to do the same thing. You get drawn into it if it's a story more than if it's just facts.

But about this difficult subject, teenage pregnancy, I asked: "Isn't it a hard thing to write about?"

Yes, it is a hard thing. But grown-ups don't give kids credit for things. We observe. We experience things in the world and some of them aren't nice, but we need to speak about them. Many of us have friends who have been or might be threatened with the problem. We need to deal with these things. We need to get our feelings out instead of keeping them inside. And this also gives grown-ups a view of what teenagers are thinking.

Julia also pointed out that although seemingly negative stories can inspire people to change their lives, her story is a positive one. Of her story, which she wrote with the help of her good friend Camille Ryan and other readers, Julia said, "I wanted to let it be known how much Rose Bell does do in the world, that there are people doing these good things for others, that there is someone there, and not to give up." At first, she said, "It sounded too much like a fairy tale, but then I realized there aren't perfect people, things don't happen like that, and I changed it to make it more real."

CRITICAL FICTIONS AND CRITICAL ETHNOGRAPHY: DECONSTRUCTING AND RECONSTRUCTING REALITY

> One of the things that's important to me is the powerful imaginative way in which we deconstructed and reconstructed reality in order to get through. (Toni Morrison, cited in Marshall, 1992, p. 181)

Scholars from a range of political and epistemological perspectives have demonstrated the importance of developing a much closer relationship between research and lived experience.[4] By validating the importance of Rose Bell's activist work, Mianne and Julia, through their storytelling, also stand as activists with her. Their stories demonstrate that writing can be social action.

As I see it, both Mianne's and Julia's stories can be seen as examples of what Mariani (1991) called *critical fictions*, stories written as part of oppositional culture, part of dissent. Critical fictions involve "the interrogation of unitary narratives, the naming of manifold identities, the exploration of multiple subjectivities, and the incorporation of ambivalence and ambiguity as elements of resistance" (p. 12). And Mianne's and Julia's stories can also be read as what McLaren (1993) described as *critical narratology*:

> reading personal narrative (our own and those of our students) against society's treasured stock of imperial or magisterial narratives, since not all narratives share a similar status and there are those which exist, highly devalued, within society's rifts and margins. (p. 205)

McLaren also suggested that those who embrace a critical narratology will:

> encourage the oppressed to contest the stories that have been fabricated for them by 'outsiders' and to construct counterstories that give shape and direction to the practice of hope and the struggle for an emancipatory politics of everyday life. (p. 218)

---

[4]Among the scholars arguing for closer relationships between research and lived experience are those from neo-Marxist, critical perspectives (Ellis & Flaherty, 1992; McLaughlin & Tierney, 1993; Apple, 1993; Lankshear & McLaren, 1993), by those particularly interested in issues of race and gender issues (hooks, 1992; Smith, 1983), by those interested in "advocacy" or participatory action research (Gonzalez, 1993; Gluck & Patai, 1991; Whyte, 1991), and by scholars in the area of literacy education who have attempted in a variety of ways to reconcile poststructural, neo-Marxist and feminist concerns in their commitments to social and educational change (Robinson, 1990; Knoblauch & Brannon, 1993; Willinsky, 1990; Schaafsma, 1993).

This process helps storytellers to "reterritorialize identity" (p. 218) by naming themselves through their stories and refusing to be named and labeled by others. McLaren's reminder to consider student stories within the context of societal inequities is important. Mianne's and Julia's stories need to be seen as potentially more than just personally empowering but as part of the struggle for social, racial and economic justice. In their stories, Mianne and Julia name themselves and their worlds, and they tell these stories themselves in *Corridors*.

I argue that the community-based stories that the girls tell, grounded in oral history interviews with a woman whose work in the community they know well and admire, may be seen as critical, fictional ethnographies, as feminist and poststructuralist tales for social change, stories that have much to teach us about research, perhaps especially about research with people in areas where residents continue to be underserved.

Residents in such areas as Mianne and Julia live are most commonly known to outsiders through romanticized or otherwise provocative journalistic accounts. In one instance of this (mis)representing, the journalist Ze'ev Chafets (1990), after returning to the city where he had grown up, begins his book *Devil's Night and Other True Tales of Detroit*, by depicting the urban area of that city as a kind of criminal and moral nightmare. He begins his book, "It was in the fall of 1986 that I first saw the devil in Detroit" (p. 1). With references to the city as "third world," his is a disparaging outsider's characterization of the neighborhood of the Dewey Center for Urban Education. Although there are more complex—and certainly more sympathetic—accounts by journalists of urban children's lives we might read, the stories we are examining here were written by Mianne and Julia themselves, students who are through their writing acting on their own and their community's behalf. As Gordimer (1993) suggested in her essay, "Three in a Bed: Fiction, Morals, and Politics":

> To be aware that the lie also can transform the world places an enormous responsibility on art to counter this with its own transformations. The *knowledge* that the writer's searching and intuition gain instinctively contradicts the lie. (p. 229)

In my work with these girls and their stories of Rose Bell, I began to ask how their writing might function against easy, monolithic and stereotypical notions, what Gordimer referred to as *lies*, of urban culture, and particularly lies or half-truths about girls and women in that culture. In my view, the girls construct selves and a culture through these stories from which others and they may learn. The particular form they choose to draw on for their research is life history, the story of Rose Bell's life as she chose to share it with them.

Certainly, stories such as Mianne's, Julia's, and Rose Bell's are a testimony to a kind of cultural sustenance. They can be seen as culture sustaining in that they address moral traditions of social and personal responsibility long recognized in their community. Inspirational stories, such as ones about Rose Bell's volunteerism, are central to the sustenance of those moral traditions.

Both stories from *Corridors: Stories of Inner City Detroit* that I retell in the context of this chapter I see as different kinds of narrative testimony to Rose Bell's activist community work, and as imaginative creations of that community; they are also a contribution to its collective memory. Besides contributing to the community tradition, the stories contribute to the tradition of student activism (e.g., Dewey Center Community Writing Project, 1989; Earl Marshall School, 1993; Williams & Mirikitani, 1989; The Willow Run/Ann Arbor Project for Homeless Youth Summer Writing Program, 1993), where students publish imaginative renderings—poems, stories, nonfiction accounts—of their own, their families' and their neighbors' lives for social purposes.

As McLaren pointed out, however, not all stories are alike. Some are valued more than others. Within the rhetorical and political confines of research, stories that are the result of attempts to just tell the facts such as Mianne's have historically been valued more than ones, like Julia's, that are more obviously speculative. Julia's story is different from Mianne's in that it is purposely fictional. As she said:

> I just can create stories in my mind, put myself in a person's life, imagine what it would be like to be there, and hopefully I can get readers to do the same thing. You get drawn into it if it's a story more than if it's just facts.

Julia's story may be seen as an example of critical fictional ethnography.

In an essay entitled "Narratives of Struggle" bell hooks (1992) spoke of the importance of the imagination in the presence of oppression. Imagination, she pointed out, can be used to sustain life and maintain critical awareness. She spoke of "decolonizing the imagination" so that we might dream of alternative realities. As she viewed it, "critical fictions emerge when the imagination is free to wander, explore, transgress" (p. 55). To imagine is to begin the process of transforming reality. Within communities of resistance, she pointed out, narratives of struggle are imaginative testimony, the purposes of which include telling what happened, strengthening faith, and developing community. I think that both Julia and Mianne are examples of student researchers who have begun to do that.

I also think that those of us who are interested in developing a critically viable approach to research would do well to consider students' community-based stories such as Julia's and Mianne's stories of Ms. Rose Bell. Although it is common to look to professional ethnographic research for new directions, or new models for committed research, I think it is also important to look closely at how students in urban settings represent themselves and their neighbors, and see how they work against conventional notions of knowledge and research to begin to create a space for themselves to participate in social and educational change. Telling, collecting, and sharing stories are just first steps in challenging the existing social and educational order, but they are one good way to begin.

POSTSCRIPT

Several Dewey Center Community Writing Project students began volunteering in Rose Bell's 961-BABY in the weeks and months after the program was completed. Some students, with Dewey Center teacher Toby Curry's help, also began publishing their writing in a regular column in Detroit's leading African-American weekly newspaper.

REFERENCES

Abu-Lughod, L. (1993). *Writing women's worlds: Bedouin stories.* Berkeley: University of California Press.

Apple, M. W. (1993). *Official knowledge: Democratic education in a conservative age.* New York: Routledge.

Atkinson, P. (1990). *The ethnographic imagination: Textual constructions of reality.* New York: Routledge.

Belenky, M.F., Clinchy, B.M., Goldberger, N.R., & Tarule, J.M. (1986). *Women's ways of knowing: The development of self, voice and mind.* New York: Basic Books.

Chafets, Z. (1990). *Devil's night and other true stories of Detroit.* New York: Random House.

Clifford, J., & Marcus. G.E. (Eds.). (1986). *Writing culture: The poetics and politics of ethnography.* Berkeley: University of California Press.

The Dewey Center Community Writing Project. (1989). *Corridors: Stories from inner city Detroit.* Ann Arbor, MI: The Center for Educational Improvement through Collaboration.

Earl Marshall School. (1993). *Lives of love and hope: A Sheffeld herstory.* Sheffeld, England: Earl Marshall School.

Geertz, C. (1986). *Works and lives: The anthropologist as author.* Stanford: Stanford University Press.

Gluck, S.B., & Patai, D. (Ed.). (1991). *Women's world: The feminist practice of oral history.* London: Routledge.

Gonzalez, R. D. (1993) *Language, race, and the politics of educational failure: A case for advocacy.* Urbana: NCTE.

Gordimer, N. (1993). Three in a bed: Fiction, morals, and politics. In C. Boylan (Ed.), *The agony and the ego: The art and strategy of fiction writing explored.* London: Penguin.

Harding, S. (1991). *Whose science? Whose knowledge?: Thinking from women's lives.* Ithaca: Cornell.

hooks, b. (1992). *Black looks: Race and representation.* Boston: South End Press.

Jaggar, A., & Smith-Burke, M. (Ed.). (1985). *Observing the language learner.* Urbana: NCTE.

Knoblauch, C.H., & Brannon, L. (1993). *Critical teaching and the idea of literacy.* Portsmouth, NH: Heinemann.

Lankshear, C., & McLaren, P.L. (Ed.). (1993). *Critical literacy: politics, praxis and the postmodern.* Albany: SUNY Press.

Lather, P. (1991). *Getting smart: Feminist research and pedagogy with/in the postmodern.* New York: Routledge.

Mariani, P. (Ed.). (1991). *Critical fictions: The politics of imaginative writing.* Seattle: Bay Press.

Marshall, B. K. (1992). *Teaching the postmodern: Fiction and theory.* New York: Routledge.

McLaughlin, D., & Tierney, W.G. (Eds.). (1993). *Naming silenced lives: Personal narratives and the process of educational change.* New York: Routledge.

McLaren, P. (1993). Border disputes: Multicultural narrative, identity formation, and critical pedagogy in postmodern America. In D. McLaughlin & W.G. Tierney (Eds.), *Naming silenced lives: Personal narratives and the process of educational change* (pp. 201-235). New York: Routledge.

Minh-ha, T. (1989). *Women native other: Writing, postcoloniality and feminism.* Bloomington: Indiana University Press.

Nicholson, L. (Ed.). (1990). *Feminism/postmodernism.* New York: Routledge.

Robinson, J.L. (1990). *Conversations on the written word: Essays on language and literacy.* Portsmouth, NH: Heinemann.

Schaafsma, D. (1993). *Eating on the street: Teaching literacy in a multicultural society.* Pittsburgh: University of Pittsburgh Press.

Schaafsma, D. (1994). What's the matter with variety?: Dora and Julia writing stories and the relationship between literary merit and academic success. In P. Smagorinsky (Ed.), *Culture and literacy: Bridging the gap between community and classroom.* Urbana: NCTE.

Schaafsma, D., & Smith, M. (1992). Autobiography and authority in composition and literature. In J. Collins (Ed.), *Vital signs* (Vol. 3, pp. 74-86). Portsmouth: Heinemann/Boynton-Cook.

Smith, B. (Ed.). (1983). *Home girls: A black feminist anthology*. Latham, NY: Women of Color Press.

Turner, V.W., & Bruner, E.M. (Eds.). (1986). *The anthropology of experience*. Chicago: University of Illinois Press.

Van Maanen, J. (1988). *Tales of the field: On writing ethnography*. Chicago: University of Chicago.

Walkerdine, V. (1990). *Schoolgirl fictions*. London: Verso.

Whyte, W. F. (Ed.). (1991). *Participatory action research*. London: Sage.

Williams, C., & Mirikitani, J. (Eds.). (1989). *I have something to say about this big trouble: Children of the tenderloin speak out*. San Francisco: Glide Memorial United Methodist Church.

Willinsky, J. (1990). *The new literacy: Redefining reading and writing in the schools*. London: Routledge.

The Willow Run/Ann Arbor Project for Homeless Youth Summer Writing Program. (1993). *Life stories*. Ann Arbor, MI: The Willow Run/Ann Arbor Project for Homeless Youth.

Wolf, M. (1992). *A thrice told tale: Feminism, postmodernism, and ethnographic responsibility*. Stanford: Stanford University Press.

12

"We Must Ask Our Questions and Tell Our Stories": Writing Ethnography and Constructing Personhood

Ann Egan-Robertson
University of Wisconsin-Madison

I know about kids on the street. I walk down the street and there's a group of boys selling and getting high. The goal of my chapter is to get more jobs, clubs, and activities for teenagers to keep us off the streets.
—Flores (in Vega Community Writing Club, 1993, p. 36)

I had the opportunity to work with a small, multiracial group of young women in a students-as-ethnographers project during the winter and spring of 1993. This project was a community writing club that I formed out of their eighth-grade English language arts class. Like other educators who work with teenagers, I am committed to finding ways of empowering students as active participants in our democracy and as readers, writers, and lifelong learners. I am especially concerned about those students, all too numerous, who act as though their living does not matter.

I began the writing club because I wanted to study how reading and writing activities in school might be used in such a way as to address the alienation so many adolescents feel today. The young women joined the group because they had an interest in researching and writing about their communities. This chapter describes the project, what we did together, what we talked about, the people the students interviewed, and what the students wrote. This chapter also raises questions about school literacy practices and personhood, alienation, and ethnography. I define personhood and alienation in the next section.

PERSONHOOD

Personhood refers to how a culture or subculture, such as a school, defines *person* and what attributes it associates with person (Besnier, 1993; Kondo, 1990). Personhood includes the ways that people construct identities in relation to one another. Personhood is not given or predetermined but is established through everyday interactions, which in turn, are influenced by historical and institutionalized contexts and narratives (DuBois, 1903/1969; Galwatney, 1981; West, 1993; Willis, 1995). More simply put, to ask about personhood is to ask, "What does it mean to be a person in a particular cultural group, at a particular time, in a particular event?"

Definitions of *person*—and related concepts such as *self, identity, individual*—vary a great deal across situations, people, cultures, and subcultures (Kirshenblatt-Gimblett, 1989). For example, the Western view of the self is usually described as a bounded, ontological unit. This definition contrasts markedly with views of the self as essentially interconnected to others found among the Bali by Geertz (1976), the Illongot by Rosaldo (1984), African women across the diaspora by Steady (1981), and the Apache by Basso (1988). The view of the individual as a distinct social and political entity that prevails in the United States (Carbaugh, 1992) and elsewhere differs fundamentally from some Eastern views of a distributed and shared existence.

Personhood also is defined by cultural perceptions about where people fit in the various institutions that make up a society. People are assigned to categories and groups, and parameters are set for inclusion and exclusion. Thus, terms such as *race, ethnicity, gender, age, economic class,* and even *academic track* (academic stream) are closely associated with personhood because, at least in some cultures and in some situations, these terms are part of a definition of *person.* For example, within classrooms, people are defined as students, as members of a reading group, and often as part of an academic track. Assessment, comparing an individual's performance to that of others and particularly to national achievement norms, is a key literacy practice that implicitly defines personhood. School literacy practices, then, are a major site for the cultural work of defining personhood. Young people in school form feelings and beliefs, roles and relationships—all elements of personhood—at least in part through the ways in which written material is used to organize activity in classrooms and through the content of what they read.

ALIENATION

Alienation can be defined as an aspect of personhood. I am defining alienation as feeling like or being treated as a stranger (an alien) in a situation in which one should not or would not expect to have that feeling and/or be treated that way. Even if one is treated nicely one can be alienated. One can be treated as a welcome stranger or one can be treated as an unwelcome stranger and even encouraged to leave.

In some cultures and social groups, some groups of people are treated as strangers and by definition may be denied personhood entirely. Denial of personhood is a terrible aspect of the legacy we all inherit in the United States and elsewhere: The genocide of one people and the enslavement of another could only happen by denying them personhood. It is no wonder that many scholars and cultural critics have argued that issues of personhood, alienation, race, gender, power, and history should be considered together. Steady (1981, 1987), for example, listed six dimensions that need to be included in studies of personhood:

1. the studies need to be cross-cultural;
2. there must be recognition of race as the most salient dimension of personhood in the United States (as is true elsewhere as well);
3. analysis should include how social, political, economic, and historical human relationships are structured;
4. with regard to African Americans, studies need to recognize values shared across African cultures (by extension, the same recognition must be extended to other cultural groups);
5. the study of personhood needs to involve a commitment to an elimination of human oppression; and
6. there should be an emphasis on (auto)biographical experiences as the basis for theorizing about social and political life.

I kept these six dimensions in mind in forming and directing the writing club, although much of the direction came from the students themselves and from the people they interviewed.

THE SCHOOL AND THE STUDENTS[1]

The Vega School opened in the mid-1970s in the city of Riverside as an urban K-6 school, expanding to include grades 7 and 8 a year before this study took place. Housed within the same building are various community programs, such as a community music school, a branch of the public library, a pool, and an adult literacy program.

---

[1]All names of people and places in this chapter are pseudonyms except mine. The Ann in the transcripts refers to me.

The members of the community writing club reflect the multiracial and multicultural diversity of the school, which is 48% Puerto Rican, 28% African-American, 23% Euro-American, and 1% other, according to school district documents. There were six students. Felicita Bermudez identifies herself as Puerto Rican; Marielis Flores as Puerto Rican and White; Shanae Lester as African-American, Cherokee, and Puerto Rican; DeLayne Monson as African-American and Blackfoot; Sandra Verne as Puerto Rican and French; and Denise Yothers as White. Clearly, school census form categories do not reflect this group of young women's multiracial identities. Each was a member of a church or community-based youth group, involved in various arts and sporting activities. All were assigned to the lowest academic track, placed there on the basis of achievement test scores and teacher recommendations. The year of the study was the first year that Marielis and DeLayne were in a regular classroom because they were part of a pilot inclusion program for special education students; prior to this school year, they had spent most of their class time in substantially separate special educational programs. The students were familiar with me in my role as participant-observer in their English language arts class, where I acted as an assistant to the teacher.

Initially, their language arts teacher, Mrs. Boulanger, and I had intended to implement the students-as-ethnographers project in the class; however, a rotating schedule and several other constraints negated this plan. Instead, we came up with the idea of a writing club, presented as an alternate activity during a free-time block. I distributed a flier to approximately 20 students who played board games or listened to music during free time, having chosen not to participate in chorus, band, computer club, or any other organized activity.

THE COMMUNITY WRITING CLUB

The flier explained that club activities would involve researching and writing about the community, publishing our writing, and making decisions as a group. Students responded with inquiries, exploring expectations and negotiating ground rules. A key factor influencing the students' initial decision to join the club was spelling. As students asked about the club, they sounded interested in the kinds of activities I sketched; nevertheless, a consistent reaction was, "Oh, but I can't write." When I probed further I discovered that this translated to "I can't spell." This early negotiation around definitions of writing was significant in that the orientation to literacy that eventually developed within the club contrasted markedly with the historical definitions of writing that the students initially carried with them. They believed that surface level features of written language were of primary importance. In the club, what mattered was commitment to engage in research and report the findings.[2]

The writing club met for an average of 3 hours per week over the second half of the school year. At first, we focused on formulating and revising research questions and plans. Then, we began interviewing community members. And, toward the end of the project, the students focused on analyzing their data and writing ethnographic reports.

The students did a lot of writing throughout the project, including research questions, interview questions, field notes, logs, conceptual memos, and an ethnographic report. Having worked as a research team, the students decided to report their findings in an edited volume, which they entitled *Life As Teenagers in the Nineties: Growing Up in Riverside*. The final chapter of their book explains how the group went about researching and includes examples of student writing from different phases of the project. The students included a favorite quotation from each community member they interviewed "so kids can see. . .music, alcoholism, what kids need, and racism from other people's eyes than our own" (Vega Community Writing Club, 1993, p. 56). They held a book signing at the school, distributing 50 copies of the book to the community members they interviewed, to the principal, several of their teachers, their families, and to staff and participants in two local adult literacy programs. The students each kept six copies of the book.

The rest of this chapter gives a detailed description of some of the key events of the writing club. These include generating our research questions, conducting interviews with people in the community, and writing ethnographic reports. Throughout the description of these events, I emphasize how the students were reconstructing their definitions of personhood, both for themselves and in general.

THE FIRST MEETING AND THE RESEARCH QUESTIONS

At the first meeting, the group read and heard my descriptions of the work of teenage ethnographers from different areas of the country: the Bronx (Mercado, this volume); Detroit (Bloome & Curry, this volume; Schaafsma, this volume); the Piedmont Carolinas (Heath & Branscombe, 1986); Saginaw (Robinson & Stock, 1990); and Santa Barbara (Santa Barbara Classroom Discourse Group, this volume).

As I told them about each of these projects, I gave a couple of examples of questions and topics that the other student ethnographers had pursued and related those questions and topics to potential avenues

---

[2]I edited the students' writing for spelling as I entered their text on the computer. The students remained concerned about their spelling, asking each other how to spell particular words.

for them. For example, tying to the Saginaw project, I said, "You might want to ask, 'What's it like growing up as a female teenager in Riverside? What's it like growing up as an African-American young woman in Riverside? As a Latina? Or as a White young woman?'" This particular wording made an intertextual link between the extant students-as-ethnographers projects and their own project that proved to be very important. Another important framing I made in this initial meeting was the particularity of my offered questions. Rather than leaving the topic at "What's it like being a young woman growing up in Riverside?" I brought to that gender category the added categories of race and ethnicity.

In making these intertextual links with other projects, I described how the teenage researchers reported out their findings. In short, from the first meeting, it was clear to the students that one of the obligations of researchers is to share in a public way what is found. I explained to them that the Santa Barbara students were recognized as co-researchers, and that the Bronx students attended professional conferences.

I made clear from the first meeting that the students, by following through and reporting their findings (in whatever form they chose), were joining a national contingent of student researchers of their own communities. They also knew that, as with the other projects, a central part of my role as facilitator of the club was to study their research of the community. In turn, they knew that I would be writing up and presenting in book format and at conferences how they went about their research and the findings.

I invited the students to decide collectively the focus and approach we would take. I also suggested that, in addition to individual questions and topics, we investigate people's reasons and methods for researching and writing about their community.

From the start, students raised and discussed such serious questions as: "Why do men rape women?" and "Why do kids call me a 'wannabe' when I say I'm Puerto Rican?" Students began field notebooks at their first meeting, recording questions and writing on topics. Although they generated many questions, each student eventually settled on one to pursue:

DeLayne: *How can you avoid becoming an alcoholic if your parents are alcoholic?*
Denise: *Is racism a problem in Riverside?*
Felicita: *How do you deal with teenage pregnancy?*
Sandra: *Does music affect the way we think and feel about people?*
Shanae: *What's it like being or having two nationalities?*
Marielis: *What can help teenagers stay off the streets?*

Felicita and Shanae researched as club members during the winter and early spring, eventually deciding that they could not continue their inquiry at the time for personal reasons. Both came to the book signing, were acknowledged in the book as co-researchers, encouraged, and were encouraged by, the group in many ways.

DISCUSSING PERSONHOOD

In our meetings, each person would provoke the group into discussion by raising a question. Often this would be preceded and/or followed by writing on the topic. Sometimes the student would read aloud what she had written; then the other students would recount their own experiences on the topic. The issue of personhood was raised by the students in the earliest discussions, especially with regard to race and gender. As Transcript 1 shows, the students were concerned and distressed by the way they and peers were sometimes defined by others; here the focus is on negative interactions around negotiating ethnic and racial identities.

TRANSCRIPT 1

Shanae: Sometimes when you tell someone your nationality, it's got to really show or they'll call you a wannabe. Like for her [referring to Sandra], she's got Puerto Rican in her but yet it's still—when she tells people that they pick on her and call her a wannabe cuz it don't look like she's Puerto Rican. Looks like she's all White.

Denise: Yeah, it's like when I hear people talking in the pod [classroom] and, they're fighting or something, they'll say "that White girl" or "that Black girl," Why don't they say their name? They know their name! They'll just say "that Black girl," you know. And it's—I don't think that's right. I mean, I could understand if they're describing the person but when they know their name or even how they look like, they don't always have to say, "that," "this," and "that." We're all people.

Shanae: Yeah, she's got something good. Does it look like I'm Puerto Rican?

Denise: Somewhat.

Shanae: Does it?

Ann: Yes. You can see the features in your eyes and . . .

Shanae: That's because I'm Cherokee and Black but on the other side I'm Puerto Rican. Some people say they can't see it but I talk it. That's why they can tell. See, she [Sandra] don't talk it.

Ann: I think it depends on how aware you are, too, of Puerto Rican culture as a blend of European, of African, and of Indian, right? And so I think honoring the African within the Puerto Rican is really important. And the Indian that's Puerto Rican.

Shanae: Um-hum.

DeLayne: I think everybody's got a mixture in them somewhere. Just like I'm Indian and Black.

Sandra: You are, too. I'm Indian.

Ann: That's why it is so important that our reading and writing, our schooling, every part of our lives reflect the wonderful, various parts of our heritage.

Shanae: Doesn't matter what your race is cuz everyone is special and everything about everyone is different.

Sandra: We all look the same on the inside.

The transcript shows the group wrestling with issues of personhood.[3] As early as the third club meeting, writing club members established that we were involved in contesting historically dominant discourses about people. Our researching became important as a way to contest negative notions about people through an examination of power and identity. Learning about oneself requires a deepened knowledge of one's culture and the underlying and often hidden or ignored aspects of culture.

From the beginning, the students began generating, describing, and analyzing various cultural terms, doing various types of semantic analysis. For example, Delayne analyzed various types of alcoholics: functional alcoholics, drunks, and social drinkers. Denise analyzed racism and racial prejudice. She wrote: "When I started researching this chapter, I had racism and racial prejudice confused." She explained how conversations with adults and peers helped her sort out important differences between the two terms. She did this by analyzing quotes, personal stories, and definitions from the group's interviews with community members. Sandra contrasts the dominant view of music as entertainment with the African and African-American view of music as a form of communication. Noting that "all music puts messages across," she presents definitions of common versus political music and discusses negative versus positive messages about people promoted in various kinds of music.

---

[3]For a full analysis and discussion of the project, see Egan-Robertson (1994).

INTERVIEWING

The kind of discussion documented in Transcript 1 set the frame for the students' interviews with community members. The students interviewed three kinds of community members. First, students as a group conducted ethnographic interviews of community researchers and writers and solicited their views on researching and writing about the community. The students were interested in probing the community members' beliefs, goals, feelings about literacy, who they are researching and writing for, and why; students also shared their own personal research topics. Second, the students as a group interviewed community members who belong to community organizations that address each of the student's research topics. For example, the group interviewed Earl Ackerman, the director of the community music school, about the interaction between music and people. They also interviewed Carlos Vega, director of the Puerto Rican cultural center located near the school. Third, each individual student was encouraged to interview a person who was a resource to them personally in the community. Marielis, for example, interviewed her youth group leader at church.

The first set of interviews, with community researchers and writers, was very powerful. One of the interviews was with Irma Ashton, who identifies herself as an actress and director within the African-American political theater. She is a founder of a local theater company and had recently performed in *Ida B. Wells* and *Joe Turner's Come and Gone*. At the time she met with the students she was in the research phase of preparing to direct *Black Nativity*, the classic play by Langston Hughes. They also interviewed Terésa Cruz, a Puerto Rican poet and playwright whose plays are performed by a local children's theater company. One of her plays explores the Taino Indian heritage of Puerto Ricans. Cruz's poetry is included in several college anthologies.

The process of conducting life history interviews with Ashton and Cruz allowed the students to ask community members to elaborate on how they saw themselves, to tell about their experiences, thoughts, and feelings, to inquire about their work for social change, and to hear community members' stories.

The following excerpt from the writing club members' interview of community member Irma Ashton is long, yet it is actually only a small piece of the entire meeting. What is important to note is the way that DeLayne responds to Ashton and to the methods for researching that Ashton conveys. Much of what Ashton says and much of what happens in the interview—the relationship built between Ashton and the students—profoundly affected the research designs the students constructed and eventually impacted what the students wrote.

TRANSCRIPT 2

1. Ashton: . . . Ask questions. Talk to people. I think that the research that you're doing in your community is dynamite. I mean, that's where you get your—some of your best ideas as writers or as performers. Where your best ideas come from. Just sittin' down the lady next door and talking to her about what was her life living in the South . . . what was that like? You know, talkin' to your grandma and talking to your mother, talking to your aunt about what their experiences were. I mean, we all know how it is. You sit around and you get to—together with a family gathering and the stories start rolling! I'm sure every single person at this table can tell a story that your grandmother told you, that your grandfather told you, or that an aunt or an uncle or a family friend told you. And that's how plays are written! You know? And there's nothing new in the world. Nobody that . . . devise a story . . . it's something that they heard somewhere and had elaborated on. I just finished a production that I performed, called Joe Turner's Come and Gone. And it takes place in 1911. And it—and it tells a part of history that a lot of people don't know about. After slavery, Black men were— were stolen and put back in slavery to work for the big industrialists in the South. Now, it's something that this playwright, August Wilson, he— he had heard—stories being told at the kitchen table when he was a kid, how, you know, Miss Ruby's husband never came home. I wonder where he is? Do you think he left her?

2. Group: [Small laugh from group]

3. Ashton: And then months and months and months would go by and they would find out that this had happened exactly to his dad. You know— you know what I'm saying? That—so it's that sort of oral history. And we come from an oral tradition. Black people do. And, um, Latino people, also. Come from an oral tradition. We don't write a lot of stuff down, but we tell stories. We're storytellers. We pass stories to one another. Another thing that inspired August Wilson to write the play was a painting that he saw by an African-American artist, um. It was a collage, muralist. And his name was, Romare Bearden. And he saw this—this painting with this Black man sitting at a table with a hat pulled down, another man coming down the staircase. And it inspired him 'cause it was just so beautiful, this—that this painting was also haunting. And he'd say, "Who are these people? I'm going to write a story. I'm going to make something up." You know? And so he—and then he goes back into his memory, what he calls his "blood memory" which means stories that he heard as a child. And create a story for these two people in the—in the painting that he saw. So there's many ways to, you know, do your research and then write it. It doesn't always—I mean, and the best place to go is your library and—and

looking things up. But that's for, you know, like the technical stuff and the dates and—and—and historical stuff. But to get the real information and what you're doing and the way you're going about it, I think, is the best way. Talking to people. And asking questions of people in your community and then in your—in your home, in your family. So why don't you tell me a bit about yourselves or—or the kind of research that you'd be doing?

4. Denise: I was wondering when you'd say that!
5. DeLayne: The things that I'm doing?
6. Ashton: Mmm-hmm.
7. DeLayne: Well, my mother told me stories my grandmother told who passed away.
8. Ashton: Uh-huh.
9. DeLayne: She told me a lot of stories about being raised . . . about the time when they had to work in the fields and stuff.
10. Ashton: Mmm-hmm.
11. DeLayne: And they—
12. Ashton: Where was your grandmother from?
13. DeLayne: . . . Um, Georgia.
14. Ashton: Mmm-hmm.
15. DeLayne: And-and my mother, she used to tell me stories about, how, um, they had to work in fields until . . . and during slavery—they had to work for White people.
16. Ashton: Mmm-hmm.
17. DeLayne: And they told me a lot! And I, like, it was very interesting— inter—
18. Ashton: Interesting?
19. DeLayne: Uh-huh.
20. Ashton: It's fascinating, isn't it?
21. DeLayne: Yeah. They had great stories—
22. Ashton: My daughter did some research, and I'm trying to get her back—into it. She started researching our family,—our genealogy, just by a little bit of information that I found out and—because we always wondered how our relatives—some of our relatives got to live in Canada. Well, we all know that the Underground Railroad went all the way up from the South, all the way up to Canada. You know? And so we kind of knew, but we didn't know the real story. That, you know, it—it had to be through slavery that, you know, that part of our family ended up in—in Old Town, Canada. And so when I went to visit some relatives near Canada in, upstate New York, a cousin of mine gave me a—a—a—book. It was like a program from an art exhibit that they had on some of the local churches, Black churches. And he just said, "Turn the page! Turn the page," and when I opened it up, there

was a picture of my great-grandfather—who I never knew about! And there's a picture of this man, and he was a founder of the Christian Methodist-Episcopal Church! I mean, I was blown away! I mean, it's an important part of American history. And an important part of my family history. You know? Because the tragic thing that has happened to African Americans in this country is that we don't know our history. We don't know our genealogy. And why? Because of slavery. Our names were taken away from us, our heritage, our culture. All of that was stripped from us. So, I mean, if you wanted to visit your folks in Africa, where would you go? You don't know. You don't even know what your name is. You know what I'm saying?—our drum was taken away from us, and that was our means of communication. The drum was—is not used as, music. I mean, it's used for music, too, but the main function of the drum in Africa is communication. So, [like] . . . telephones out in the interior, you know? And so one group of people had to communicate if somebody was sick and they needed help. Somebody whose baby was born and there was going to be a celebration, and somebody was getting married or somebody just needed to get a message to another clan member. That's why they called it "the talking drum." Our drums were taken away so that there could be no communication between the—the different tribes that were being brought over. So we lost all of that. So it's very—it's extremely hard to try to figure out where we're from—where we're from, you know? Um. That's another part of—I mean, it—it can definitely happen, believe me. You can find it out. It's so—it'll just take a lot of time. And if you're willing to put in that time, it will be wonderful. Wouldn't it be great if we could find out exactly who we were, what our clan was?

At the time of the interview with Ashton, I thought DeLayne had misunderstood Ashton's question to her about her topic. However, I argue that this is not what happened here. DeLayne keeps the focus on the collective question about community research practices and signals her and her family's position within these traditions by virtue of their ongoing engagement in the practices Ashton has described (see Transcript 2). In turns 7, 9, 15, 17, and 21, DeLayne positions herself as a member of a family and culture of storytellers, encouraged at each point by Ashton's backchannelling (Mmm-Hmm; Uhh.). DeLayne establishes the social significance of what Ashton has laid out, saying in essence, that her mother and grandmother are/were oral historians. DeLayne shows that she has learned about what life was like growing up during slavery through the stories her mother and grandmother told "around the kitchen table." During the interview, Ashton acknowledges that the kind of research the students are engaged in is culturally appropriate because it is based in the community and in community practices, and she positions African-American family members as theorists and oral historians. The role of narrative within the community as serving these functions and meanings is discussed by Ashton and recognized by DeLayne, who puts a coda on the accounts she has heard. She does this in turn 17, with her comment about the sheer amount of accounts rendered, and in turn 21, with the evaluative comment, "They had great stories."

DeLayne refocuses Ashton on the topic of community reasons for and ways of researching so that in turn 22, Ashton "tells a great story" of research practice within her own family, positioning herself here as a mother who is passing on the practice to her daughter. Ashton lays out what Foster (1992) and Galwatney (1981) called a world view and moral message in response to DeLayne's comment. In turns 12 and 22 she asks specific questions about genealogy to teach about the relationship between African-American family history and U.S. history—each important and constitutive—of the other, and the tragic legacy of slavery: "Our names were taken away from us, our heritage, our culture. All of that was stripped from us."

Ashton emphasized the use of narrative to teach about history and culture and the importance of reclaiming them. DeLayne used this community way of researching. She found a neighborhood family to sit around the kitchen table with her and talk about alcoholism and how it had affected their lives. Her hope, and theirs, was that by providing an insider's account more might be done to address a critical community problem.

During her interview with the students, Terésa Cruz (see Transcript 3) explained how to use knowledge as a way to create personhood by defining who one is as one contests dominant oppressive social conditions and views about race and ethnicity.

TRANSCRIPT 3

Terésa Cruz: I grew up in the South East Bronx. Every topic that you touched on was part of my growing up. It was really scary and I didn't feel safe. I started writing to create safe places for myself. I think art is a way of healing. I felt very insecure. I had so many problems. I experienced racism. When I moved into a primarily White neighborhood as a Latina, kids would make fun of my accent. I'd get that feeling of being an outsider, like you don't fit in. Because I had White skin, kids would say "You don't look it." Like I don't look Puerto Rican. I'd say to them, "What do you think I'm supposed to look like?" Then I'd tell them about the history of Puerto Rico and that the first people to live there were Tainos and then the Spaniards came as colonizers, then the Africans. So when you are Puerto Rican you really have the blood and cultures of Tainos, Spaniards, and Africans. We are really the Rainbow People. The Tainos named the island after themselves because they traveled all the way from South America. From Venezuela and the Orinoco River. They traveled to the island. They settled there 1,500 years before Columbus. And people are telling us that Columbus discovered the Americas. He was an invader and a colonizer. The original settlers were the Tainos.

Cruz addresses the same tensions the students had raised from the beginning of the project (compare with the students' earlier discussion about group identity). In lines 8-17, she tells how she uses her knowledge about the community's culture and history to contest racist attitudes. Acknowledgment of personhood as a central, ongoing issue, wound up inextricably with everyday interactions, was a predominant theme stressed by community members in their responses to students' interview questions. Here Cruz uses a personal narrative to convey the idea that, beginning with the first encounters between Europeans and the indigenous American peoples, racism has characterized individual and institutional social relationships and cultural practices in this country. These factors, according to Cruz, continue to mediate the relationship between school literacy practices and the social construction of personhood for students. Cruz acknowledges that the content of knowledge learned in her school was harmful, and even dangerous, to the sense of personhood among the community's youth.

The themes and comments developed by Ashton and Cruz reoccur throughout the students' writing. Although the students interviewed several other people in their community, the interviews with Ashton and Cruz were especially powerful. These two interviews provided the students with a framework for researching their communities, helped them understand the importance of narrative, and provided emotional support. Ashton and Cruz took an active interest in what the students were doing and in doing so validated their research activity. The students could affiliate their research and writing activities with the efforts of Ashton and Cruz.

As often happens in ethnographic research, one activity led to another activity that could not have been planned in advance. Ashton told us about a group of local high schoolers, who, through its Health Peer Education group, was examining similar issues and writing a play. The writing club members went to a rehearsal and a performance of the play.[4] After the rehearsal, the students interviewed Marsha Davidson (see Transcript 4), the director. The transcript of that interview with Davidson shows the repetition of the themes brought up in the interviews with Ashton and Cruz.

---

[4]See McLean-Donaldson (1994) for a study of a similar Peer Education project, making connections between community health issues and racism.

TRANSCRIPT 4

DeLayne: Is there a connection between alcoholism and racism?

Marsha: Racism has an effect on how a student behaves. Students who are treated poorly by teachers, whose history and culture is missing from the curriculum, who are put into tracked classes become disinterested in school. Uninterested students often drop out and turn to drugs because they are bored. Alcohol is a drug. That's why the Peer Education Group is establishing a performing company. They are developing a repertoire of plays because these issues are connected: alcoholism, drug abuse, and racism. One of the implications of racism for students of color is poor self-esteem. When you are constantly put down, you begin to feel bad about yourself. For example, Native Americans have a very high rate of alcoholism. They were pushed off their land and onto Indian reservations. This caused so deep a hurt. They turned the hurt inside and then turned to alcohol to numb the pain.

Davidson describes how she and the peer educators/playwrights see everyday interactions between teachers and students as a site for maintaining or contesting dominant cultural views of personhood, which are destructive to students of color.

Through their interviews and through discussions within the group, the students were investigating their research questions, coming to see community-based ways of knowing, using language and literacy, and solving problems—such as those used by Ashton, Cruz, and the Health Peer Education Group—as essential sources to school knowledge, language and literacy practices, and as necessary strategies for addressing the problems they faced as adolescents. Each community member conveyed the importance of researching the community's history, language, and culture as a primary tool to challenge institutionalized and internalized notions about persons based on race and gender. Terésa Cruz put it this way in a letter she wrote to the group:

> [W]e must not be silent. We must ask our questions and tell our stories. We must learn our true history. Learning about our families, our culture, our language empowers us to better understand and celebrate ourselves.

STUDENT WRITING

The following excerpts from Sandra Verne's notebook give a sense of the issues and themes raised across interviews as well as the feelings of affiliation and alienation that the students felt as they conducted the project.

March 13, 1993[5]

Irma Ashton told us about her trip to Africa and how when she got there everyone was kind and emotional They came up to her and gave her hugs and told her welcome back and that they loved her.

She told us about some of her plays.

She also told us about how her daughter traced her family roots by making a couple of phone calls and how her great grandfather started a church.

She also told us that her two cousins were famous ballerinas.

May 2, 1993

Today I'm going to write down some questions for Teresa Cruz

Question #1. How did you go about tracing your roots?

Question # 2. At what age did you realize that you wanted to trace your roots?

May 15, 1993

[Questions for and Field Notes from Carlos Vega Interview]

Why did you start writing/investigating racism?

Explain what you mean by racism?

Did you ever think about what the world would be like without racism?

Wouldn't have violance

Could like people for who you are

it would be great equal oppertunity

How do you think you might stop racism? How did you find out?

Do you think racism is connected to kids dropping out of school?

Racism is part of why people drop out of school. Yes when they are treated differently and are looked at as on the outside. They feel unwanted .

What does the P. R.C.C. do?

1. to provide culturel programs not to forget came from culture

2. adult education program to get education

Goals as a director of Agency

to make sure community learns about Puerto Ricans

develope a center where people can come and see art history people. The P. R. Community.

Sandra takes Ashton's strategy of "tracing your roots" and frames it into a question for another community member, cross checking its

---

[5]Spelling, punctuation, and capitalization are as they appear in Sandra's notebook.

importance. She asks Vega for a definition of racism, for his vision of a future without racism, his ideas on how he found out how to fight it, and his opinion on whether racism or sexism is worse. In addition to the strategy of reclaiming your cultural heritage, the other strategies elicited from Vega include the importance of learning your history, analyzing multiple forms of oppression, and acting for social justice through your everyday interactions.

Ashton's comments also reappeared in the students' reports. Sandra wrote about music, focusing on the difference between music as entertainment and music as communication. The title of her report was "Does Music Affect the Way We Think and Feel About People?"

> My goal for the chapter is to let people know what music really is because teenagers seem to think that music is just something to dance to. I'm trying to provide them with information that I have found by talking to people and researching . . .
>
> Music is used as a form of communication. The Indian and African tribes used the drums to warn if there was danger. Some ways you used music is to signal for help or to tell someone there is a celebration, like on the drums. When the Americans went to Africa, took people as slaves, and brought them to America they took away their drums because the Americans found they were using the drums as a form of communication. . .
>
> I found two different kinds of music. Common music and political music. Common music is what we hear on the radio, on MTV, all the time. Some people call this popular music but I can't call it popular because it's not popular with a lot of people when it talks about women that way. I call it common music instead. Political music is music that gets people to do something about the problems of the world. At first I thought cultural music was a third kind of music. Then I decided that cultural music is a kind of political music because it brings back your culture. . . . For some people, your culture was never written in books. Cultural music tells you how your own history was. . . .
>
> It's not just music that's sexist or racist; it's television, too. When you turn on the T.V. and you see an African American, he/she is either a drug dealer or user. When you see a Latina, she is either a hooker or a drunk mother who has lots of kids and can barely make the rent. Every time you see old movies, the woman was always at home, a housewife. . . .

As with the work of the other student ethnographers, Sandra's writing reflects community members' ideas about the importance of examining your own experiences. By sharing what she learned with friends, family members, peers, and other researchers, she provides an explanation of how negative messages about people and entire communities are learned. She is saying that these images impact her vision of herself and the way others sometimes view and treat her. In the process of sharing, she creates positive cultural, social, personal and political identities for herself and others. Through her writing, she extends the invitation to her readers, which was extended to her by community members, to examine their experience in order to generate the knowledge needed to change negative models of personhood.

The way students wrote up their ethnographic reports was profoundly influenced by the literacy practices they encountered through their inquiry: seeing the Health Peer Educators' play, and hearing about Ashton's and Cruz's work in the political theater. The students also had the opportunity to work with Ashton as they wrote up their research. All of these activities led the students to write monologues, skits, and poetry. The students' writing reflects recent changes in ethnography, moving toward interdisciplinary perspectives and paying more attention to writing style (e.g., Holloway, 1991). Their writing is based on what they learned about themselves and their various communities as they did the ethnography. As they wrote, they used the community practices they accessed during their inquiry.

Ashton read the students' book prospectus prior to meeting with the group. When DeLayne asked Ashton, "What's it going to take?" to write up the research, using techniques from the political theater, Ashton responded: "Well, you've done your research and you remember everything that was said, right? So you speak the way that they did to you, the people that you interviewed. Just tell their story the way they told it to you. It's almost like just pretending that you are them. Or that the situation is yours, as opposed to someone else's." Thus, Ashton directed DeLayne to take on roles of researcher, recorder, storyteller, and actor in order to accomplish her intent. Ashton then asked DeLayne if she could read aloud from DeLayne's writing and notes. Ashton read it dramatically, displaying DeLayne's accomplishments as a researcher who has engaged in the community literacy practice of collecting stories around the kitchen table, which is exactly where DeLayne gathered a family together for her research session.

DeLayne wrote stories, presented in the form of letters, from the perspective of various family members who were writing to each other: the youngest daughter, Martha, who wanted her mother to know how she felt about her drinking; the mother, Elsie, who was raised in an alcoholic family, treated badly by her husband, and juggled three jobs to pay the rent while raising six kids alone; the older sister, Laticia, who got pregnant as a teenager to escape the house. Here's the mother's letter:

Martha,

I can only tell you, I've had problems in my life. I had a husband who did not appreciate me, and that was hard for me. I could not do the things I wanted to do for my kids. And the only thing I thought was consoling me was the alcohol.

Alcohol doesn't do a thing but destroy you. Alcohol is not a thing that'll help you 'cause you still got the problem when you get off that high. You drink to try to forget the problem but the problem faces you more so after you get sober.

I deal with my problems today by trying to take them day by day, you know? I can deal with them better than I used to, and my kids are helping me out.

I am trying not to take a drink. But I can't do it by myself. I have to go to AA and get some help.

Once you are an alcoholic, you're always an alcoholic. Alcohol is a disease. Get that taste, you want more. Once you get addicted to alcohol, it's hard to get the taste out of your mouth.

DeLayne told the mother's story just as it was told to her in one of her interviews, dropping her own voice as the interviewer who asked questions such as "How did you get started drinking? Did anyone force you into it? How are you dealing with your problems today? Once you're an alcoholic, are you always an alcoholic?" By structuring her ethnographic report as a series of letters, Delayne was able to maintain the voice of the people she interviewed following Ashton's advice "to tell their story the way they told it to you." If Delayne had placed information she gathered from her interviews in a traditional ethnographic report and academic genre she may have distorted what she found by not "pretending that you are them. Or that the situation is yours, as opposed to someone else's." Just as anthropologists such as Galwatney (1981)[6] and Myerhoff (1978) have had to seek new ways to communicate what they learned through their ethnographic studies, so too did the students have to find appropriate genres for reporting.

---

[6]Galwatney presented his ethnographic report as a series of narratives, collected in communal gatherings, without interpretation. Calling for a "theory of native anthropology," Galwatney argued that the narratives rendered by the African-American participants provide theorized examinations of the struggle for personhood within U.S. society. Survival itself, in a culture characterized by racism, requires engaging in ethnographic analysis of views of humanity and parameters for inclusion and exclusion. As part of her study of an elderly Jewish community, Myerhoff (1978) included an imagined conversation between herself and a member of that community who became a close friend but who died before the study was completed. She also included a dream and some of her memories of growing up.

Ashton asked Marielis, who wrote about the problems of teenagers, to envision someone giving her $500 or $1000 to open a club. "If you were given the resources . . . [h]ow would you go about it?" Marielis wrote:

Marielis' New
Mix-A-Lot Fun Club

What I would have in my club to have kids stay and have fun:
- a swimming pool
- a basketball court
- I'll have places to dance. Kids love to dance. On the dance floor, there'll be a lightning ball. It makes it more exciting.
- arcades-In my club kids would have fun in the arcades without using or selling and not using or selling.
- hair salon-I'll have a time and place in my club for kids to get their hair cut or fixed. I know how kids feel when they need a hair cut but they don't have any money or hair clips.
- I'll have an ice cream bar so kids can have ice cream. Kids love ice cream.
- a place where you can go just to talk. There would be a meeting every day on drugs.

So many things. Kids would change their ideas about drugs.

As she did with each student, Ashton asked to read aloud what Marielis had written. This provoked animated response. It became apparent that Marielis was triangulating her data. She was concerned about whether to include arcades because a neighbor, who read her draft, told her that drugs were sold at a local arcade. She decided to address this by adding the caveat, "Kids would have fun in arcades without using or selling and not using and selling"; redundancy here underscores her message.

Denise, who explored the topic of racism, explained to Ashton that "I had to change my opinion. I had racism confused with prejudice. And I thought only Blacks and Whites were affected by it. I found out I was wrong. It was actually the Whites who started the racist-racial tension." Ashton rejoined, "There's your beginning. You just open it up, so you can set it up. And then talk about what the process was. How— what kinds of things happened to make you see more clearly? What kinds of things happened to you during this process that made you change your mind? What things did you learn about Black people that are not true? Myths that you need to expel." Ashton then read a portion of a transcript from Carlos Vega that Denise had highlighted for inclusion in her chapter. Ashton told Denise it was important to make people aware of how racism hurts. She asked her to write a skit about how racism hurts. Denise wrote about a racist incident she had witnessed in the classroom 2 years earlier. When she finished, Ashton read it silently, then said, "You set up the conflict. Now how does it get resolved?" Denise said, "But I wasn't there" to which Ashton responded, "You don't have to be there. How would you resolve it?" When she finished the second skit, Ashton read both aloud, indicating her pleasure with both. She encouraged Denise to write a third skit in which she confronted an adult with the information she had learned from her research, suggesting that she might talk to a teacher. Denise included all three pieces of writing in her final chapter. She also followed Ashton's suggestion that she write about her own process of change.

> When I started researching this chapter, I had racism and racial prejudice confused. This is how I got racism and racial prejudice confused. When the writers' club interviewed Teresa Cruz, the topic of racism came up. She asked, "Has anyone experienced racism?"
>
> Some answered, "Yes."
>
> "Explain how."
>
> I started saying I did by being called, "That white girl," "Honky" and "Gringa." Then I found out that is not racism! What that is called is racial prejudice.
>
> The real definition for racism is a form of oppression. Oppression is when you are pushed down or let down because of your race. . . . Like Marsha Davidson said in words teens can understand, "Racism = prejudice + power" . . .

In her ethnographic report, Denise summarized her newfound understanding of racism and racial tensions. The inquiry process helped her gain an awareness of ethnocentric attitudes and actions, reformulate her response to her personal experiences, and gain ideas on how to intervene when a racist incident occurs. As she wrote in the introduction to her chapter: "I would like teens to look at who we are and to get rid of the idea 'I'm superior because I am White.' . . . The purpose of my chapter is to say do not judge a person by their skin color and to show you can change yourself." The quote she includes here, and within the body of the chapter, is a definition of racism given by a student in the Health Peer Educators' play.

For the "Connection Chapter" of their edited volume, Sandra wrote:

> I feel out of all these topics racism ties them all together. . . . Racism is in the media and in the schools which causes kids to drop out of school. When they drop out most of them turn to alcohol. The pressure makes people drop out. . . . Racism causes a lot of problems.

She reported the implications of "being made to feel like a stranger" for students, for families, for teachers, for schools, and for communities, that she had learned from the people the students talked to during their inquiry. The students came to see the problems they investigated as connected with many serious urban issues.

CONCLUSION

It is impossible to separate the students-as-ethnographers project from what the students learned, felt, and wrote. From the beginning of the project, the students addressed the issue of personhood. The students found that personhood was explicitly addressed in the communities in which they did their work and by the people the students talked to, influencing what and how the students wrote. Students' research and writing built on community ways of knowing, problem solving, and using language and literacy, which were inseparable from taking action against the various forms of oppression faced by the students and their communities.

The personhood that students constructed in their writing was grounded in their discussions with community members. The students' questions provoked the community members to raise several themes and strategies, which include the importance of: reclaiming your cultural heritage; learning history from the community's point of view; analyzing multiple forms of oppression; acting for social justice through your everyday interactions. The community knowledge students accessed and gained from interviewing community members challenged school-based knowledge and ways of interacting. In essence, community members argued that when personhood is not directly, intentionally, and consciously addressed as a cultural construction in school, a default definition of personhood is established, one which, by failing to acknowledge the culture and history of students of color, too often results in their feeling like strangers in school.

The students wrote in a variety of forms, not just in traditional ethnographic genres. Their writing reflects the fact that the ethnographic endeavor itself involves a construction of personhood and a search for appropriate genres in which to write.

The students' ethnographic research can be viewed as a kind of "native anthropology" such as that called for by Jones (1988) and Galwatney (1981). Rather than exporting knowledge of a community for use by others, ethnographic research becomes a way for people to reflect on their own communities by developing a better understanding of the cultural dynamics in which they live. But the methods and theoretical frameworks that might be used in a "native anthropology" cannot be merely imported from outside, they must be recreated. This is what the students did and what they needed to do in order to address the issue of personhood as it presented itself to them as students, community members, and as ethnographers of their own communities.

REFERENCES

Basso, K. (1988). Speaking with names: Language and landscape among the western Apache. *Journal of Cultural Anthropology, 3*(2), 9-130.

Besnier, N. (1993). Literacy and feelings: The encoding of affect in Nukulaelae letters. In B. Street (Ed.), *Cross-cultural approaches to literacy* (pp. 62-86). Cambridge: Cambridge University Press.

Carbaugh, D. (1992). *Cultural communication and intercultural contact.* Hillsdale, NJ: Lawrence Erlbaum Associates.

Du Bois, W.E.B. (1969). *The souls of black folks.* New York: Signet. (Original work published 1903)

Egan-Robertson, A. (1994). *Literacy practices, personhood, and students as researchers in their own communities.* Unpublished doctoral dissertation, University of Massachusetts, Amherst.

Foster, M. (1992). Sociolinguistics and the African-American community: Implications for literacy. *Theory Into Practice, 32*(4), 303-311.

Galwatney, J. (1981). *Drylongso: A self-portrait of black America.* New York: Random House Press.

Geertz, C. (1976). From the native's point-of-view: On the nature of anthropological understanding. In K. Basso & H. Shelby (Eds.), *Meaning in anthropology.* Albuquerque: University of New Mexico Press.

Heath, S.B., & Branscombe, A. (1986). "Intelligent writing" in an audience community: Teacher, student, and researcher. In S. Freedman (Ed.), *The acquisition of written language: Response and revision* (pp. 16-34). Norwood, NJ: Ablex.

Holloway, K. (1991). The Thursday ladies. In P. Bell-Scott, B. Guy Sheftall, J. Royster, J. Suns-Woods, M. DeCosta-Willis, & L. Fultz, *Double stitch: Black women write about mothers and daughters.* New York: Harper.

Jones, D. (1988). Towards a native anthropology. In J. Cole (Ed.), *Anthropology for the nineties: Introductory readings* (pp. 30-41). New York: The Free Press.

Kirshenblatt-Gimblett, B. (1989). Authoring lives. *Journal of Folklore Research, 26*, 123-149.

Kondo, D. (1990). *Crafting selves: Power, gender, and discourses of identity in a Japanese workplace.* Chicago: Chicago University Press.

McLean-Donaldson, K. (1994). *Racism in U.S. schools: Assessing the impact of an anti-racism/multicultural arts curriculum on high school students in a peer education program*. Unpublished doctoral dissertation, University of Massachusetts, Amherst.

Myerhoff, B. (1978). *Number our days*. New York: Simon & Schuster.

Robinson, J., & Stock, P. (1990). The politics of literacy. In J. Robinson (Ed.), *Conversations on the written word: Essays on language and literacy* (pp. 271-318). Portsmouth, NH: Boynton/Cook.

Rosaldo, M. (1984). Toward an anthropology of self and feeling. In R. Shwerder & R. LeVine (Eds.), *Culture theory: Essays on mind, self, and emotion*. Cambridge, England: Cambridge University Press.

Steady, F. (Ed.). (1981). *The black woman cross-culturally*. Cambridge, MA: Schenkman Publishing Co.

Steady, F. (1987). African feminism: A worldwide perspective. In R. Ternborg-Penn, S. Harley, & A. Rushing (Eds.), *Women in Africa and the African diaspora* (pp. 3-33). Washington, D.C.: Howard University Press.

Vega Community Writing Club. (1993). How we went about researching and writing this book. In *Vega Community Writing Club, Life as teenagers in the nineties: Growing up in Riverside* (pp. 54-64). Riverside: Author.

West, C. (1993). *Race matters*. Boston: Beacon Press.

Willis, A. (1995). Reading the world of school literacy: Contextuality in the experience of a young African American man. *Harvard Educational Review, 65*(1), 30-49.

Author Index

A

Abu-Lughod, L., 243n, 257
Acosta, N., 222, 239
Adger, C., 171, 178, 183
Agar, M., 3, 25
Alvarez, L., 173, 180, 184
Anderson, G., 7, 25
Anderson, J., 193, 211
Andrade, R., 94, 96, 97, 112
Anthony, M., 163, 166
Apple, M.W., 11, 25
Aries, P., 94, 96, 112
Arvizu, S., 6, 30
Atkinson, P., 3, 243n, 257
Atwell, N., 88, 92
Au, K., 18, 25
Avery, V., 154, 163, 165

B

Barton, D., 19, 21, 25, 28
Basso, K., 19, 25, 262, 284
Bauman, R., 11, 25
Belenky, M.F., 243n, 257
Benedict, R., 2, 25
Bennett, A., 20, 31, 146, 166
Bhatt, A., 194, 211
Bloome, D., 16, 19, 21, 25, 32, 38, 40, 57n, 57
Bloor, T., 211, 211
Bogdan, R., 100, 112

Borko, H., 23, 25
Bourne, J., 195, 211
Boyarin, J., 19, 25
Brannon, L., 254, 258
Branscombe, A., 24, 28, 43, 57, 265, 285
Brilliant-Mills, H., 124, 138
British Broadcasting Corporation, 148, 153, 165
Brodkey, L., 7, 14, 25-26
Bronfenbrenner, U., 111, 112
Bruner, E.M., 145, 165, 243n, 259
Bruner, J., 145, 165
Burgess, T., 146, 166, 196, 214
Burns, A., 95, 113

C

Cahan, E., 94, 96, 112
Calkins, L., 116, 138
Camarillo, A., 100, 112
Cameron, D., 195, 211
Carbaugh, D., 262, 285
Carrasquillo, A.L., 100, 113
Carter, R., 194, 211
Cazden, C., 22, 26
Chafets, Z., 255, 257
Chambers, J., 208, 214
Chandler, P., 196, 212
Cheshire, J., 194, 196, 197, 207, 210, 212

Chomsky, A., 218, *239*
Christian, D., 4, *32*
Clark, R., 172, 184, *193*
Cleary, L., 167, 168, *184*
Clifford, J., 243n, *257*
Clinchy, B.M., 243n, *257*
Cole, J., 6, *26*
Cole, M., 21, *30*
Coles, R., 94, 97, *113*
College Composition Committee on Language Statement, 168, *184*
Collins, E., 118, *138*
Collins, P., 204, *212*
Cook-Gumperz, J., 22, *26*
Coupland, N., 208, 209, *212*
Cran, W., 90, *92*
Crystal, D., 195, *212*
Cullingford, D., 95, 107, 109, *113*
Cummins, J., 23, *26*

D

D'Amato, J.J., 95, *113*
Davies, B., 14, 18, 26, 124, *139*
Dei, G., 18, *26*
Delamont, S., 22, *26*
Delpit, L., 69, *92*
deMause, L., 94, 96, *113*
Department of Education and Science, 193, 195, 196, 199, 200, 210, *212*
Detwyler, J., 171, 178, *184*
Dewey Center Community Writing Project, 244, 245, 256, *257*
Diaz, R., 18, 29, 72, 85, *92*
Donmall, B.G., 172, 184, 192, *212*
Donmall, G., 172, *184*, 192, *212*
Dorsey-Gaines, C., 21, *31*
Doughty, P., 192, *212*
Du Bois, W.E.B., 2, *26*, 262, *285*

E

Earl Marshall School, 256, *257*
Eckert, P., 9, 23, *26*
Edelsky, C., 85, 89, *92*

Eder, D., 22, *26*
Edwards, A., 22, *25*
Edwards, C., 6, 9, *32*
Edwards, V., 195, 196, 197, 205, 207, 210, *212, 213*
Egan-Robertson, A., 268, *285*
Eisenhart, M., 23, *25*
El'konin, D.R., 112, *133*
Elsasser, N., 20, *26*
Erickson, F., 6, 20, 26, 30, 96, *113*
Ernst, G., 18, *26*
Everhart, R.B., 12, *26*

F

Fairclough, N., 13, 27, 172, *184*, 193, 194, 195, 211, *213*
Ferguson, C., 3, *27*
Fernie, D., 124, *139*
Fine, G.A., 98, *113*
Fine, M., 13, *27*
Firth, R., 3, *27*
Floriani, A., 125, 131, *139*
Florio, S., 6, *30*
Fonseca, N., 222, *239*
Foster, M., 18, 22, 27, 274, *285*
Foucault, M., 14, *27*
Freire, P., 75, *92*, 235, *239*
Furlong, V., 22, *26*

G

Gadsden, V., 20, *27*
Galton, M., 22, *26*
Galwatney, J., 262, 274, 281, 284, *285*
Garcia, O., 4, *27*
Garrett, P., 172, *184*
Geertz, C., 10, 27, 243n, *257*, 262, *285*
Gibson, M., 16, *27*
Gilbert, P., 14, 18, *27*
Giles, H., 201, *213*
Gilmore, P., 21, 22, 27, *30*
Giroux, H., 11, *27*
Gluck, S.B., 254, *257*
Gmelch, G., 51, *57*
Goldberger, N.R., 243n, *257*

Gonzalez, R.D., 254, *258*
Goodenough, W., 9, *27*
Goodnow, J., 95, *113*
Goody, J., 20, 27
Gordimer, N., 255, *258*
Gordon, W., 45, *57*
Graddol, D., 3, *27*, 194, *213*
Graff, H., 20, *27-28*
Graves, D., 56, *57*
Green, J., 5, 22, *27*, 32, 118, *139*
Greenbaum, S., 210, *214*
Greenberg, J., 95, *114*
Grillo, R., 3, *28*
Gumperz, J., 11, *28*

H

Hamilton, M., 19, *28*
Hammersly, M., 3, *28*
Harding, S., 243n, *258*
Hargreaves, A., 3, *28*
Harkness, S., 17, *28*
Harris, R., 161, *166*
Harry, B., 171, *184*
Hart, S., 23, *28*
Hawes, J.M., 96, 106, *113*
Hawkins, E., 172, *184*, 197, *213*
Heath, S., 3, 5, 16, 19, 24, *27*, *28*, 43, *57*, 70, 72, 85, 92, 265, *285*
Hemmings, S., 154, *166*
Heras, A.I., 125, 131, *139*
Hernandez Cruz, V., 90, 91, *92*
Hillier, H., 4, *31*
Hiner, N.R., 96, 106, *113*
Hoban, R., 163, *166*
Holland, D., 9, 10, *28*
Holloway, K., 279, *285*
Hood, L., 21, *29*
hooks, b., 254, 256, *258*
Hsu, O.B., 44, *58*
Hudson, R., 207, *213*
Hughes, H.A., 208, 210, *213*
Hymes, D., 2, 11, 22, 25, *26*, *28*, *29*, 118, *139*

I

Irvine, P., 20, *26*
Irwin, H., 163, *166*
Ivanic, R., 19, 21, 25, *28*, 172, *184*

J

Jacobs, L., 16, *31*
Jagger, A., 245, *258*
James, C., 172, *184*
Jenks, C., 96, *113*
John, V., 22, *26*
Jones, A.P., 192, *213*
Jones, D., 9, *29*, 197, *213*, 284, *285*
Joyce, B., 45, *58*

K

Kantor, R., 124, *129*
Keefer, C., 17, *28*
Kirshenblatt-Gimblett, B., 262, *285*
Kirton, E., 16, *31*
Knoblauch, C.H., 254, *258*
Kolker, A., 180, *184*
Kondo, D., 262, *285*
Kotlowitz, A., 99, *113*
Kozol, J., 98, *113*
Kreeft Peyton, J., 97, *114*

L

Labov, W., 3, 4, *29*
Ladson-Billings, G., 18, *29*
Lancaster, L., 192, *213*
Lankshear, C., 254, *258*
Lass, R., 207, *213*
Lather, P., 18, *29*, 243, 243n, 244, *258*
Lave, J., 70, 72, *92*
Lawlor, S., 196, *213*
Lee, L., 154, *166*
Leech, G., 210, *214*
Letwin, S., 196, *213*
Lin, L., 124, *139*
Linguistic Minorities Project, 196, *213*
Lund, N., 167, 168, *184*

M

Macaulay, R.K.S., 203, *213*
Macedo, D., 75, *92*
MacNeil, R., 90, *92*
Magandzo, A., 227, *239*
Malinowski, B., 2, *29*
Mannheim, K., 100, *113*
Marcus, G.E., 243n, *257*
Marenbon, J., 196, *213*
Mariani, P., 254, *258*
Marshall, B.K., 254, *258*
Martin-Jones, M., 172, *184*, 193, 194, *211*
Maybin, J., 19, 27, *29*
Mayorga, G., 236, *240*
McClendon, J., 49, *58*
McCrum, R., 90, *92*
McDermott, R., 21, 23, *29*
McKinney, K., 218, *239*
McLaren, P.L., 12, *29*, 254, *258*
McLarney, B., 239, *240*
McLaughlin, D., 254, *258*
McLean-Donaldson, K., 274n, *285*
McMurray, P., 124, *139*
McPhaul, J., 218, *240*
Mead, M., 2, *29*
Mechling, J., 94, 96, *112*
Mehan, H., 22, *29*
Michaels, S., 21, *29*
Miller, J., 146, *166*
Milroy, J., 170, *184*, 195, *213, 214*
Milroy, L., 170, *184*, 195, 208, *213, 214*
Minh-ha, T., 243, *258*
Minor, H., 50, *58*
Mirikitani, J., 256, *259*
Moll, L., 18, *29*, 72, 85, *92*, 94, 95, 96, 97, *112, 114*, 146, *166*, 238, *240*
Montero Barrantes, F., 221, *240*
Montero-Sieburth, M., 226, *240*
Montgomery, M., 3, *29*
Moss, B., 21, *29*

Moss, G., 18, *30*
Myerhoff, B., xvi, *xx*, 279n, 281, *285*

N

National Association for the Teaching of English, 194, *215*
National Curriculum Council, 144, *166*
Newsum, H.E., 3, *30*
Nicholson, L., 243n, *258*
Noyes, P., 196, *212*

O

Ochs, E., 11, *30*
Ogbu, J., 9, *30*
Ong, W., 20, *30*
Open University, 164, *166*
Orton, H., 207, *214*
Owen, B., 163, *166*

P

Palmer, P., 220, 221, 222, 223, 224, 230, 236, *240*
Patai, D., 254, *257*
Peacock, J., 8, *30*
Pearce, J., 192, *212*
Philips, S., 16, *30*
Powesland, P., 201, *213*
Purcell, T.W., 218, *240*
Puro, P., 40, *57*

Q

Quinn, N., 9, 10, *28*
Quirk, R., 210, *214*

R

Reder, S., 21, *30*
Richmond, J., 144, *166*
Ringgold, F., 116, *139*
Robinson, J.L., 43, *58*, 254n, *258*, 265, *285*
Robinson, W.P., 196, *212*
Rockhill, K., 18, *30*
Rogers, T., 21, *31*
Romero, A., 108, 110, *114*

Rosaldo, M., 262, *286*
Rosen, H., 196, *214*
Ryan, E.B., 201, *214*

S

Salazar, M., 236, *240*
Sanchez, J., 236, *240*
Sandstrom, K.L., 98, *113*
Santa Barbara Classroom
    Discourse Group, 22, *30*, 118,
    124, 131, *139*
Sapir, E., 2, *30*
Saravia-Shore, M., 6, *30*
Saunders, G., 146, *166*
Saville-Troika, M., 11, *30*
Savitsky, F., 161, *166*
Schaafsma, D., 244, 246, 254n, *258*
Schieffelin, B., 1, 21, *30*
Schulz, C.B., 106, *113*
Scollon, R., 19, *30*
Scollon, S., 19, *30*
Scribner, S., 21, *30*
Shaw, G., 163, *166*
Sheikh, F., 163, *166*
Sheridan, T.E., 100, *114*
Sherzer, J., 11, *25*
Shultz, J., 6, *30*, 96, 106, *113*
Shuman, A., 11, *31*
Slobodchikov, V.L., 254, *259*
Smith, B., 254, *259*
Smith-Burke, M., 245, *259*
Smitherman, G., 4, *31*
Sola, M., 20, *31*, 146, *166*
Solomon, P., 14, *31*
Solsken, J., 15, *31*
Spindler, G., 6, 9, 15, *31*
Spindler, L., 6, 9, 15, *31*
Spradley, J.P., 93, *114*
Spradley, J.W., 118, *139*
Staton, J., 97, *114*
Statzner, E., 18, *26*
Steady, F., 262, 263, *286*
Stierer, B., 3, *27*
Stock, P., 43, *58*, 265, *285*

Street, B., 19, 21, *31*
Stubbs, M., 4, *31*
Super, C., 17, *28*
Sutton-Smith, B., 94, 96, *112*
Svartvik, J., 210, *214*

T

Tannen, D., 11, *31*
Tarule, J.M., 243n, *257*
Taylor, D., 21, *31*, 96, 100, 109, *114*
Taylor, R., 192, *213*
Taylor, S.J., 18, *27*
The English Centre, 154, *166*
Theodorou, E., 40, *57*
Thornton, G., 192, *212*
Tierney, R., 21, *31*
Tierney, W.G., 254, *258*
Trudgill, P., 4, *31*, 195, 197, 198,
    201, 203, 208, 209, 210, 213, *214*
Trueba, H., 18, 22, *26*, *31*, 72, 85, *92*
Turner, V.W., 243n, *259*

U

University of London, 192, *214*

V

van Maanen, J., 73, *92*, 243n, *259*
Varenne, H., 9, *31*
Vega Community Writing Club,
    261, *284*
Velez-Ibanez, C., 95, *114*
Venger, A.L., 112, *114*

W

Wakelin, M., 207, *214*
Walkerdine, V., 243n, *257*
Wallat, C., 5, *28*
Walsh, C., 18, *32*
Watt, I., 20, *27*
Weedon, C., 14, *32*
Weil, M., 45, *58*
Wells, G., 70, *92*
Weltens, B., 195, 197, *213*, *214*
Wenger, E., 70, 72, *92*
West, C., 262, *286*

White, S.B., 94, 96, *112*
Whiting, B., 6, 9, 32
Whittle, P., 197, 207, 210, *212*
Whyte, W.F., 254, *259*
Wigginton, E., 43, *58*, 181, *184*, 237, 241
Wikelund, K., 21, *30*
Willett, J., 16, *32*, 57, *58*
Williams, C., 256, *259*
Williams, R., xvii-xviii, *xx*
Willinsky, J., 19, *32*, 254, *259*
Willis, A., 262, *284*

Willis, P., 12, 32, 254, *259*
Willow Run/Ann Arbor Project, 256, *259*
Wolcott, H.F., 2, *32*
Wolf, M., 243n, *259*
Wolfram, W., 4, *32*, 170, 171, 175, 178, 181, *184*
Woods, P., 3, *28*

Z

Zaharlick, A., 5, *32*
Zuman, J.P., 226, *241*

Subject Index

A

Abductive reasoning, 45, 51, 52
Academic learning, 18, 41, 108, 215
Access, 12, 22-24, 34, 237
Afrocentricity, 18
Alienation, viii, 22, 60, 104, 199, 216, 261, 263, 275
Anthropology
  cognitive anthropology, 9-10, 118
  cultural anthropology, xiv, 8
  ethnography of communication, xiv, 4, 11
  functionalism, 9, 12
  interpretive ethnography, 10-11
  language of anthropologists, 119, 120, 125, 138
  nacirema, 51
  native anthropology, 9. 216. 279, 282
  psychological anthropology, 9
  social anthropology, xiv, 9
  sociolinguistic ethnography; see Ethnography of communication
  structuralism, 9, 12
Appropriateness, 159, 195
Attitude, 22; see also Language, Language Attitude
Autobiography, 154, 263; see also Language, Language autobiography

B

Bilingualism, 4, 96, 105-112, 146, 156, 193, 229
Biliteracy, 73, 89-91, 98, 100, 105-107
Black English; see African American Vernacular English

C

Critical theory, 9, 11-12, 254
Culture
  cross-cultural contact, xv
  cross-cultural miscommunication, 11, 109
  cultural bias, 17, 18, 21
  cultural diversity, 24, 38, 42
  cultural heritage, 90, 92, 100
  cultural ideology, 17, 18, 19
  cultural practices, 20, 21, 238
  cultural production, 11
  cultural reproduction, 16, 23
  cultural transmission, 17, 19
  definitions of, 7-14, 244
  students' cultural background, 18, 22
Curriculum, x, 35, 56, 67, 143, 145, 159, 224, 225, 226-229, 238
  cognitively oriented curriculum 44, 49-50, 52; see also planning model

curriculum as inquiry, 59, 68, 115, 119, 142, 169

curriculum development, 147, 219, 224, 228, 237, 246

language arts curriculum, 141, 167, 169, 170

national curriculum, 143-144, 159-160, 191, 193, 194, 195, 196, 210, 225, 226, 227, 238

D

Democracy, 71; see also Ethnography and democracy

Dialect, v, 3, 16, 20, 141, 148, 169, 189, 191, 205

dialect awareness, 170, 172-183

ethical considerations, 181

dialect discrimination, 170, 171

dialect grammar, 190, 195, 197, 206, 210

dialect leveling, 197, 206, 207, 210

dialect literature, 211

dialect pronunciation, 189

dialect rights, 168

dialect study, 170-172

dialect vocabulary, 190, 195, 206

dialect writing, 204

dominant dialects, 3

eye dialect, 169

habitual be, 176-177

prestige dialects, 3, 203

r-lessness, 176, 179

Survey of British Dialect Grammar, 194-198, 207, 210

Dialogue journals, 34, 93, 94, 97-107

Directory of English Dialect Resources, 205

Discourse, 14

E

Education

community-centered education, 16-17, 57, 219

definitions of, 15-18

school-centered education, 15-16, 57

English as a second language, 146, 193

Ethnography

British ethnographic studies of education, 3

classroom ethnography, 118, 120

critical ethnography, 7, 254, 257

cross-cultural comparison, 6, 49

cultural history, 49-50

cultural relativity, 51

definitions of ethnographic research, iii, iv-vii, 2-7, 1-25, 70

emic perspective, 6, 45, 51, 52, 96

ethnography and democracy, 25

etic perspective, 6, 45, 51, 52

ethnography of communication; see Anthropology

field notes, 63, 82, 126, 232, 265; see also Writing, notemaking, notetaking

participant observer, 129, 264

thick description, 10

traditions of inquiry, 2, 141

writing ethnography, vi-vii, 6, 24, 43-57, 73-92, 243, 265, 278

documentation, 84

field notes, 73-76, 119, 120

Eurocentricism, 17

Evaluation, 21, 49-50

student self-evaluation, 45, 82, 123, 129, 135-138

Folklore, 51

Foxfire, 43, 181, 215, 217, 228, 237-238

Family, 16, 21, 38, 39, 40, 44, 46, 51, 57, 70, 72, 91, 99, 119, 141, 158, 273

G

Gender and schooling, 18, 22

Gender issues, 18, 148, 149, 156, 157, 254, 267

Grammar study, v, 167, 176

H

High/Scope Educational Research Foundation, 44
History, 135; *see also* Writing, Writing History
Homework, xiii, 53, 66-67, 78, 127, 129, 130, 131, 133

I

Identity, 34, 71, 144, 146, 149, 155, 156, 160, 195, 198, 199, 203-204, 216, 227, 228, 229, 235, 255, 262, 267, 274, 278
Instruction/instructional practices, xx, 124, 125
Intertextuality, 52, 266
Interviewing, 64, 219, 222, 224, 229, 230, 231, 232, 244, 246, 269-275

K

Knowledge
    academic knowledge, iii, 33, 52, 70, 116, 121, 135, 215
    community knowledge, xii, xiii, xvi, xvii, 16, 33, 40, 44, 45, 46-50, 52, 53, 55, 60-61, 215
    common knowledge, 138
    control of knowledge, 25
    definitions of, 16, 70, 115-116, 119, 121
    disciplinary knowledge; *see* Knowledge, Academic Knowledge
    funds of knowledge, 93, 238
    knowledge about language, 34, 143-144, 159-160, 191-211
    knowledge and bias, 17
    reproduction of knowledge, xii, 33, 116
    student knowledge, 39, 125

L

Language
    African American Vernacular English (AAVE), 4, 171, 176, 178, 179, 182
    community language(s), 141
    knowledge about language; *see* Knowledge
    language across the curriculum, 193
    language and power, v, 70, 144, 149, 153, 160, 194, 202
    language attitude, 201-202
    language autobiographies, 141, 144, 148, 153-156, 158
    language awareness, 146, 172, 192-193, 196, 197
    language change, 90-91, 179, 197
    reinventing English, 90-91
    language community, 21, 181
    language development, 144, 146, 160
    language differences; *see* Linguistic diversity
    Language in the National Curriculum (Linc) Project, 194
    language loyalty, 110-111
    language practices, 143, 144, 145, 146, 153, 159
    language socialization, 11
    language study, xv, xx, 141, 192-198
    associate tradition of, 168
    grammar tradition of, 167, 169
    language usage tradition, 167-169
    language use, 4, 141, 147, 156
    language variation, xv, xx, 4, 141, 142, 144, 159, 169, 170, 172, 176, 178, 197, 205
    Li'l Abner Syndrome, 169
    linguistic diversity, 24, 42, 75, 197, 198-205, 210
    linguistic insecurity, 203, 204
    linguistic prejudice, 100, 179, 180
    linguistic rules/grammatical rules, 168, 175, 177
    multiple languages, 4, 141, 143-165

prescriptive grammar, 141
racist language, 156
register, 141, 160
sexist language, 156, 157
talking proper, 141, 148-150,
    156, 159, 197-200, 203
Life history, 269
Literacy, 18, 19-21, 22, 118, 254,
    269; see also Reading, Writing
academic literacy, 69, 71, 72
community literacy, 94, 97, 105
family literacy, 21
"Great Divide" theory, 20-21
illiteracy, 21
literacy and power, 20, 91
literacy events, 19
literacy practices, 19, 20, 21, 87,
    145, 158, 169, 261, 262, 278
Literary study, 168

M

Marginalization, 142, 218; see also
    Community, Marginalized
    communities
Metaphor, 45, 53
Motivation, 70, 71, 76, 85
Multiculturalism, 18, 19, 235

N

Narrative, vi, 19, 21, 39, 77, 127,
    132, 144, 154, 162, 243-257, 262,
    274
Nonverbal communication, 150, 232

O

Oral history, 217, 219, 220, 222,
    227, 228, 229, 230, 231, 235, 236,
    238, 246, 255, 272

P

Parents, iii, 16, 33, 37, 38, 41, 51,
    59-62, 68, 91, 95, 105-107, 116,
    120, 215, 229
Personhood, xvii, 14, 71, 216, 261-
    283

Planning model; see Cognitively
    oriented curriculum
Portfolios, 135-138
Poststructuralism, 9, 14
Power relations, 11, 12
Praxis, xix
Principles of language learning, 235
Problem solving, 45
Procedural display, 40-57

Q

Qualitative research, 75, 130, 219,
    220, 227, 228, 230

R

Racial issues, 22, 104, 156, 170, 171,
    218, 235, 254, 263, 267, 273
Racism, vii, viii, 157, 216, 265, 268,
    274, 277, 279, 280
Reading, 18, 19, 21, 34, 37, 38, 40,
    43, 63, 69
learning to read, 16, 21
oral reading, 108
reading as a social process, 19, 146
reading in a second language,
    108, 110
reading scores, 69
Reflection, 79-82, 93, 112, 116, 121,
    123, 136, 137, 144, 145, 156, 215,
    230, 231, 232; see also Writing,
    Writing to reflect
Representation, 74, 130, 243, 255,
    256; see also Research,
    representing data
Research
action research, 254
classroom research, xii
definitions of research, xii, xiv,
    24, 244
ecological approach, 96
ethics, 75
feminist research, 18
inquiry, xx, 59, 120, 121, 122, 123,
    136, 138, 142, 171-172, 215, 216

multiple perspectives, 125
observation, 125-131
phenomenological approaches, 96
planning, 76-79
point of view, 125-131
representing data, 126, 130, 131
researchers and the researched, xiii, 12, 25, 93-94, 120
researching children, 95-96
sharing research, 82-88
theory and research, 1, 2, 7-8
Resistance, 12, 13, 41, 237, 254, 256

S

Scaffolding, 145, 157, 158
Schools
    educational equity, 24, 70, 170, 171
    tracking, 23, 264
Silencing, 13
Social action, viii, x, 12, 59, 215, 244, 254
Socialization, 17, 23, 96, 145
Social reproduction, 12, 17, 23
Social practices, 145
Socioeconomic class issues; see class issues
Sociolinguistics, xiv, 3, 141, 142, 145, 197, 210
Standard English, xv, xx, 3, 91, 149, 162, 168, 169, 172, 178, 182, 191, 195, 196, 197, 205, 207, 210
Sociolinguistic ethnography; see Anthropology, Ethnography of Communication
Stigmatization, 198-199
Storytelling, vii, 245, 246, 254, 272, 278
Synectics, 45, 52

T

Talamanca, 215, 221-224, 228, 229, 230, 231, 234, 235, 237

Talamanca Community Research Project, 217, 219, 220, 235
Text production, xii, 41-42, 43, 52-53, 56
Text reproduction, xii, 33, 41, 42, 43, 55, 57, 215
Time, 78, 80, 82, 92
Tools, 78, 82, 117, 118, 124-135, 142, 275
Transcribing, 150, 230, 231, 232
Turn taking, 153

V

Voice, 13, 52, 56, 69, 71, 92, 123, 138, 154, 235, 238, 244

W

Whole language, 38, 42
Women's history, 64-65
Writing, xvi, 27, 38, 40, 42, 43, 118, 204, 216, 243-257
    academic writing, 42, 43, 44, 45, 52-56
    argumentative writing, 156
    authentic writing, 67, 97
    community of writers, 85, 87, 118
    community writing, 21, 261, 264-267
    genres, xvi, 25, 45, 71, 130, 131, 279
    informative writing, 144
    learning to write, 16, 21, 37-57, 232
    notemaking, 125-131
    notetaking, 125-131
    spelling, 264
    story writing, 163-164, 244
    writing development, 89
    writing ethnography; see Ethnography
    writing history, 131-135
    writing in a second language, 109
    writing to reflect, 80, 118
    writing workshop, 56

Printed in the United States
65223LVS00004B/202-219